TEACHING HISTORY

TEACHING HISTORY

SUGGESTED THEMES FOR THE CURRICULUM IN WALDORF SCHOOLS

Christoph Lindenberg

Translation by Peter Luborsky

Published by Waldorf Publications at the Research Institute for Waldorf Education

Published by:

Waldorf Publications at the
Research Institute for Waldorf Education
38 Main Street
Chatham, NY 12037

Title: *Teaching History*
    Suggested Themes for the Curriculum in Waldorf Schools
Author: Christoph Lindenberg
German Text © Verlag Freies Geistesleben GmbH, Stuttgart
Originally published as:
    Geschichte lehren: thmat, Anregungen zum Lehrplan
ISBN # 3-7725-0243-1 NE:GT
Translator: Peter Luborsky
Editor: David Mitchell
Designer: Robin Brooks
© 1989, revised 2004 by AWSNA
Reprinted 2014 by Waldorf Publications
ISBN # 978-0-962397-80-6

ACKNOWLEDGEMENT

The editor wishes gratefully to acknowledge the financial support provided by The Waldorf Institute of Southern California and the *Freunde der Erziehungskunst Rudolf Steiners* for the translation of the text.

Special thanks to Dr. Wolfgang Schad of the *Pädagogische Forschungstelle*, Stuttgart, for his encouragement and help.

May, 1989
Ekkehard Piening

CONTENTS

PREFACE

This book has been written for practicing teachers as well as for parents with an interest in history and education. Principally, however, it is addressed to my colleagues in history teaching at Waldorf Schools, both class teachers and upper grade teachers. The task I have set myself in this work is to join two elements: an approach to history instruction that is appropriate to the various age levels (following the Waldorf School curriculum), and a view of history based on Rudolf Steiner's symptomalogical approach. An introduction to this view of history can be found in the paperback *Zur symptomatischen Geschichtsbetrachtung*, which is to appear soon in the series *Rudolf Steiner — Themen aus dem Gesamtwerk*. A listing of relevant literature is also provided there.

This work does not concern itself with the current specialized discussions concerning history teaching. I have expressed my views on this topic in my book *Die Lebensbedingungen des Erziehens*, in the chapter "Geschichte, Schule und Gesellschaft" (Reinbek, 1981)

Let a heartfelt thanks be said to all who have helped further the work on this book. Here I will mention but a single name to stand for all those through whom I have learned history: Professor Dr. Hermann Heimpel of Goettingen, whose handling of source material and art of narration have always remained models for me. I would also like to remember my colleagues at Waldorf Schools who have contributed to this work with their stimulating suggestions and questions. Special thanks goes to the "Rudolf Steiner Fonds für wissenschaftliche Forschung," whose gift to the Pädagogische Forschungsstelle beim Bund der Freien Waldorfschulen supported the work on this book.

July 1981, Zarten bei Freiburg
Christoph Lindenberg

1

HISTORY FOR TOMORROW

We meet the future every day. It faces us in the children we bring up as parents or educate as teachers. We know that the fourteen-year-olds who sit before us learning mathematics or history will be thirty-three when the century ends. The world they will live in then can scarcely be visualized concretely today, but we know intuitively that it will be moved by quite different questions and tasks than those concerning us today.

A teacher of history does not wish merely to communicate interesting facts to the younger generation. He wishes to tell them about experiences of humanity that might have significance tomorrow as well. Many themes that have been assiduously elaborated by historians during the last few decades — the evolution of the Federal Republic (West Germany), the National Socialist regime, the Weimar Republic — will soon occupy only the specialist's attention — at least in the form in which they seem significant to us today. Nothing gets old faster than current events.

A history teacher who puts his imagination to work will be able to tell that in the future for which he educates, certain themes will have grown in significance. Hence he will try to choose his subject matter with a view towards these themes. He will attempt to recast his old knowledge into a new form that can still speak to the adult of the year 2010. One of the fundamental themes that undoubtedly will outlast our century is the relationship between man and nature. The "ecological" and "environmental" problems beginning to be noticed today — in reality, problems of our society and of our interaction with the oceans, forests, soil, and air — will be among the burning issues of the year 2000. And this issue will have a history. If Auschwitz is still on our minds today, in the year 2000 the North Sea will be, and we will be asking how this could have happened. Another issue will be the relationship between man and technology. It will not be just a matter of how we deal with

11

technology, but also of how technology in turn affects human societies and the individual human being. And these two questions will be joined by a third: what future can be envisaged for the way human beings live together and for their inner health, their health of soul. Some dangers are clearly visible. For instance, we already see devices being developed for monitoring human beings by computer and directing their behavior by a variety of means.

Thoughts like these, however, grasp the future only one-sidedly. For over against the looming dangers and dismal prognoses stands the will of human beings — our students among them. When fourteen- and fifteen-year-olds begin to be aware of the dangers now threatening humanity and nature, they will spontaneously ask what can be done for the future of the individual and of mankind; what can be done for the preservation and care of nature. The teacher who looks into the future with these students will explore the prospects and the tasks that can already be seen from our vantage point today. The catastrophes resulting from man's past abuse of nature demand new ideas about nature — ideas that can give rise to a nurturing relationship with the foundations of our existence. Indeed, the catastrophes themselves contain hints about the path to take. Similarly, the pathological aspects of today's society can also teach us what human, democratic forms of social life are. Total regulation, control, and social welfare programs deprive human beings of initiative, make them ill. A web of life whose interrelationships remain surveyable, where there are problems to be solved and room for initiative, where the state extensively limits its sphere of competence and gives citizens scope for individual responsibility overcomes anonymity and challenges us to work together. This is something that interests both students and teacher.

Certainly, such a future-oriented approach to history teaching cannot anticipate the future or tell us how to deal with it. Yet the teacher will make every effort to present the experiences of the past in such a way that the students develop imagination and power of judgment. With these, they will be able to understand and judge historical developments of the future with an eye towards humanness, freedom, and brotherhood.

It is only after such considerations that the teacher will finally ask: What should I teach? What do I want to teach? The difference between history and mathematics (or one of the natural sciences) will have be kept in mind. As a teacher of mathematics, if I have learned my subject well once I will always be able to turn back to what I learned earlier. Wherever possible I will try to set about teaching it more effectively, with more truth to its spiritual reality. I will seek to penetrate more and more deeply into the arithmetical and mathematical operations out of a knowledge of the power of historical imagination as well as the power of human understanding. Yet essentially, mathematics remains what it has been for decades and centuries, and what it will be in the future. Not so history. Significant parts of history must be re-written and re-reviewed for each new generation. This applies particularly to whatever topic may have interested us most on the *abitur* (university entrance qualifying examinations at end of high school) or during our training — the most recent history. As in any other field, in history we are inclined to teach what we have once learned well, since we know it. This is how our own history teacher proceeded, which is why Bismarck is still asked on the abitur. Teachers who are forty or fifty years old today will have a tendency to go into detail on Bruenings Emergency Decrees, the Empowerment Act, or the Conference of Potsdam. These things are believed to have had an important impact on the course of history; and, indeed, they did play an important role in their time. In the year 2010, however, when our students are forty-year-old adults actively engaged in life, these issues may be no more than historic curiosities, very much as the revision of the Ems Telegram is today.

In our attempt to arrive at a meaningful selection of themes for our lessons, we will seek to understand the task of history. We may start with the premise that history is the study of the human being: anthropology. Historical anthropology shows us — in a different way than ethnology — the development and growth of the human being and humanity as a whole. For as we look at historical action and the configurations that take form in the course of history, we begin to see what is "within the human being." Thus, to pursue history means to garner the active and passive experiences of mankind. The idea of viewing history as anthropology can give the teacher a certain breadth of vision. He will focus on what is symptomatic and characteristic, on what has given an impetus to history. Which ways of life, which actions, which social forms reveal possibilities, trials, or enhancements of the human condition? How does history mold or challenge the human being, and how do human beings in turn shape history? Such are the questions he will ask.

History, and history instruction, can exemplify or epitomize such characteristic experiences of humankind in certain individual personalities. In this it is different from sociology, anthropology, and ethics. The impact of the Migration of the Peoples on life in the Roman Empire, for example, finds individual expression in the figure of Augustine. Similarly in Gutenberg, history actually illustrates the fate of an inventor in a town of the late Middle Ages, or in Robert Owen the lot of a social reformer. In this way we get beyond empty generalizations and learn to develop what, along with C. Wright Mills, I would call social and historical imagination. This imagination has the capacity to grasp pictorially the meaning of general processes in the fates of individuals. Terms such as the "Migration of the Peoples," "social misery," and "unemployment," are replaced by definite pictures that enable us to visualize human experiences and sufferings as well as historical and social struggles.

Social and historical imagination becomes the basis of a power of judgment that applies not just to the past. When it is cultivated as a habit, it also enables us to visualize the fates of human beings living in the present and to think concretely about the future. This is because it does not deal in general formulae. It has been trained on history. It has learned to observe how high and noble principles — rationality or equality, for example — take effect in individual lives and societies. Such imagination orients itself on the human being: what is within him, what motivates him, and what comes of it. It looks at the socially formative forces in statu nascendi, and at the way they take hold of social reality. Do we find a dictatorship that claims a monopoly on the truth, or human beings working to make the world a more livable place? Thus we see that the anthropological approach is not concerned with principles, but tries, through imagination, to learn to see the social reality — an ability so often lacking today.

As a further result of the anthropological approach, history teaching will not be needlessly fixated on lists of facts and rather unhelpful details of the kind that are handed down from generation to generation out of mere habit. What we present to our students should be of general human significance — not things that would strain even a specialist's memory. It hardly makes sense to inculcate our students with material that will be completely forgotten in a short time. What, of our instruction, will have a lasting impact upon the students? Only what is able to

grow with them as time goes by; what tells them something about themselves; what enables them to see the world in a different light; what
sends them out with riddles and questions — ones that are not quickly
resolved in the very same lesson, but that must be carried with them.

The elements that are significant in an anthropologically oriented
approach to history are those which, in the long run, are able to stimulate the power of historical imagination as well as the power of human
understanding. Let us now briefly introduce some of these elements.

Time

The first and fundamental suggestion regards widening the students' horizon. Especially the younger ones are inclined to believe that
conditions in the world have always and everywhere been the same as
they know them. Through history, however, they learn of entirely different peoples and living conditions. These far-removed cultures give them
a sense for the meaning of time, in the historical sense. First of all, a feeling for the remoteness of the ancient cultures must be cultivated in the
history lesson. Temporal distance must be brought home to them
through examples that they can experience directly. The parents of these
children were born at a time when our cities were quite a bit smaller and
there were no skyscrapers. When their grandparents were born, the sight
of an automobile would bring people running, and airplanes were practically nonexistent. Before World War I, when their great grandparents
were born, there was no electric lighting and scarcely any running water.
Their great-great-grandfathers witnessed the building of the first railroads and factories. Thus, by going back five generations, we see what
incisive changes 150 years have wrought on the face of the world. When
a whole class of thirty-three students stands in line, each representing a
generation, we reach back a thousand years. We arrive at a time when
Germany was largely covered with forests, when hardly any towns and
certainly no roads existed, and when very few churches built of stone
could be seen. In such a way an idea of temporal and cultural distance
begins to develop. When we come to speak of the time when the
Egyptian pyramids were built, we will be able to make "four and a half
thousand years ago" a vivid experience. At the same time, a basis has

been laid for communicating the entirely different way of feeling, seeing, and experiencing in that distant age.

What relevance does this have today? Today's humanity comprises people who, outwardly regarded, all live together in the twentieth century. Yet right in our own times — in New Guinea, for instance — we find stone-age people who are culturally and intellectually removed from us by thousands of years. Even where technological culture has spread, as in Japan and China, people think and feel in an entirely different way than we. Remnants of an ancient culture are still alive today in India. Each of these cultures has a value of its own. By expanding our temporal horizon, we also lay the groundwork for an understanding of the other cultures alive in our own time. In yet another respect we are helping towards an understanding of the present: the particular quality of our own times becomes clear only against the backdrop of history. Thus at each age level, again and again it will be important to vivify historical time in other ways of thinking, acting, and living together. And this again implies that life and thinking will be different in the future. The future, made imaginable through rightly understood history, is not an extended past: it is something new.

Development

The twentieth century has shown itself to be an epoch of accelerated development. The tempo of history is increasing. Prehistory was a period of comparatively slow development. The high civilizations of ancient times endured for millennia almost unchanged in their essential traits. Not until Greek history do we find development in the real sense. The same could be said of Roman and medieval history. Today, however, the human race is consciously pushing development ahead. This is why, after historical time, development is the second important category for which we must prepare an understanding.

There are simple examples that shed light on the present situation in particular. Modern technology developed out of an experiment-oriented natural science. We can follow how the successful experiment results in the development of a machine or technical procedure; how this in turn makes possible a factory; and the factory then changes the living condition of human beings. A certain way of thinking and investigating brings about an institution, and the institution in turn affects social conditions. Thus, a development can be seen to pass through successive stages and spheres of existence; and only when it has finally reached the social life, do we recognize what was hidden in the germ. When developments are traced from their origin to their social effect, an idea comes into being that stimulates social imagination. Encouraged by this idea, the imaginative mind will begin to seek for developments that move beyond the field it first focussed on, into other fields.

Ideas

Just as one must learn to perceive developments, one must also try hard to evaluate justly the influential ideas that are conceived in the course of history. Some ideas penetrate almost unnoticed into human thinking, altering people's attitudes and the way they see things. Often, however, ideas are fascinating and convincing; they demand realization and action. The direct implementation of ideas can cause nameless misery; and it is in this misery that we begin to see the spirit in which the idea was conceived, how it lived in human beings. Hence not every idea can be taken for what it pretends to be.

Perhaps a very simple distinction may prove helpful here. Some ideas are put into practice by their own proponents. They themselves do practical work, possibly staking their fortunes as well. I am thinking here of Robert Owen, of Pestalozzi, of Henri Dunant. They perform the actual labor, the translation of the idea into concrete measures. They may founder in the attempt; but the human intent of the idea is not lost. In many areas of life such reforms prove to have a beneficent effect for many years to come. The picture may be quite different, however, when new ideas are introduced directly from above — especially when a political administration brings pressure or even terrorism to bear. Very few meaningful reforms have been introduced directly from above, and those few did not create specific programs. They were reforms, undertaken in the name of freedom, that made self-governing citizens out of vassals. This, however, is not the imposition of an idea from above; it is a ruler's retraction of his own imposed will.

Setting

Our attention is drawn in quite another direction when we turn our practicing gaze to the outer circumstances of life: the setting, the conditions, and the structures within which human activity takes place. What has it meant for France and French history to have a natural and historic center in the city of Paris? What is the significance for Russia of having such vast land at her disposal, with the immense hinterland of Siberia? What does its location in the Mediterranean basin mean for Rome? Holland proper is an example of a land that required the greatest efforts of its first inhabitants to secure the land and to keep it dry through dike-building and other measures. At the same time, its situation on the North Sea opened up the possibility for global seafaring and trade. The self-confidence of the Dutch is a result of their own achievements. Knowledge of the world and dealings with the most varied peoples bring them a pragmatic tolerance. Thus we see a commonwealth form with republican institutions, with a culture all its own, and with a science belonging to the modern era.

We have quite a different example of the conditions for human action when we consider the possibilities for opposition under totalitarian dictatorship. In either case, however — whether we view the natural or the social conditions that must be faced — the student learns to develop an *imagination for reality*. It is an apparently paradoxical concept. Yet to grasp reality demands a mobile imagination. And precisely such an imaginative faculty will be called for in the future, with the ever more complex realities it will entail. The external conditions will have to be considered together with the answers that human action can provide for them. Today's social conditions and environmental problems require human action that should be approached, not from general principles, but rather with plenty of imagination.

View of History

Among the most powerful forces shaping Western history are the views of history that particular societies have held. Through these views the human being orients himself in time; within them he understands

himself and his tasks. The character of the Middle Ages was determined
by a Christian concept of history, especially by that of Augustine. Hence
rulers and knights, bishops and monks all considered it their mission to
work towards the City of God. Humanism found its ideal in antiquity,
and with it affected education for a long time. The Reformation saw as its
task the restoration of Christianity to its original form. These views of
history gave direction and purpose to the whole of life.

In the modern age a specifically political, secularized interpretation
of history takes its place alongside the earlier views. The English
Revolution justified itself by pointing to the origin of the kingdom, especially to the Magna Carta, and interpreted the historical tradition in
terms of the liberties sought by Parliament. The Age of Enlight-enment
saw history as progress in *this* world and within the human being, and
regarded itself as the beginning of a radiant, enlightened age in which
man will have come to himself. Seeing itself as the executor of these
ideas, the French Revolution marked this beginning by introducing a calendar of its own.

With Marxism yet another view of history gained political significance, a view that claims to know the origin and goal of history. Marx
regarded his own time as the last period of history before the advent of
the classless society, or in Engels' terms, the reign of freedom. It was this
conception of history that supplied Lenin and Mao Tse-Tung with a basis
for their actions. Significant as the various conceptions of history are in
providing a meaningful basis for action, their results can often be highly
problematic in particular cases — especially when such views are taken as
prognoses or prophecies. Talk of the decline of the West or other somber
visions of the future may prove to be a self-fulfilling prophecy. Untold
wrong can be done in the name of a better, utopian society.

Human beings of the present cannot avoid seeing their own existence between the background of history and the horizon of the future.
Yet history also helps us to recognize the dangers of any form of chil-
iasm. History knows that every society is subject to development and
metamorphosis. It recognizes that there are no perfect solutions to the
problems of society, only acceptable ones. With this in mind, we will not
abandon humanity's highest ideals, those of freedom and of living
together in brotherhood, as goals for the future. We will, however,
renounce prophecies and look with scepticism at systems for utopia,
aware that the future cannot be planned or invented. Furthermore, since

we know that any attempt to implement an idea or ideal directly from above only leads to dictatorship and thus perverts the ideal, we will reflect upon other approaches to the future.

Here we can learn from Montesquieu. He formed his ideas of a future state by observing the functioning of the English political system (even if his vision was not accurate in every respect), and in this way he came to a very few, but practical, proposals. The measures he proposed do not aim to fix society in a particular state or establish a particular ethic. Rather, the division of powers he proposed is "merely" intended to create conditions that would allow people to make reasonable decisions and live in a manner worthy of human beings. At the time of Montesquieu, the issue was how to break the absolute power of the monarch and replace it with a procedure by which decisions could be made collectively.

Our society suffers under more weighty problems than did absolutism at the time of Montesquieu. If we hope to work for a more human future — and today the question of the future can no longer be pushed aside — then we must proceed as Montesquieu did. We must ask how to create the right conditions for more reasonable action. To be sure, we would first need an exact description of the pathological symptoms manifested by today's society (something that cannot be offered here): among them, the disenfranchisement of the citizens, a system of collective irresponsibility, the burdening of society as a whole with the consequences of individual and collective action, and a merely administrative or economic response to all problems. If we seek a future in which action is guided by reason, we must seek for the conditions under which responsibility can be reestablished, under which the individual will again be confronted by the consequences of his own actions, under which the problems of society can be solved by free initiatives. The measures necessary to this end could consist in nothing other than a definite limitation of the state's sphere of powers, in uncoupling the systems of society, in the creation of societal freedom.

History as Anthropology

The contribution of history to this shaping of the future and to orienting our thinking about it cannot be put in the form of direct suggestions or indications. Understood as anthropology, however, history can be of indirect help by furnishing a basis for forming judgments. If we are consistent in approaching history as an expression of what is in man, so that in the course of historical development we see the evolution of the human being, then we will be able to find words for the questions and requirements of the human condition today. It first must be understood that man is an historical being. Unlike the creatures of nature, man and humanity undergo change and metamorphosis in and through history.

In order to see this more clearly, we need an approach that is able to see the various historical formations and events as an expression of the gradual evolution of man. The history of freedom is one aspect of this evolution. Beginning with man's emancipation from nature, it moves on to freedom of thought, finally reaching freedom of action based on knowledge. Another aspect is the history of societal forms. This takes us from the theocracies of the ancient Orient through the city-states of antiquity — where the freedom of the citizens was dependent on the work of slaves — up to present-day society with its division of labor, global trade, and communication that bring together human beings of all races and levels.

Hidden but active within these phenomena is a soul-spiritual development, the symptoms of which can be discerned in art and philosophy, state and economy. Thus, the art of the Renaissance reflects a growing self-awareness in human beings. The political struggles of the modern age reveal the growing concern for the individual and his rights. The literature of our century shows us ever more complex and individual personalities, while the growth of technology signifies a widening of the individual's scope of action. Increasing freedom, increasing rights, increasing contacts and relationships, increasing inner complexity and sphere of influence: all of these characterize the extremely difficult situation of contemporary man. The human being unfolds in history and must be seen in its context; for it is with this human being, with all his requirements and abilities, that we shall be dealing in the future.

Through the various aspects I have mentioned — time, development, setting and structures, and view of history — a sense for history and a social imagination develop. Furthermore, these aspects show us a social and historical life of many layers, within which significant phenomena become noticeable at different points in time. When we look at the beginning of the modern era, for example, we find Renaissance and

Reformation, the sciences and humanism, the voyages of discovery and social upheavals, all speaking to us of a new way of seeing, thinking, and acting. A changed humanity reveals itself in a variety of symptoms, some of them perhaps contradictory to the superficial gaze.

It is here that historical anthropology seeks to penetrate to deeper levels and grasp the motives or impulses that moved human beings. The central concern of historical anthropology always requires that we approach historical facts — like any other expression of the human being — with a view towards their sense and meaning, towards the inner posture they reveal. Historical understanding takes historical events symptomatically; it is not content with mere reconstruction or enumeration of facts. Pedagogically speaking, after all, to present the bare facts is senseless. Events that took place in former years do not repeat themselves and do not yield pragmatic maxims to apply to life. What makes eminent sense, on the other hand, is to practice anthropological contemplation with understanding; for through it one learns something of what is in the human being. This approach to history aims towards an historical symptomatology. In the following chapter the basis of it will be described.

2

HISTORICAL SYMPTOMATOLOGY

The idea of historical symptomatology was developed by Rudolf Steiner. He uses this term in order to draw attention to the basic difference between the pursuit of natural science and that of insight into history. The idea of a symptomalogical approach to history — if not the word symptomatology itself — occurs as early as 1886 in his *Grundlinien einer Erkenntnistheorie der Goetheschen Weltanschauung*. Steiner, continuing Goethe's thinking, shows that when we try to gain knowledge of phenomena in the physical realm, our thinking apprehends the conditions of their appearance by seeking these in the phenomenal world itself. The cognitive approach here consists in ascertaining these basic conditions by experimentally tracing more complex phenomena back to simpler ones. The simplest phenomena Goethe calls archetypal (or "ur-") phenomena. Pursuing knowledge of the organic realm, the investigator meets the living form: the *type*. In order to apprehend the type, first the whole type and the functions of its members or parts must be understood in the context of its way of life and natural environment; and second, the metamorphoses of the type must be traced in their various forms (e.g. egg-caterpillar-butterfly). Thus in the organic realm too, the experience of knowledge is achieved through processes which occur as phenomena.

To gain insight into the inner world of the human being or into history, however, is quite another matter. A simple example can make this clear. When reading, we normally do not attend to the letters or their forms; rather, we penetrate through the words and the sentence to the meaning. As a rule, what the writer wishes to communicate cannot be found on the acoustic or optical plane. We understand what is meant in the sentence by activating within ourselves experiences, mental images, and ideas that can disclose its meaning to us. At the same time, the phenomena of language (e.g. letters, words, voice) are by no means unimportant in this process. What we bring out of our inner world towards these phenomena must meet them so completely as to totally absorb them. Until this has happened, we cannot feel satisfied that we have understood the sentence. Thus letters, words, and all expressions of the human being challenge us to activate and engage our inner world in a definite manner.

The comparison with reading is instructive in other respects as well. Some texts are written in scripts unknown to us: we can do no more than describe the form of the characters. The investigator finds himself in this position in the face of many prehistoric structures — those of Machu Picchu and Carnac, for example, or the monuments of Easter Island. He knows that the "characters" of these "scripts" are of human origin and that they are meaningful, but he does not even perceive the language they speak. On a further level of understanding we succeed in deciphering the script, but the language at first remains unintelligible. At that point we try gradually to get behind the meaning of the expressions by approaching them with conjectures. We ask: What might the subject of this document be? Is it a sacred text or are these practical records of some kind? Such attempts at deciphering are applied to structures like Stonehenge, or to the Pyramids. It is possible to set up certain well-founded hypotheses. We have single words before us, but the meaning of the whole remains hidden. On a third stage of understanding, the text can be deciphered and translated, as is the case with the Egyptian Book of the Dead. And yet even here, the critical researcher is aware that in a deeper sense he still has failed to understand the text. He understands certain words and sentences, but does not know the world to which they refer. It is the situation of a translator without any knowledge of chemistry, who translates a technical text on the manufacture of a new synthetic material. Since he understands nothing of the subject, the translation is likely to be inaccurate. In this sense, to understand a document requires that we can decipher the script and language, and also that we can meet such a text transmitted from earlier times with an understanding of the subject matter involved. Indeed, in many cases it is the understanding of the subject that is crucial; for only when we have that can we interpret the characters and content of the text with certainty.

History, unlike a modern scientific text, does not present us with subjects, contents, or phenomena that can be easily explained by a living specialist. It confronts us with content, views, and behavior that are foreign to us, that we cannot fully explain. Even in our day, we already find it difficult to relate inwardly to nineteenth century ideas of honor. The real religious life of the Middle Ages, with its prolifically attested miracles and visions and the severe, penitential practices of its monks, is not understood but simply disparaged as superstition. And as to the construction of the Pyramids or Stonehenge, the knowledge and conceptions that lay behind it are a riddle to us indeed. The more carefully and exactly research inquires into the heritage of ancient cultures, the greater the riddles become; for the facts themselves rule out crude and simple explanations.

Thus the historian faces a task that is still hardly seen. He must expand his accustomed ways of thinking and knowing; he must acquire new ways of seeing and sensing if he wishes to understand the ancient cultures rather than to "explain them away." It is evident that in the course of history a change in consciousness takes place; and the historian will be able to do it justice only if, for his part, he expands his own consciousness. This expansion of the consciousness is not to be brought about by controlled experimentation (e.g. drugs), but by a "schooling" of the consciousness that involves deepening our own inner experience.

In his anthroposophical portrayal of history, Rudolf Steiner has presented us with the results of historical research based on just such a schooling and extension of the consciousness. The first historical work proper in which he applied this cognitive method to historical events was *Das Christentum als mystische Tatsache und die Mysterien des Altertums* (1902). In this book the ancient Mysteries and Christianity are not treated — as is customary in religious history — by tracing back motifs and ideas to their inception, by noting traditions, influences, and similarities. Rather, the emphasis is placed on understanding the essence and content of the Mysteries and of Christianity in the light of the author's own mystical experience. Rudolf Steiner said: "No one can actually understand the historical truth of documents such as the Gospels who has not first experienced their mystical significance within himself."[1] Today's investigator of religious history will object here that such an approach to knowledge carries the danger that an interpretation derived from extremely subjective experiences could be imposed on the ancient Mysteries. In principle this danger can never be dismissed. In each case, however, one will always be able to distinguish whether the

---

[1] R. Steiner: "Die Übersinnliche Welt und ihre Erkenntnis (1904); now in: Luzifer-Gnosis 1903-1908. Gesammelte Aufsätze, Dornach, 1960, p. 147.

insight rooted in actual mystical experience reveals the content of the text in a meaningful way, without violating it, or whether a mere subjective opinion is being attached to the document. At the same time, the historian of religion will also have to admit that his own interpretation (perhaps one that regards Christianity as a synthesis of various ancient beliefs) is based on a certain subjective opinion regarding the nature of religion — unless he simply limits himself to classifying data without considering their meaning. Here it is methodologically more appropriate to express one's premises and preconceptions, as well as the goals and conditions of the research, and consciously to incorporate these into the cognitive process.

Needless to say, the understanding of mystical and religious texts is not the only task of historical inquiry. History also harbors within itself the general soul-spiritual development of humanity, one expression of which appears in the development of philosophy and art. Looking at the various philosophies from this point of view, we see them as different ways in which the soul seeks to understand the world and itself; and so we are able to recognize the questions and problems of philosophy as an expression of the development of the human soul. Rudolf Steiner wrote such a history of the "inner" development of Europe: *Die Rätsel der Philosophie* (1914). To be sure, this work by no means regards the philosophies and philosophers as agents of this development. Rather, their thinking reflects the changing relationship of the soul to the world and to itself in the course of the centuries. Philosophy by its very nature shows the development of thoughts and of thinking, while music, painting, and poetry manifest changes in ways of seeing and feeling. Both art and philosophy, however, despite all special developments and regional differences, express a most fundamental, general development that also sheds much light on social and political developments. Still, it would be wrong to try to derive the one development from the other. History must be considered as a whole, and all phenomena within it as the expression or the symptom of an integral development.

Before these thoughts are applied to the whole of history in the hope of understanding its social, political, and economic developments, a possible misunderstanding must be forestalled. The symptomatic view of history makes us aware that historical insight depends on knowing and penetrating all the particular facts in question; it seeks the deeper impulses lying behind the symptoms. These general impulses, however, cannot be derived a priori from certain principles of historical knowledge, nor can a general knowledge of soul development be directly applied to the historical facts. History is an empirical science, and in each individual case the historian will have to decipher the language of the symptoms anew. Applying all means of exact study to the sources — that is, through the historical phenomena — he will try to approach what lives within them. Allowing the phenomena to be his teacher, he will seek to recreate and bring to life in his own soul that which gave rise to them.

Thus without any doubt the first task of the historian is exact description of the factual circumstances. This is considerably more difficult in history than it is in the natural sciences, because the attempt must be made to reconstruct the facts using the most varied sources. History is not a given in the way that natural phenomena are. Reconstruction of history shows that the course of events is influenced by highly diverse factors. Natural events break in upon history as from without, setting off or accelerating historical processes. Fixed, established forms of life and stereotyped modes of behavior in time become types that repeat themselves thousands of times by iron necessity. Such life-forms stabilize history; movements that arise relatively suddenly are indicative of new moods, new states of consciousness, crises. They are easily recognizable symptoms.

External Influences

Having reconstructed history with some degree of certainty, we notice that there are quite different types of events, phenomena, and conditions. First, there are events that occur as natural phenomena and yet can have historical significance. Three examples: A torrential flood inundates large areas of dry land and forces the people living there to flee. Perhaps it was such an event that set off the migration of the Cimbri and Teutons. Or: The river that flows by a center of trade becomes choked with silt, and the technology to make it navigable again is lacking. Under certain conditions this trading center will lose its importance, as was the case with the city of Bruges. Or: A disease is introduced into a country, turns epidemic and claims countless victims. In the year 1347 this happened with the plague, which then raged throughout Europe for decades.

It led to a sharp decline in population and left a deep mark on the minds of contemporaries. In these cases, historical events were in fact brought about by natural causes, but the way in which human beings reacted to them shows that such causes turn into something quite different when they enter into history. The actions and changes in attitude towards life that are caused by the natural occurrences enter into the sphere of historical events, and here they no longer follow natural laws: now they are experienced, meaningful deeds and sufferings that are directed within the human consciousness.

The Historical Type: A Life-Form

Secondly, ways of life go through such powerful changes in the course of history that these changes — themselves symptoms of the first order — give rise to certain typical manifestations. The adoption of a sedentary way of life, a particular type in human communal existence, gave rise to the farm village. The high civilizations brought forth the city; the industrial revolution gave birth to factories. As enduring orders of life, these phenomena remain changeable, but they are also quite definite forms and can be recognized in limitless metamorphoses. Moreover, they are also symptoms of a particular cast of mind. One example of an historical type is the towns which began to be founded anew in medieval Europe. Surely these are symptomatic in themselves. This renewed founding gave rise to a particular form: the medieval town. Despite individual and regional variations, the type, with similar inner organization and outer appearance, can easily be recognized. Medieval history knows a great number of such typical formations: the village, the monastery, the castle with its chivalric life, the medieval university. These are forms of life that have become historical; forms which in their every occurrence and in their stages of development can rightly be taken as symptoms, as the expression of an historical impulse. As forms of life, as types, such structures show considerable stability.

There are two starting points towards understanding these symptoms. On the one hand, when the conditions make themselves clearly recognizable, the founding impulse can be examined. In the case of the monasteries a good example is the founding of the Benedictine Order by

Benedict of Nursia. Here the underlying impulse is revealed in the statutes of the order, particularly in its principle of "ora et labora." Through this principle, monasticism, hitherto a flight from this world, is joined to earthly labor. There emerges a well-defined life-form that proves durable. At the same time, the foundation of a monastery creates a space apart from the secular world. The significance and forward-looking quality of this impulse become apparent when we see that later, the Benedictine monasteries everywhere become cultural centers — centers which, by taking up earthly and spiritual tasks, laid the basis of Western European culture. In their buildings, their scriptories and convent gardens, their hospitals, they created islands of peace in a savage world and spheres where the spiritual could become concrete.

The second approach to an understanding of these symptoms is to trace the development of such a life-form. Applying this to monastic culture, we find that it continuously rejuvenated itself by assimilating new impulses — the reforms of Cluny and Citeaux, for example. The towns of the Middle Ages are similar in this respect.

Movements

As an entirely different kind of symptom, we can look at the movements, small and large, that engage or engulf human beings. One may think of the Crusades, the devotio moderna of the later Middle Ages, the witch-hunting mania of early modern times or the less eye-catching movement of Pietism, and also the youth movement of our own century. Such movements are often guided by religious feelings. When we study the Crusades as a symptom, we cannot avoid becoming aware of something questionable, even sick in their driving impulse. The Crusades arose in a Europe shaken to its foundations by the struggle between emperor and pope, a struggle preceded by the West's first dispute over the nature of the Eucharist (Berengar of Tours). The Christians of the West hoped to find in the East something they had lost. Hence the papal summons set off a mass movement — a movement whose questionable character quite early became apparent in the persecution of the Jews at Mainz and Cologne, Speyer and Worms. Cruelty and plundering reached their heights after the storming of Jerusalem in July 1099.

A completely different picture would present itself if we were to study the movement of the Brothers of the Common Life (the devotio moderna). Thus the symptoms visible in historical movements clearly have a superindividual character that stamps the entire movement.

Understanding the Inner Impulses

To understand what is expressed in historical symptoms requires that we gain a comprehensive view, taking in the total setting of the symptom and the consequences resulting from it, be it a movement or a change in a way of life. Attention to the field surrounding the particular phenomenon lends the historian assurance and shows him that he is not chasing after shadows. Ultimately, however, all depends on grasping what underlies the symptom.

For example, when we study the middle years of the nineteenth century — the period from 1830 to 1870 — we find researchers turning with utmost zeal towards a materialistic approach to knowledge. While European thinking had previously pondered and speculated upon the way things in the world are interconnected, now it turned away from grand, comprehensive views to the tangible, to microscopic detail. In 1836 Theodor Schwann discovered the protein-digesting function of pepsin; in 1838 Schleiden established cell theory; in 1839 Schwann discovered the nucleus; in 1841 Köllicker described the fertilization of the egg; and finally, around 1858, these preliminary stages led to Pasteur's bacteriology and Virchow's cellular pathology. It is better known that Marx began to develop his materialistic view of history during these years (starting around 1848); that Darwin published his theory of origins, which Haeckel then linked to the biogenetic principle; that Gobineau propounded his racial theory; and that Büchner, Vogt, and Moleschott preached their crude materialism. The list could be continued. Now, if we wish to go beyond merely registering such symptoms externally, we will try inwardly to re-experience this course of development as it leads from the breadth of the *human* world-view advocated by Humboldt, by Schelling, by Pestalozzi and Owen, by Hegel and Goethe, to the materialistic conception established by such thinkers as Virchow, Haeckel, and Marx. In this process of inner reenactment, we notice not just the transition from idealism to factualism, nor just the contraction of a vast compass of thought to a one-sidedly naturalistic interpretation of phenomena, but also, above all, we notice the combative zeal, the well-nigh religious fervor with which the new dogmas were proclaimed.

Here we see an impulse appear in quite diverse, superficially even contradictory directions of thought. In philosophy, it appears both in the ideas of Eugen Duehring (in drastic form) as well as in those of his opponent Friedrich Engels. It occurs in the social Darwinism of Winwood Reade, for example, and finally triumphs in the late philosophy of Nietzsche. When we contemplate the nature of this peculiar impetus, we become aware that it is not the sort of thing that results from a sober assimilation of the facts brought to light by science. It begins to appear much more as the expression of a will that takes possession of humanity like a spiritual epidemic, and then takes on popular form in the turn towards *realpolitik*, exaggerated nationalism, imperialism, antisemitism, and materialism in both thought and practice.

Looked at in this way, the impulse active in history is not merely a problem in the history of philosophy. We experience it as a total change in ways of thinking and seeing and also as a force that possesses the soul, evoking very strong feelings and judgments and finally resulting in a cast of mind that sets its stamp on human action.

Changes in the View of History

The dominant views of history look at it as a large network of causal links, thus assuming that what came earlier causes what comes later. It is in their weighting of the different factors that the various views differ. The materialistic conception of history sees economic processes and structures as the factors that actually shape history — the political institutions and ideas of an age are viewed as a political and ideological superstructure. To overstate it slightly, according to this paradigm the Reformation can be seen "as the ideological expression of radical changes in the European wool market." An idealistic approach to history, on the other hand, will seek the causes of the Reformation in certain ideas, tracing these in the history of thought back to Wycliffe, Hus, and the nominalistic stream of thought, and emphasizing Luther's development before the Reformation. In any case, however — even in more complex views of history — the earlier is taken as the cause of the later. Both Hegel and Marx see history as a development that is "lawful" in this sense — a development which, despite dialectic reversals and leaps, is ultimately continuous. This concept of connection and causality also gives rise to the notion that with sufficient knowledge of the historical factors one can predict future developments.

Over against this view Rudolf Steiner, in his lectures on historical symptomatology (1918), stresses the discontinuity or "openness" of history. As an idea this is easy to understand if one starts from the premise of freedom. Assuming men were free beings, capable of making their own decisions, taking responsibility, and acting freely, then — when freedom is a reality — causality would necessarily be interrupted. Through freedom, new impulses would continually flow into history. Certainly, such argumentation by hypothesis is insufficient for an analysis of history. Nevertheless, an historian who proceeds empirically can also arrive at a view that comes very close to that of Rudolf Steiner in this respect. Geoffrey Barraclough, in the introduction to the book *Tendencies of History in the 20th Century*, writes: "In my view continuity is by no means the most striking feature of history. Bertrand Russell once said that the universe is composed wholly of points and leaps [*The Scientific Outlook*, 1931, p. 98], and my impression of history is almost identical. At each great turning point of the past we are faced by the chance and unforeseen, the new and dynamic, the revolutionary. As Herbert Butterfield once pointed out, at such moments the usual arguments of causality are by no means alone sufficient to explain the next stage, the next development, the next turn in events."

An exact analysis of the historical process could describe how people make decisions. First, one would have to examine the situation requiring a decision; second, one would have to find out how the person or group who had to reach the decision was informed of the situation; and third — which is where it becomes interesting — one must discover how, based on this information, the situation was perceived and evaluated. It is no secret that human beings will understand one and the same report in very different ways. Situations are not necessarily straightforward. One can misunderstand situations or meet them with a routine reaction; one can also attach hopes or fears to them. The decision on a course of action is often linked up with all kinds of intentions. We are impelled by motives. Motives vary from person to person. Their influence is already felt in the way a situation is perceived, and works on in the actor's intention. The actor, however, does not know the future. In a stable situation the behavior of others may be in part predictable. Previous experiences, particular opinions or theories will provide a halfway reliable orientation in deciding the course to be taken. In a complex situation, however, or in one that is rapidly changing, where new forms are entering existence, the consequences of one course of action are hardly calculable. Hence assuming the action is not taken on impulse — which is quite often the case — one can only say: the actor is motivated by certain definite expectations and intentions, and these determine his interpretation of the situation. And that is precisely why mistakes can happen and why it is difficult to foresee the results of the action. Thus the notorious capitalist orients his decisions not to profit per se, but to the expectation that one or another course of action will bring profit. Yet careful observation would disclose that such unequivocal motivations are rare. Without doubt, an economic action can be guided by the motive of security, of responsibility to a firm and its employees, *and* by desire for profit. Fiascos and bankruptcies, however, prove that the situation is often evaluated "wrongly." It is even more difficult to plan or calculate actions that are intended to make politics and history on a grand scale. The French revolutionaries of 1792 certainly had something rather different in mind than the advent of Napoleon. Napoleon, for his part, "mis-"calculated the consequences of his Russian campaign.

Thus in history we are not dealing with clear-cut facts that have definite effects; we are dealing chiefly with the factor of human consciousness. Consciousness constantly interrupts what comes at the human being from the outside. Through this break, situations and facts lose any singleness of meaning; for they are apprehended by human beings with different ways of seeing and thinking, with different intentions and dispositions. This becomes especially interesting to observe at times when new ideas move men, giving their seeing and thinking a new orientation. In a relatively short time, old situations once felt to be normal and acceptable may be given a wholly new valuation. The more general and basic such new ideas or feelings are, the less we can foresee what their effects will be when they have turned into practical guidelines for action.

The significance of ways of thinking and seeing can also be read in the history of the various peoples. Thus, wealth or poverty can be taken in quite different ways. Under certain circumstances, poverty leads to ever increasing misery and helplessness. People feel their want and poverty acutely and expect help from the outside. Yet when it comes, if it is merely accepted passively, it brings no improvement. At the same time, poverty, like necessity, can be "the mother" of invention and industriousness. People can respond to need and poverty with a spirit of inventiveness and hard work. History also shows us situations where great amounts of money or gold, or credit, have flowed into a region or nation. In one instance this wealth becomes the foundation for general affluence; in another it fails to be utilized productively, and after a while the nation is poorer than before.

A further and very important observation can be added to these — one that clearly shows that history is by no means shaped by the causes stemming from the past. Some societies that developed a definite form and order in the past, after a time, decay. The old structures become brittle and the forms of behavior lose their hold. History provides examples of such slowly crumbling or stagnating societies. On the other hand, there are examples of societies that have repeatedly renewed themselves. As a rule, the renewal takes place in this way: A few human beings conceive in thoughts and feelings an idea of a new society, a new order. They make themselves a practical picture of the future and stake new aims. With few exceptions such new aims do not stem from the past, even though the group bearing the new goals may present them as a restoration of a supposed old order. In such a way, a society can renew itself again and again through future-impulses, impulses grasped through the moral and social imagination of human beings.

Finally, a further circumstance deserves mention here. In physics, causality is spoken of in terms of the law "action = reaction," i.e. the effect corresponds to the cause. In history, however, different planes of existence always interact. Small causes can have great effects. A tiny fire destroys a whole city — that is a physical process. A minor human inattentiveness can bring death to more than a hundred people. A murderer can kill a statesman for personal reasons and so, perhaps, thwart a process of social conciliation. Thus, causes that appear small from the physical point of view can have enormous repercussions on the social and human level. The opposite is true as well: actions undertaken with monumental effort and expense can in many ways remain without effect.

The scheme below, though it is naturally an oversimplification of the many-dimensional interplay of forces, impulses, phenomena, and goals that go into the *vortex of history*, might provide a helpful overview to teachers as well as to students in the upper grades:

impulses
inventions
new ways of seeing

foundations prerequisites inherited structures		goals, intentions necessities of the future, hopes

external influences, e.g.
natural catastrophes
isolated actions
diseases

Each of these elements gives rise to totally different kinds of formations, forces, obstacles, and effects. *Impulses, inventions,* and *new ways of seeing* can lastingly transform the life and thinking of human beings. *Goals, intentions,* and *hopes* motivate individuals or groups. Here we can speak of success or failure, and here quite unintentional side-effects can develop. The *foundations* must never be underrated: without a centrally located capital like Paris, the French Revolution would have taken a very different course; without the Nile, no Egyptian culture; without coal and iron ore, no industrial revolution in England. Of themselves, however, the foundations can bring forth nothing: they are the necessary basis upon which history "plays." *External influences* can be of a human or a natural kind. To European culture, the invasion of the

Hungarians, Mongols, and Turks was an outside influence. For Japan and China, the breaking of European-American culture into their history was an outside influence. At the same time, we must also count the gradual drying up of the Sahara since 10,000 B. C., or the plague in the fourteenth and fifteenth centuries, among the outer influences that have had a significant effect on history.

Thus history appears altogether as a loosely knotted rug whose irregular patterns and pictures speak of human development, of spiritual impulses — some helping, some hindering — which are revealed and at the same time hidden in the pictures.

In a scientific treatise, these observations would be given more extended and exact treatment. The historical significance of preconditions, causes, reasons, goals, ways of seeing, attitudes, and motives would be discussed in greater detail. For history instruction in school, we are concerned first with the practical insights they provide. Having freed ourselves of the idea that history is a continuous process of cause and effect, we will feel freer to concentrate on those themes which we consider important, i.e. symptomatic. We will not think it impossible to take up the Reformation without having first worked through the Middle Ages. We find the courage to "leave out." And we will not be tempted to construct "causal chains" of the kind that were popular after 1945. At that time, Hitler was traced back to Bismarck, Bismarck to Frederick the Great, and Frederick the Great to Luther ("Germany's misfortunes began with Luther"). Rather, we will restrict ourselves to certain representative themes and leave as much time as possible for them.

Beyond practical help, this approach opens a further possibility for the teacher. He can say: Not all of history speaks to me to the same degree. Certain occurrences or processes interest me tremendously; something I experience in them still occupies me on the feeling level, something I can understand in a deeper way than many other things. If I begin my private preparations on these themes and in good time, through them I will learn to grasp history personally, to penetrate from the symptoms to the impulses that shape it. And with the passage of time, the teacher's interest will broaden. What is crucial for the students is to experience a teacher, and through the teacher, history: history that has inner meaning, that speaks to the human being and generates enthusiasm.

In this way ultimately a kind of history teaching can arise in which historical insight deepens human insight, since history will be illuminated by the inner discoveries and experiences of the human soul. Then the great battles and developments of history will not appear as indifferent facts that are required knowledge, nor will they simply serve as examples for interpreting political events. Rather, they will become material on which the soul can awaken, in which it can discover itself and its will.

3

AN EXAMPLE OF THE SYMPTOMATIC APPROACH: HISTORY AS SOUL DEVELOPMENT

Sentient Soul and Intellectual Soul

The life of the human soul can be regarded from various points of view. One of these is to trace the emergence of independence and inwardness in soul-life. Certainly this is not meant to imply that the soul is "built up" one stage at a time. The soul-life is always a whole, and the entire soul is always alive within it. Nevertheless, it is only slowly and gradually that the soul gains a consciousness of its functions. From this point of view, the first prerequisite for an independent soul-life is the forming of mental images *of one's own*, which the soul is able to retain and then recall. Note that we are speaking here of mental images of one's own, not of mental images generally. In a second stage, the concepts living within these mental images emerge and are connected with one another according to their thought content. In this stage, the soul frees itself from the mental images through a process of abstraction. Finally, in a third stage, the soul recognizes itself as the creator of its own thoughts. It now seeks consciously and independently to give form to these thoughts from within, to apply them to the world, and also to orient itself according to such self-created thoughts.

Rudolf Steiner, who employed this view of soul-life and described it is his works *Theosophy and Occult Science*, designates the three stages as follows: The first stage towards independence, when the soul still orients itself on the sensory content of mental images and is one with this, he calls the sentient-soul. The second stage, when the thought emerges from the mental image, when thinking becomes conceptual, Steiner calls the intellectual-soul. And the third stage, when the soul is able to consciously structure its own activity, he names consciousness-soul.

When we turn to history and wish to study the corresponding phases of cultural development, it is good to begin by observing the stages of soul-development in ourselves. Tracing the formation of mental images, we find we can distinguish two kinds. In one case, mental images take form from without. Phenomena make their impressions upon us. We experience cold and rain, wind and sun, field and woods. And we learn to designate certain things or processes with words, naming them bear, creek, or tree. In the other kind of mental image formation, in addition to naming, our own activity enters in. A person who has turned the garden with a spade or worked with an axe knows more about "spade" and "axe" than one who has only looked at them. Whoever has built a table or made a clay pot really knows what a table or pot is. The more we are connected with things through doing and making, the more developed and clear our mental images become. Similarly, when we model or draw an object, at very least we absorb its form into our own activity and our mental images grow concrete and rich. On the other hand, whenever we merely give names or dwell within the phenomena, our mental images gain little concreteness; we have not really made them our own. A concrete mental picture born of our own activity is always accompanied by a feeling for the thing or matter, an intuitive knowledge of the way it functions.

A mental image produced from without is linked only with naming. What it experiences of things is essentially their effects: we feel cold or warmth; we sense taste; the world affects us pleasantly or unpleasantly; we feel drawn toward certain phenomena, while others repel us and we flee them. On this level, knowledge of the things is linked with their directly experienced presence. Indeed, since we still have no inner space of self-created mental images into which we can withdraw, the impressions made by the world may be experienced with much greater intensity. A mental image that we have created through our own activity can be held, stored for us in our memory: we have it even when the object is not there. Indeed, on the model of such mental images we can form an entire world-conception, filled with figures that act purposefully and vividly and so give form to the world. In other words, we have a world made by gods who act in their own manner and give it form. Thus, over against the impressions from the world we set mental representations and pictures of our own, and in these we assert ourselves.

In history, the first real development of "own" mental images is found in the ancient cultures. These ancient cultures have the distinguishing feature of creating cities, a realm rich in human activities and removed from nature. Around the city, the irrigation of the land is planned and regulated; canals and dikes are built. Within the city the numerous different crafts develop: smiths, cartwrights, weavers, masons, and millers are at work here. Stones are dressed; artists create statues and paintings. And most significantly, pictographs serve to record what needs to be recorded. One example of such a culture is Egypt. Indeed, we have visible evidence of the Egyptians' concrete mental images: the numerous paintings and sculptures found in graves and temples give a pictorial rendition of practically every aspect of their lives. Furthermore, the pictographs (or hieroglyphs) — even when they are used as phonetic symbols — are also representatives of an inner pictorial world. The figures of the gods as well were pictured in a wealth of images. Once they achieved finality, forms were preserved and handed down for centuries with a precision that itself testifies that this was a culture of mental pictures. Images and types, once conceived, were retained in a definite form: the image of the pharaoh, the image of the state, the image of the gods, the representations of the afterlife — all remained stable for millennia.

This constancy stems from a world that was fashioned ever again by the same procedures, by artisans and farmers, by builders and priests. The shape of the world was known through many individual involvements with work; and from particular aspects, it was preserved in images — very much as the human form itself was preserved through mummification. However, no concepts were formed. Since water was known in the form of the Nile alone, all water occurring elsewhere was simply "the Nile that comes down from the sky to cast waves on the mountains like an ocean and moisten the fields." The Tigris and Euphrates, which flowed from north to south and not — like the Nile — from south to north, were "the circling waters that flow downstream by flowing upstream." The picture of the world takes shape from the phenomena, and goes no further than the phenomena as they take form in mental representations.

When we wish to observe how our soul life develops from representation to intellect, we need but detach activities from their concrete, traditional forms and examine them as to their function. Action is then perceived as a causing, forming, or resisting done with respect to intentions, aims, and purposes; and the particular form of action appears as a means to the end. It is now possible to imagine that educating or governing can be done in different ways. Similarly, one and the same thing can now be recognized in various forms: water as ice, as steam, or as liquid. The moment this is possible, it is also possible to enter into conversation about the appropriate form of action, to discuss and compare, to imagine possibilities and see alternatives. In this way a world of thoughts comes into being. In the realm of nature, we recognize not only things, but also principles and conditions of creation, growth, and procreation; we recognize classes, commonalities, and differences. From the visible, we learn to infer the invisible: since all things are created, we infer an underlying source of all creation. And the rules behind such deduction and argumentation can be formulated as laws: logic is born.

When we have reached this degree of mental freedom, we can think of different ways of portraying and expressing things; we are no longer bound to traditional ways. We proceed from a theme conceived in our minds, and seek to give it form again and again in new ways. Thus we become acquainted with the forces that create expression, and we naturally regard these creative forces as more important than what they create. Whoever has acquired such an ability to perceive creative forces, expression, and design in human activity is then able to wonder about what acts creatively in the world, and may perhaps inquire after the "plan" that underlies everything and manifests itself in expression and symbol. Still, at this level of development the highest aims and purposes of action are experienced as given, as necessities of nature. Just as the simple craftsman sees his work as following natural laws or the thinker sees himself as grasping natural forces in thought, we apprehend the highest aims and purposes as God-given or dictated by human nature. Certainly, it is possible to have doubts about particular purposes — skepticism is possible — but in principle we are convinced of the objective validity of universal laws, the objective validity of an ethic, and the objective existence of God, even if particular doubts and divergent representations arise.

Historically, this stage of soul development is met with in the Greeks, Romans, and Jews, as well as in medieval times. When Thales asserted that water is the basic element of the world, he was following the workings of water through all its forms. When Heraclitus recognized that it is the word through which all human beings communicate, on which they orientate themselves, and in which they find the law that guides action, he recognized the ordering principle of thinking in the word. Solon, with his carefully considered legislation, gives us a remarkable example of rational planning at work in his drafting of the Athenian constitution: the law was carefully designed to meet the city's needs. Ninety years later Cleisthenes was to reform this law, adapting it to new needs. It is significant that the Athenians placed trust in such regulations based upon agreement, that they were willing to be ruled by the law rather than by a man. They relied upon the achievements of the intellect. In art, too, it was not a matter of retaining tried and true conceptions, but of constantly inventing new things. The themes of the ancient legends take on ever new and different form in the hands of Aeschylus, Sophocles, and Euripides. In sculpture, the portrayal of the human being changed. Often such works of art — in the Parthenon, for example — reveal an intellectual meaning, an idea, or in any case a composition.

In this culture of reason, after a certain time of preparation, the intellect was publicly cultivated in democratic discussion and trained in school. In Aristotle's philosophy the rules of reasoning, of logical thinking, were also understood. Such facts make it clear that life-forms and ideas were in accordance, both being determined by the principle of reason. At the same time, it is evident that a notion of values and an inner attitude of respect towards them were a natural, unquestioned element of life in this culture. The oracles and mysteries were revered. The instructions sent forth from Delphi and other places were widely observed; and significantly, they were heeded by such a questioning thinker as Socrates, who had developed the human faculty of reason to its full.

In the culture of Rome, reason was now applied to the social realm. The significance of law and legal process was recognized. As the Greeks had brought logic to its flowering, so the Romans developed a sense for legal and political procedures. Knowledge of the law, instilled by rote into the children at school, was taken for granted. Above all, however, Roman civilization put the intellect to the service of practical endeavors. Roads, aqueducts, thermal baths, giant sewage systems, and houses with heated floors were constructed, making life comfortable. In addition, there was was an imperial postal service, a food-preserving industry, and much else that demanded considerable thought and planning. While the intelligence of the Greeks was directly chiefly towards cosmic events and common social processes, among the Romans it was applied to concrete and practical interests. In Rome the subjective rights of the individual citizen, stable and useful architecture, and the *commercium* (trade) were developed in grand style. Finally, among the Jews the intellectual element manifested itself in a religion of law.

During the Middle Ages intellectual knowledge was re-acquired in a most remarkable manner, as the authors of antiquity gradually became known once again. Under the sign of Christian religion, the entire body of antique thinking was rethought: it was sifted, ordered, and eventually brought into a system. The procedure was meticulous. For each question, major or minor, a collection was made of all the known statements of the ancient philosophers, the Bible, and the church fathers, including council resolutions. By means of a yes/no procedure, the sentences were then either accepted or rejected, or freshly interpreted. Thus, through careful discussion of all important questions, a new thought-picture of the world emerged out of the old body of ideas. What is significant about this process is that at this stage of development the ideas are no longer derived naively from nature, as it were, but appear as thoughts that have been thought before. Their truth is no longer tested against nature, but is determined according to Christian dogma. In this way the world of ideas acquires an historical dimension: every thought has its author or authors, its history, its friends and foes. The ordering principle of thought has shifted inward: the cosmos of thought no longer aligns itself with the natural phenomena; rather, truth is determined through the revelation of the spirit inherent in the Christian religion.

The social life of the Middle Ages evolves through various phases. At first we see forms of culture which in many ways are still at a very early stage of development. The assimilation of culture, however, and the evolution of social life were influenced by certain historically inherited thoughts. Thus, we see a desire to renew the Roman Empire — the title "kaiser" for emperor is derived from Caesar. The week is introduced from the Judeo-Christian realm. Monasticism, with its strict adherence to the rules of Benedict of Nursia, is a form of life dating back to late antiquity. The Christian orientation of thought manifests itself quite clearly in the Crusades. Adoption of the Roman legal tradition is recognizable in canonical law. The most impressive embodiment of inherited thought, however, is to be traced in the conception of the Gothic cathedrals. In them everything — from the floor plan to the form of the roof, from the lighting arrangements to the figures and column — is charged with thought and meaning.

The Development of the Consciousness-Soul

The sentient soul, in its activity of forming mental images, is still completely given over to external stimulation through sense impressions. It forgets its own activity, seeing the object as the sole determining factor. The intellect too is outward directed: stimulated by observations and mental images, it believes that it draws the thoughts from the objects. The criterion for truth is whether the thoughts correspond to objective reality or not. It is not until the stage of the consciousness-soul that a new insight slowly dawns: it is our own activity, our own way of seeing and hearing, our own thoughts that give things their particular profile in our apprehension of them; it is our dealings with and relation to things that elicit that characteristic of them that we put into thoughts. The reversal of attention towards this personal activity amounts to a veritable Copernican revolution. Through it the outer world takes on an entirely different significance. To be sure, this new consciousness only slowly gains a foothold in us, especially since the other attitudes of soul live on. The first thing we become aware of is the significance of our own inner attitude altogether. In all I do and think — so we feel — the important thing is that I myself stand behind it, that I am identical with my action, that I am convinced of my thoughts, that I am really able to carry out what I think. We further notice that each individual regards the world from a different standpoint and that things have many different aspects; and we would like to explore them with this in mind. As our self-awareness is heightened in this way, it leads to unconventional actions, each of them following particular plans of our own. Then, at a further stage, we wish to recreate the world ourselves, while before we primarily looked at and inwardly processed it. No longer satisfied with nature alone, we want to shape it according to our own thoughts and intentions. Particularly at this point, the danger arises of falling back into the attitude of the intellect: forgetting there is an activity on our own part, forgetting our conscious, questioning experimentation, we believe that our thoughts portray the world just as it is.

As soon as this self-awareness is fully developed, a new difficulty presents itself, manifesting in two forms. The self-conscious ego (or "I") now reflects, wondering as to its position in the world. One question is: How do the thoughts that I produce from within me relate to the world? Do they have any significance for the world? How do I arrive at all at forming thoughts about the world? Do my thoughts portray the world or are they something that exists independently within the things? The other question concerns the coexistence of the many independent "I's" in the world. If the chief concern of the "I" is our personal conviction and independent action in freedom, how are individuals supposed to live together in society; how can it be organized? Is free unfoldment of the individuality consonant with life in society? At this point of development it is crucial that the consciousness-soul experience the "I" within it not just as the producer of self-determined activity; rather the "I" must come to experience its own contents more consciously. Out of the "I," out of this point of freedom, new intuitions must be born that lead beyond the individual "I." In contrast to rational constructions and thoughts about reality, here the power of the "I" must bring something new to the world. The organ for grasping new intuitions is the imagination. When we consciously experience a community, for example, our imagination can give birth to an intuition as to how this community of equal and free individuals might be newly shaped through activity of our own and of all in common. The imagination forms a picture of the individuals in the community and of their hidden possibilities, asking how these possibilities might be coaxed out and promoted. Social intuition born out of imagination in this way is able to create something new, something that has arisen consciously from the human "I" and yet is part of the real matter at hand. Out of the spirit of freedom and an inner perception of others, such imagination shapes new social realities.

Similarly, imagination can try to help and shape the process of nature. In freely conceived pictures, it can visualize how to heal an ailing landscape, shaping the natural processes in such a way that man and nature, wood, meadow, field, tree, bush, and animal all complement one another in harmony with human life and work. By such creations of the spirit, the human being imbues the world with a spiritual content. New possibilities are lured out of the being of what exists already. Out of the spirit, a wholesome future is drawn into the present. This future is not simply an extension of the past, as the intellect sees it (or as it is described in "futurologies"): it is the future born from within the "I," a human world reborn. In anthroposophical study of the human being, the "I" that absorbs the spirit of the world into itself in this way is called the "spirit-self." The consciousness-soul can develop further only when it opens itself up to the spirit-self in the way we have described.

When such future-oriented development is not possible or is not sought, evolution takes a problematic course. True, the demand for the different freedoms remains alive in the soul, and one seeks access to the world; but the means for realization are those of the intellect (though now it makes use of the fruits of the consciousness-soul: technology), and the search for integration into the world finds fulfillment in the exercise of power or in self-gratification. In this way one finds one's own will mirrored in the world, and one realizes one's own wishes by directly seizing all that one wants. When this does not succeed, and when freedom is not consciously shaped either, the consciousness-soul sinks into loneliness, dissatisfaction, and melancholy. It falls into a state of dull brooding: subjectivity and wretched stewing in its own juices.

The Development of the Consciousness-Soul as Mirrored in History

In history, the development of the consciousness soul falls into quite definite phases. These developmental stages can be studied in the course of historical events; yet at the same time history in turn casts a certain light on the inner development of the individual.

a) Upheavals before the appearance of the consciousness-soul. Before the actual appearance of the consciousness-soul, one notices a remarkable process of dissolution, even self-destruction, of the hierarchical social systems that were the outer reflection of the mental order of the intellectual-soul. First we see emperor and pope — both of them representatives of the highest principles of order — fighting one another until the old universal empire collapses (1250). Then the papacy, having formulated its universal claim to supremacy in the bull "Unam Sanctam" (1302), itself falls prey to a particular power: it comes under the influence of the French king and its seat is moved to Avignon in 1309. Finally, in 1378, we arrive at the great schism: two popes are elected, one in Rome and the other in Avignon. To the medieval mind, this signified nothing less than the world had first jumped off its axis and then fallen to pieces. Confusion spread its tentacles. What was one supposed to take as a guide now? The center of the system, the capstone of the whole edifice was in jeopardy. This disintegration of church authority was rounded off with a mighty basso profundo by an event of elemental fury which, over the next two centuries, repeatedly shook Europe to its very core: In 1347, the plague had crept into Europe by way of Genoa. The withered hand of death reached mainly into the big cities. Often a third of the population succumbed within a few months to the deadly breath of the pestilence.

The psychic effects of these experiences is revealed in a new phenomenon: the picture of death in the arts. Everywhere in Europe there appeared frescoes, woodcuts, sculptures, and written works on the theme of death. One may think of the *Triumph of Death* by Francesco Traini on the Campo Santo in Pisa, of the *Danse Macabre*, a woodcut by Holbein, of the *Everyman* drama enacted throughout Europe; of the *Ackermann aus Boehmen* by Johannes Tepl, and of hundreds of other works all revolving around death. In fact the decay of the body, the frailty of the world, and the death experience are the basis of the actual development of the consciousness-soul. After the upheaval in church tradition, the loss of trust in the pope and other high dignitaries of the Church, and the lesson that "nothing stands before the scythe of death," the hitherto valid forms of consciousness lost the ground they stood upon. Neither Church nor nature promised lasting security. Each single individual had to fall back upon himself.

One of the first symptoms of this new state of the world is found in John Wycliffe's (1320-1384) interpretation of the Holy Sacrament. Wycliffe could no longer believe that bread and wine were objectively transformed into the body and blood of Christ during Holy Communion. Thus he denied the real presence of Christ in the bread and wine. This was the beginning of the view that holds the significance of

Holy Communion to lie within the subject: each individual's memory of the Christ's Last Supper makes the bread and wine outward symbols of the Communion, but the latter takes place essentially through subjective memory. Thus Wycliffe provides an example on which we can directly observe how the human being was forced to fall back upon himself and his own inner resources. What is more, here the connection between the new condition of soul and the shaking of papal authority by the schism can be demonstrated especially well.

b) First Symptoms. The individual, cast upon his own resources, now began to reorient himself in the world from his own viewpoint. Early art endeavored to paint things "the way they are," emphasizing their objective meaning. A personal standpoint or way of seeing things did not come into play. Now, however, painters began to apprehend things from their own standpoint. The result was perspective, which describes the objects in space from the painter's particular standpoint. Beyond this, the desire awakened to explore the world on one's own. Ancient and medieval navigation had been essentially coastal navigation. Now, with better measuring devices and new astronomical knowledge and theories, it was possible to calculate one's own position on the open sea. Here it is impossible to see where one is located: it must be calculated on the basis of theories, knowledge, and measuring instruments. Thus, action is no longer guided by the immediate data of the senses, but by thinking. Africa was circumnavigated and America discovered in this way; and the pride of self-awareness was alive in these discoveries. This feeling of self, this self-confidence, finds expression in self-portraiture and autobiography. Self-reliance is also manifested in a figure like Martin Luther. Despite some hesitation, he dared to stand up against emperor and empire, pope and Church, protesting council decisions and the whole of tradition. He remained steadfast in convictions drawn purely from within himself: the soul is responsible directly to God; it needs no mediator. The echo that he found showed that hundreds of thousands now thought as he did. Their conviction was gained from the Bible alone, by recourse to the original sources. They too no longer needed a go-between, a priest; for they could read and interpret the Holy Scriptures themselves.

In the domain of social life, the idea of human rights appeared for the first time. The idea of universal human rights was unknown to ancient times and early Christianity, both of which had affirmed slavery. Now every single human being, every "subject," had a claim to respect. In their Twelve Articles (1525), the peasants demanded that the community be allowed not only to choose its priest but also to depose him should he fail to preach the Gospel in a pure manner. They also — chiefly — demanded no longer to be vassals, since Christ, in shedding His precious blood, had freed and saved the least among them no less than those of noble birth. Thus the hierarchical thinking that grasps and orders society "from above" encounters the impulse "from below" — the impulse of social self-determination through freedom and equality.

c) From the outside to the inside. This new spirit, this new attitude, led to new investigation. The mind was not satisfied to look at the known and explore the unknown from its own standpoint. There was a will to penetrate the depths, to get behind the phenomena. It was only the foregoing experience of death which had made this possible. The world of appearances was fallible: it was no longer seen chiefly as the miracle work of God, as the book of nature in which we are to read and whose revelations we are to accept. No, this world belongs to death. A dead world can be examined: one can dissect it and experiment with it. During the Renaissance, Leonardo Da Vinci and a few others had already begun studies in anatomy. In 1543 Andreas Vesalius presented the first great anatomical work: *De Humani Corporis Fabrica*. Then, in 1618 William Harvey discovered the dual system of blood circulation, and in 1628 this discovery was published in his work: *De Motu Cordis et Sanguini.*

It is characteristic of this kind of research that it first penetrates through the sensory appearances and then seeks to mentally reconstruct what was dissected. The new astronomy proceeded analogically. To begin with, Copernicus advanced a theory that — contrary to all appearances — the earth and planets move in orbits around the sun (*De revolutionibus orbium coelestium*, 1543). Kepler then corrected this thesis in his *Astronomia Nova* (1609), describing the planetary orbits more exactly — as ellipses — and formulating the laws of motion mathematically. Finally Newton, in his *Philosophiae naturalis principia mathematica* (1687), demonstrated the mechanical, material nature and dynamics of these movements through the laws of inertia, force, impulse, and gravitation. The old picture of the world, like the dissected body, was thus externally destroyed and then reconstructed mentally. This reconstruction is particularly clear when, as with Kepler and Newton, it is formulated purely in mathematical laws: out of its own activity the soul creates a completely new picture of the cosmos. In this thought process, which constructs nature anew out of pure concepts, the human being experiences himself as the creator of his own thoughts.

Hence it is no coincidence that in the century of Kepler and Newton such a man as Rene Descartes was living. Descartes too was a mathematician and natural philosopher. As the creator of analytic geometry, which describes the world mathematically from a single point, he had described movements mathematically. It is in this activity of mental construction, which one produces oneself and gets neither from without nor from tradition, that the conscious ego dwells. And so it is that Descartes arrived at the statement: "It is thinking alone that cannot be separated from me. I am, I exist; that is certain. But how long? Well, as long as I am thinking!" So the self-awareness of the "I" grasps itself, in conscious mental construction of the world — and to Descartes it was an external world of space (res extensa), a dead, mechanical world.

In these events we recognize the first appearance of the con-sciousness-soul. Because it separates itself from living nature and confronts it, the soul perceives nature as "dead," as merely mechanical. It draws a line between this dead world and its own inwardness. And inwardness par excellence is pure thought, as it occurs in the activity of mathematical construction: this has not been taken from a process of modeling or picturing external nature, but solely from the inner activity of the soul.

In social life as well, derivations of this form of self-consciousness occur. Absolutism, in the political realm, is the attempt to construct the life of the state in the same way as physics had mentally constructed the world. In this system the king appears as the absolute "I," constructing the world anew out of itself: he has streets, canals, and factories built; he organizes foreign trade, establishes a uniformed standing army, and — most significantly — constructs a bureaucratic apparatus dependent on and taxable by him alone. In accordance with this idea, any other power is suppressed, declared dead. Absolutism rises on the ruins of ducal power and the destroyed independence of the Huguenot cities. Even the architecture of the streets of Versailles, which all run towards the center of the royal castle, symbolizes the rule of one single "I." Needless to say, in social reality this principle of absolute rule had its limits and did not function.

In England the attempts of the king to import the French system foundered as the many "I's" rose up against the single "I." Following the principle "my home is my castle," each one of them demanded its own freedoms, its own inner space. In Germany the corresponding period was marked by the Thirty Years' War and its consequences. In it one can recognize the crisis of a will to independence that still lacks a content that might orientate it and lead to new social forms.

d) New depth and abstraction. The search for new social forms, once under way, did not remain in the hands of the few. Beyond criticism of the old existing social forms, which went hand in hand with ever more radical criticism of traditional religion, wide sections of eighteenth century society also knew a lively ferment of ideas concerning the new state, the state of the future. Two thinkers stand out: Montesquieu and Rousseau. Montesquieu, in the interests of freedom, undertook to draft a thought-picture of the new state and arrived at the idea of the division of powers. Rousseau, on the other hand, proceeded radically. In his *Contrat Social* he constructed a new commonwealth based on the principle of equality. This construction rests upon axioms and unconsciously follows the thought-scheme of the natural sciences of that time. In the French Revolution, however, the attempt to construct a social reality out of Rousseau's conceptions foundered: the bloody terror of Robespierre and his followers finally ended with the rule of Napoleon. Montesquieu's more sketchy recommendations, aimed at a few practical measures, have demonstrated the possibility of social modeling. His recommendations became the basis for a constitution in the United States that is still functioning today, albeit in amended form. Subsequent developments, however — in particular the unjust conditions found everywhere (not excluding the United States) — have made it clear that the task of creating a community of free and equal human beings on a foundation of brotherhood is still with us today.

While the French Revolution was attempting to fundamentally transform society, dissolving old bonds of sovereign authority and shaping new relationships, the natural sciences began to delve deeper into nature, also dissolving bonds, separating, and making new connections. It no longer sufficed to reconstruct mathematically the movements of solid bodies. Experimentation made it possible to analyze substances and create new syntheses. The era of chemistry had begun. In 1766 Cavendish discovered hydrogen; in 1771 and 1774 Scheele and Priestley discovered oxygen; in 1772 Rutherford discovered nitrogen; and soon thereafter the true nature of combustion was recognized. The gate to chemical analysis and synthesis had been opened. Another chain of investigations led still deeper into nature. The discovery that was being made in stages was that of electricity, and to the eyes of the the romantic nature-philosophers it already appeared as the fundamental principle of the world. When, in 1831, Michael Faraday succeeded in producing electric currents by means of motion, by changing the magnetic field, access was gained to a force hitherto hidden in nature. A force of which no direct sensory perception whatever is possible could now be produced at will and transformed in many ways. All energies known up till then — wind, water, fire, and coal — were somehow of an objective nature: they appeared openly in nature. Here, however, an energy had been created that was intangible. As it turned out, it could be transported through wires to distant points and transformed into heat or cold, movement or light. It was capable of stimulating chemical processes and carrying information. Was this not the universal key to nature, the highest possible abstraction of all natural phenomena?

Simultaneously with this progress in natural science, the exploration of the human spirit had also advanced, passing by way of Descartes' principle "I think." Taking Kant as their starting point, the philosophers Fichte, Hegel, and Schelling had arrived at the gate of the pure ego. They had discovered that the "I" creates itself through its own activity, forming the power of thinking from within. In those years Novalis had jotted a note to himself: "Fichte has taught — and discovered — the active use of the organ of thought. Has Fichte perhaps discovered the laws of active use of the organs altogether?" And in another note: "The active use of the organs is nothing other than magical, miracle-working thought — or willful use of the physical, bodily world — for will is nothing other than magical, forceful thinking ability."

Thus, one had come upon the universally transformable energy, electricity, believing it to be the universal key for the domination and exploration of nature. And just as natural science had thus left all "tangible" energies behind, in philosophical development the self-conscious ego had also reached a new point. Vivid, active thinking that goes beyond a mathematical understanding of nature was now ready to grasp the realm of the living and to work upon forming the social organism. This tendency can be recognized in Goethe, Lamarck, and later also in Darwin and Haeckel: the theme of their research was the living. Incipient social science and the science of history* showed a similar tendency: now the desire arose to really investigate society and history in order to affect and shape them. Thus, knowledge of nature and self had reached a stage where the vanguard of humanity had liberated itself from natural and traditional bonds and now stood at the threshold of freedom, about to take the shaping of life and the world into its own hands.

e) The crisis of the consciousness-soul. When we view the situation of European humanity in the years following Hegel's death and the discovery of electricity, we see that the world still stood at the beginning of industrialization and its consequences. The social contrasts had not yet broken forth to the extent and with the severity that characterized the decades after 1870. Large-scale military confrontations had ceased with the end of the Napoleonic Wars; materialism had not yet taken root in human souls; in western Europe political enlightenment had progressed to such a degree that the observation of human rights and a liberal constitution were widely looked upon as reasonable. Even nationalism still had a human face in the first half of the nineteenth century: the peoples of Europe looked upon themselves as members of a larger community of nations. Thus, no fateful decisions had yet been made, no hard-to-solve problems created. In other words, the situation was such that a reasonable plan for social action might have a prospect of success.

In this situation of relative freedom, an opportunity was open to the consciousness soul to create social forms out of its own being, to give society a form in keeping with its inner nature. At the same time, this situation of freedom meant that the new could not be created out of the old. The human being had to create out of nothingness, out of his own will. This is precisely the point where creative imagination has to become active, where human beings must consciously grasp the intuitions alive in them if they are to act in the face of the situation.

In a lecture of October 25, 1918 (published in the lecture series *Geschichtliche Symptomatologie*) (*From Symptom to Reality in Modern*

*History was and still is considered a "science" in Germany. [transl.]

History), Rudolf Steiner points to the decisive nature of the mid-nineteenth century. He explains that in in 1845 the first fifth of the consciousness soul period had run its course. At that point it was incumbent upon the bourgeoisie to translate the totally abstract ideas of liberalism into shaping social life. "All ideas that were alive then, that wanted to enter into the historic development of mankind, were without exception intensely abstract ideas, sometimes mere word-husks! But that did not matter: in the era of the consciousness-soul humanity had to pass through abstraction. The leading ideas of humanity had to be put once in such abstract form." Steiner further explains that in the thirty-three years from 1845 to 1878, the bourgeoisie ought to have had time to make the liberal ideas into political and historical reality. A look into history reveals that in 1847, 1848, and 1849, the bourgeoisie did set about realizing the liberal ideas, and that the bourgeoisie and the early proletariat at first worked together in the fight for a constitution, justice, and freedom. In England, one bearer of these aims was the Chartist movement; another, those who worked on a solution of the Irish problem. In Germany these efforts culminated in the Paulskirche movement; in Italy, in figures such as Garibaldi and Mazzini, in the battle for Rome. By 1850 a certain amount had been accomplished: constitutions had been introduced, popular representatives elected, and constitutional government as well as freedom of the press had been largely secured. And yet history writers declare — rightly — that the revolutions of 1848 failed. This evaluation discloses a strange paradox; for the further development shows liberalism taking great strides in western and central Europe after 1850. In 1871 general suffrage and secret ballot were introduced in Germany, and in 1884 for all practical purposes in England as well. Freedom of the press was to a great extent accepted as a fact of life, the workers were granted more and more rights, and social security was increasing. Clearly, however, this development was not decisive. First of all, the failure of the revolution can be seen from the figures who now assumed leadership: Napoleon III, Schwarzenberg, and Bismarck. In the second place, one sees that large circles of the bourgeoisie turned away from politics and shifted their interest to commerce and industry. And most crucially, certain factors of power remained unchanged: the Prussian army, for example, remained under the supreme command of the Kaiser; in the East, the position of the nobility as great agrarian landowners remained unshaken; and at the same time, the power of industry grew. Life of the spirit took an increasingly materialistic turn, especially in the natural sciences. The leading minds are now not Fichte, Schelling, or Hegel, but Darwin, Haeckel, Helmholtz, Bunsen, Virchow, Kirchhoff, Lyell, Thomas Huxley, Foucault, Kekule, and Marx. Certainly one cannot deny (nor would one wish to) that this natural science represents a significant advance, both in the abundance of its content and the exactness of its researches, when it is held up against the speculative natural philosophy of the Romantics. But the social ideas that grew out of this way of thinking were to prove most unwholesome in practice. Similarly, the social classes that continued to hold the reins of leadership sent forth no socially healthful impulses either. Thus one can say the bourgeoisie missed its chance.

What followed were indeed symptoms of illness, and a few spirits — Hobson, for example — understood this too. Under the banner of imperialism and exaggerated nationalism, the conquest and plundering of the earth began, along with an arms race on land and sea. Joseph Schaumberger quite rightly characterized this imperialism as atavistic: it brought out old behavior patterns of the robber knights and adventurers, while all kinds of foundered existences influenced or even determined the politics of states. In the non-European world, old established social and economic forms were blindly annihilated. A country such as China was plunged into chaos for decades. Through technology and politics the black peoples of Africa found instruments placed in their hands that were alien to them and undermined their way of life. In Europe imperialistic tensions led to World War I. The end of that war revealed the extent of the weakness and helplessness of those in ruling positions: they were unable to create a real peace. What followed in the wake of the Treaty of Versailles was a continuation of the war by other means. This became clear in the political developments following the peace treaty.

f) The present stage of consciousness-soul development. The example of atomic physics shows vividly that technological physics has penetrated still deeper into the realm of natural forces. The very unleashing of these hitherto unknown energies points to the special nature of nuclear technology. At the same time, it is clear that humanity is not yet in a position to deal safely or sensibly with this energy. This very simple fact draws the eye back to the inner development of humanity. We now observe numerous attempts to take hold of and understand the human being, the

human soul. From behaviorism, through the whole gamut of psychoana-
lytic directions, to Eastern meditative practices we see a desire to guide
the soul or penetrate its depths. Without evaluating the quite various
results of these endeavors, one is forced to see that no healing social
development has yet emerged from them all. On the one hand, this has to
do with the content of these techniques. For example, when human
behavior is interpreted in terms of the frustration-aggression hypothesis,
the very hypothesis already contains a socially destructive element.
Moreover, it becomes evident that in these practices the soul makes no
progress in taking hold of itself, since this penetration into the recesses of
the soul occurs under the guidance of an analyst or guru. The soul largely
fails to develop self-control, self-knowledge, and the ability to direct and
shape its own development.

A contradiction thus exists between humanity's vast capacity for
invasive interference with nature and our own inner development. Self-
knowledge, self-cultivation, and the faculties for human mutual understanding have not kept pace with the increasing exercise of power, with
the unleashing of natural energies and the controlling of nature. This is
by no means merely a theoretical or ethical problem; for our whole relationship to nature and our fellow human beings is ultimately determined
by us ourselves as human beings — by our knowledge, insight, and attitudes. For this reason the consequences of deficient knowledge and inap-
propriate attitudes come to meet us from without. A chance for
self-correction would be found if humanity could learn to understand
the outer developments that meet it as consequences of its own way of
acting and thinking.

Until now, however, the attitude of the fully industrialized countries has been to suppress the consequences of their own actions by
pushing them off onto the future. This can be done by entering into
debt, by rapidly exhausting the natural resources of the earth, and by
leaving such problems as oceanic pollution or disposal of atomic wastes
up to the future. Furthermore, the problems that arise in the "Third
World" — deforestation of the tropical forests, erosion, and hunger, for
example — are given no more than superficial acknowledgement.
Finally, people refuse to see that the complex of drug-related problems
and unrest among the youth has anything to do with their own way of
life. This attitude will come up against a limit in the years and decades to
come.

Unfortunately it cannot be taken for granted that people learn from difficulties and catastrophes. In particular, we by no means always learn the right thing from what happens to us. Hence a great deal will depend on giving our thinking a certain direction today. Today the consciousness-soul is in a position to overcome the kind of thinking that puts reasoning to the service of personal interests and tries — inwardly and outwardly — to fend off all that is disagreeable. Today the consciousness-soul has reached a stage where it can enter into what comes at it from the outside world. It can find its bearings within present experiences, base its thinking on past ones, and perceive the consequences of its own deeds in the world.

Applying this to the social domain, this means that one human being can learn to think from the other's point of view, to listen to and really understand him — instead of trying to explain him psychologically. In our relationship with nature, this means that ways must be sought to nurture it, to consider its conditions instead of exploiting it. This way of thinking represents a most timely expansion of consciousness and reversal of the will. Until now, human beings — all of us — have been thinking from their own standpoint: we have seen mainly our own rights, our own demands. We have considered what would be advantageous or harmful to ourselves and developed our thoughts accordingly, creating a technology. Should this way of thinking and acting be pursued further, it will lead to catastrophes, no matter how clever our schemes for postponing the problems. The world is too densely populated today, and the possibilities for wrecking havoc so great that rational egotism will spell its own end. In contrast, a consciousness that forms thoughts and judgments out of the full range of experience and orientates itself upon that experience, demands of us a willingness to listen to nature and the social world. Such concern and observation require the kind of sensitivity once reserved for our own selves. However, as soon as we discover that as human beings we are not separated from the world, that we truly live in it and can feel with it, then we feel the need to remove the limits from our own consciousness: the human being becomes an organ in which the world can begin to express itself.

4

HISTORY IN THE DIFFERENT AGE LEVELS[1]

The preschool child listens with joyous anticipation to the same story told over and over again. Indeed, to the child's mind the story is wrong if it is not told exactly the same way as it was the first time. He looks forward to certain words and expressions that he may not even understand intellectually, but in whose rhythms and form he feels great significance. After the sixth or seventh birthday, interest begins to grow in a *new* story. New images can be absorbed. The child expects the figures in the story to reveal their inner being in the way they appear. Though inwardly he can tell how the story will end, he follows with suspense as the good and clever overcome all obstacles. In the ninth year of life the child begins to ask something else of stories: they must be "real." He asks if the story is really "true." This question shows that the child now differentiates. He confronts the adult and asks: "Where does this come from that you are telling me?" Along with this questioning attitude comes a new ability to experience the adult, the forms and characters that appear in the world. The child now begins consciously to distinguish individual beings; their appearance and demeanor take on importance to him. When we think back to that age between nine and ten we notice that, out of our memory, figures emerge with real character. We remember certain qualities or peculiarities that seemed significant to us as children. This kind of youthful apprehension opens up the new possibility of telling stories from history. These will be stories that center on characters and events; they will not yet aim to show historical connections, far-

---

[1] Rudolf Steiner's statements on this question are collected in: "Verzeichnis der Äusserungen Rudolf Steiners über den Geschichtsunterricht", by Erich Gabert, Stuttgart, 1969.

Cf. also: Christoph Lindenberg, *Die Lebensbedingungen des Erziehens.* Reinbeck, 1981, p. 43-82.

reaching consequences, or cultural influences. Such themes cannot be fully understood until a sense for causal relationships begins to awaken around the twelfth year of life. In terms of the interest of ten- and eleven-year-old children, what sort of history instruction is appropriate for the fifth and sixth grades?

Remembering stories that we absorbed ourselves at that age, we see that at nine or ten quite a lot can be imagined and understood if the events are presented in a pictorial and biographical way. Anyone who had the good fortune at that age to hear stories from history told by a gifted storyteller will still remember the details decades later. There is no need to keep the stories especially simple or tailor them to children. On the contrary, details make a great impression. What is most important is to offer, not judgements, but imaginative pictures. To present judgements means that instead of concrete details the narrator speaks of a character as "very good," "very clever," "especially cunning," "simpleminded," and so on. Such words do not leave a lasting impression. But speak of "gray hair that has almost turned yellow," of "flashing eyes that shone even in the twilight"; indicate the energy of a character by saying: "Even uphill he took long and vigorous steps — he was always ahead of the others and never allowed himself any rest until he had reached the crest of the mountain...," and the children will understand that. Indeed, they can understand many difficult things in this way. Above all, actions speak a clear language. Thus, the seductive power of the sirens is reflected in the preparations (recommended by Circe) that Odysseus and his men make before sailing by them. Inner matters, emotions, are expressed in bodily gestures. Instead of a romantic expression such as "she cried bitterly," it is more vivid for the child at this age to hear: "She cried so, that her handkerchief became soaked and even her collar was wet with tears." This is something in which the teacher must train himself. He must use his language consciously, trying to expunge phrases like "very big," "very nice," "very courageous," and replace them with concrete comparisons and specifics: "The shields were so large that they covered the men from head to foot and offered sure protection."

This need has to do with the fact that children of ten or eleven are not yet capable of free, purely inner feeling and judging. For them, feelings and impressions are connected with pictorial forms and concrete mental images. By "pictorial" we do not mean merely "inwardly viewable." For something to become pictorial in this sense, it must connect the hearer with certain qualities, with human achievements, with inner feelings, and with spiritual relationships. For the Greek historians, the very size of the Persian army was an expression of its inhumanity: this army, thirty miles long, destroying wide stretches of land by its sheer advance, was an expression of the masses who followed the sovereign as slaves. When the Persian king commands that the sea be whipped because it has demolished the bridge, we are presented with a picture of barbaric thinking.

Thus, a presentation that is pictorial in this sense certainly engages the children's feelings and stimulates their judgment. But these feelings are not abstract; the judgments are not separated from the appearances. Considering this, it does not yet make sense to formulate thoughts, connections, and causalities in an abstract way. In very much the same way, in ancient times history knew of human encounters and deeds instead of connections and causes. The Greek sages journey to Egypt to learn from the priests. Aeneas flees from burning Troy and takes with him the city's most sacred possession, the Palladium, which at long last reaches Rome. Thus we see how, up to the age of twelve, history can be taught in a pictorial fashion, bringing in human deeds and biographies.

This pictorial quality in fact remains valid for history instruction after the age of twelve, continuing to carry and enliven it right through the twelfth grade. This is not to suggest that the teacher would do well to begin teaching abstractly after the twelfth year! A pictorial and concrete presentation of events is the soil out of which thoughts and judgments grow. Thus the seventh-grade teacher who is recounting the travels of the explorers will certainly not simply state: "In the fourteenth century, people began to build seaworthy vessels capable of venturing across the Atlantic." Here as well, such a ship would be described in detail. This would best be done by describing how such a craft was built, what kind of timbers were used, how the hull was tarred, how large the quarters of the crew were, how big the captain's cabin was, and how tall the ship's mast. It would be well to explain particular circumstances, to point out, perhaps, why the timbers had to be well dried. The difference between instruction in the fifth and sixth grades and that of the seventh is that the seventh-graders might now be asked to explain why such ships were built in the Hansa towns, or why different seafaring techniques and boats were used in the Mediterranean. Once this has been clarified, the pupils can be motivated to figure out the further necessities of high-sea navigation. Further connections can be brought out in this same sense by asking: "What caused the

Europeans to search for a sea-route around the Horn of Africa? How could Columbus arrive at the idea of seeking a passage to India by way of the Atlantic?" Questions like these do not reach into a void when pupils can develop thoughts on the basis of pictorial, concrete knowledge.

In the seventh and eighth grades, it is a matter of acquiring a working knowledge of connections and causalities in a field where definite causalities really exist in a physical sense. The industrial revolution in England could serve as an example for a meaningful examination of causes. The foundation for this revolution lies in England's coal and iron ore deposits, both of which are close to the surface and were at first easily mined. The necessity of coal mining resulted directly from the lack of wood: in the course of the centuries, the English forests had been depleted for shipbuilding, among other things, and the cold, wet climate made heating a necessity. After some time of strip-mining, deeper lying deposits had to be brought up, and in the process groundwater flowed into the pits. This water had to be pumped out. Up to this point we have strict causality. We are dealing with a sequence of natural facts. Of course, donkeys or horses might have been used to work the pumps. But the need to pump water was met by human invention — by a scientific development that leads from Denis Papin to Thomas Savery and Newcomen, as they build the precursors of the steam engine. Here we are dealing not with a causal, but with a final, i.e. goal-directed, development. This interplay of causality and purposeful human action can be observed throughout the industrial revolution, and it would be good if this difference could be clearly brought out in teaching. We are dealing here with an historical paradigm of the first order.

The students can also comprehend other historical circumstances in their necessary connections. I remember how at the age of twelve — it was in the fall of 1942 — I looked at the map of the world and, after viewing the United States, the British Empire, the Soviet Union, and the other opponents of the Axis powers and Japan, I came to the conclusion that Germany had a chance of losing the war. This thought was absolutely taboo in Germany at that time; everywhere we were told of the splendid things awaiting us Germans after the final victory. But this idea, once conceived, left me no peace, and I started to form my own picture of the situation by listening to radio transmissions from abroad. In much the same way, the twelve- or thirteen-year-old student can also understand historical processes. He can understand, for instance, why England was victorious over Spain in 1588, how its situation as an island favored its rule of the sea and acquisition of colonies, and why German industrial development began so much later. Further, the student is quite capable of understanding why the prohibition of printing in Turkey contributed to that country's intellectual and cultural decline, or what implications urbanization at the end of the nineteenth century had for social life. These are all demanding themes, themes which reveal social and historical connections. The student who learns such things has the satisfaction of really being able to understand the "laws" at work in history. He sees that he is advancing from stories to historical insights. He feels that he is being taken seriously. The gently awakening intellect is being engaged.

From the methodological and didactic point of view, it is as important not to ask too little of the pupil as it is not to ask too much. Certainly it would be too early if geographical and social structures were made the explicit object of instruction in the fifth grade. Yet a causal, reasoning approach to history should not begin too late, either. At age twelve or thirteen, causal observation is fun. The student feels that now he really has to comprehend and formulate something. Thus it is not without reason that Steiner referred the teachers of this age-group to such authors as Buckle and Lecky; for though their content is dated now, their approach is aimed precisely at the causal, "lawful" processes in history. Events, colorful as they may be, must be given a foundation and put into a context. At the same time, the teacher should see to it that the facts dealt with are "solid," "tangible" ones. The lessons will deal with geographical facts, with the effects of the introduction of printing, the origin of the modern metropolis, and the consequences of factory work. Here, the discussion is oriented around visible facts, not yet around purely inner motivations such as the ideas of the French Revolution. Some teachers will feel it as a sacrifice of sorts not to enter into such topics as freedom and equality or into political problems in a narrower sense. But to do so would be psychologically premature: the students would make use of these concepts without feeling their full weight.

In the ninth grade, recent history is taken up once again, this time from the viewpoint of the inner motivations, ideas, and themes of the different centuries. Observing the students, one clearly sees their realistic interest giving way to an interest in ideas. In the eighth grade, a number of students would still give elaborate descriptions of the inventions and achievements of Daimler, Benz, Diesel, Edison, and Ford. As a rule these interests now fade into the background. A student who shows a one-sided interest in these things, perhaps even wanting political problems to be solved by technical devices, "sticks out" in class and is not taken quite seriously. Frequently, the students are now struggling to grasp ideas: freedom, justice, equality, humanity, and peace become the themes of their thinking. Yet they have a strange experience with these themes. With a word like freedom, the idea lights up within them, but it is hard to grasp or formulate and hard to make concrete in historical situations. When technological and industrial developments were discussed in the eighth grade, this was a matter of external contrivances. These could be described clearly and easily or — depending on the student's ability — with some exertion. Now this becomes more difficult, because something from the inner world is asking expression. A description of the external world does not betray much of one's own thoughts and feelings. Boys of this age do not have an easy time expressing themselves. When it comes to questions about ideas and feelings, they are hesitant to open their inner world. On the other hand, every class has several girls who are eager to get involved here and openly voice their feelings and ideas. They are ahead of the boys, and it is not until the eleventh grade that the boys have caught up with the girls again.

In this grade, history should help students clarify the ideas they experience within themselves. First, the ideas must be discussed simply as ideas. For instance, one can discuss the idea of freedom. One can make it clear that every human being has the freedom to develop his own thoughts, but that when someone has formulated a thought, he would also like to communicate and discuss it and finally see it realized. Thus we come out with three stages: the inner freedom of thought, freedom of speech, and freedom of action. With a preliminary glance at history, it can be shown how these three stages of freedom were won. The freedom of thought and belief originated when the church's monopoly on truth was broken, allowing a new conception of the world to be born. Freedom of speech developed step by step, first in the form of free speech in parliament, then through free discussion in the drawing room. The freedom of action has many aspects, but as freedom of vocation and freedom of assembly it can be observed in the nineteenth century. In the form of free collective enterprise, we see it realized today in the independent schools. Through such a discussion, the idea of freedom has been brought into clarity before history itself is approached.

The teacher can treat the idea of equality in a similar way, beginning by showing that inequality was once the rule, that there was once unlimited power and privilege. One of the first steps towards equality is the curbing of power, the establishment of equality by rule of law, and the protection of property and dwelling place. A second step on the way towards equality is the limitation of economic power, the creation of social forces equal in weight to it. The creation of equal opportunity in education is a third attempt to bring about equality. As before, these stages in the development of equality can be developed in a preview.

Finally, a third preview is useful. The ideas of freedom and equality are mutually contradictory. Equality necessarily limits freedom, and when there is absolute equality there is no freedom. The enjoyment of freedom continually leads to inequalities. How can these contradictions be understood? Where do the ideas find their limits? Are they valid without limitation? No! In which realm, then, can they be valid? What results when these ideas are linked with the idea of brotherhood? It would be of tremendous benefit if the teacher succeeded in discussing these ideas theoretically in class and clarifying the limits of their domain of validity, before entering into history itself. In this way the students can see history in the light of the idea, and the historical struggles appear in their symptomatic character.

These ideas now become the basis for understanding the characteristic ideas of the various centuries. For example, the theme of the eighteenth century is formulated as "the effects of the ideas of the Age of Enlightenment on historical development." When the students hear this, they can now understand the ideas of the Enlightenment in terms of their understanding of the more general ideas. The great themes of the different centuries connect the general ideas with historical events. The idea of enlightenment itself is an intermediate concept. It is nourished on the high ideals of equality and freedom. The step by step realization of these concepts is seen by the Enlightenment as progress, as a brightening: as "enlightenment." And in fact the eighteenth century shows this progress: its beginning is still marked by a figure like Louis XIV, while its end finds the ideas of the French Revolution seizing Europe. For ninth grade students it is important that such facts of history be linked in this way to ideas and inner motives — that they are not treated as bare, brute facts to be learnt and known.

Most especially this is true for our own century, in which a new culture is preparing to emerge while the old technological, materialistic culture plunges itself into ever more serious crises. To describe the new culture of the twentieth century, a new concept of freedom is needed. Enlightenment conceptions of freedom culminated in the radical freedom of the individual, the "subject." The new freedom, in contrast, lies in the individual's transcending his subjectivity, grasping the world through his knowing and feeling, and out of this insight creating culture. One example of transcending individual subjectivity would be the new understanding of the environment that has been developing over the last decade. If earlier the individual had the freedom to exploit the environment, then the new freedom consists in his being able to listen to its needs, because he recognizes its laws and its significance. This new freedom creates the basis for meaningful action and the development of a new, human, pedagogical, and ecological culture.

Inner clarification of the ideal impulses that flicker up in the student at this age should become a help for the soul. At this age the students begin to judge the world. They judge constantly, though at first they have little ability to guide their own judgment. The faculty of judgment overpowers them. But once they learn that absolute freedom in social life — in the economy, for example — only gives power to the most powerful while other people are pushed aside, they recognize the limits of this principle. They learn to deal more carefully with judgments. The story of economic liberalism, ending in the misery of the working classes, lets them see where absolute economic freedom leads. The example of Robespierre helps them recognize how an individual who sets up his own judgment as absolute and declares himself the organ of the general will, can unleash a terrible tyranny of the idea — a tyranny that costs hundreds of thousands of lives and finally destroys the tyrant himself. The inner drama of this development can be experienced by the students if they first become enthusiastic about the ideas of Rousseau and Robespierre and later, in the struggle between Danton and Robespierre, they inwardly follow the events down their course to catastrophe. Georg Büchner's depiction of this conflict is a model of a unique and living portrayal.

A power of judgment oriented towards ideals has reached its full development when the student sees how ideas really can become practical. The example of Robespierre illustrates only the failure. But in the ideas and measures of the division of power, in the right to work, and in the establishment of trial by jury the student can see that the realization of ideas calls for social inventions that do not realize ideas in an immediate way. Important social inventions always realize ideas "mediately": they create means, institutions that permit the idea to be realized without directly putting it into action. The purpose of such practical institutions and procedures should therefore be treated quite pointedly in the ninth grade and later as well. Again and again the question, "What is the sense of a practical institution?" should be raised as a kind of exercise. In this way the power of judgment is drawn closer to the world.

In the tenth grade this new motif in history can be continued in quite a different way. In his lectures of 1921 to the Waldorf teachers — appearing under the title "Menschenerkenntnis und Unterrichtsgestaltung" — Rudolf Steiner explains that, after sexual maturity, it is a question of bringing the soul's subjectivity into relation with the objectivity of the world. The objective world in this sense is, first of all, the physical world of space, but at the same time it is what is objectively alive, the world of life that surrounds us. In the ninth grade, the instruction served to free the young person's soul. Under the banner of ideals, the student rose above the mere factual aspect of pictorially-grasped external developments. Thus there is by all means a freeing; but at first, since the judgment cannot yet be properly dealt with, this freeing brings unrest and turmoil. The student rebels: the world is not the way it should be. Neither, of course, is the student himself. At this stage of development, it is well to remember the words of Steiner, who in the pedagogical course of 1921/22 said: "This turmoil has to exist, and throughout the whole preceding education one must be looking towards this turbulence which must necessarily arise. People who perhaps have an overly elegiac bent may believe it would be better to spare the human being all this turmoil. To do that, however, would be to make oneself one's own greatest enemy. The human being should not be spared this turmoil. The entire previous education should be designed so that it supports the inner working of the soul-spiritual on the human being at this point."

In the tenth grade, the way from the turmoil of subjectivity to a new orientation in the objective can no longer be mediated by the teacher's authority at all. The students demand reasons for everything. They want to know why things have become the way they now appear. Only insight can mediate the way to a new objectivity. And such insights must first be gained from clear paradigms. As we now proceed, in accordance with the curriculum, into the relation between history and geography, the geographic facts provide a clearly objective foundation. On the one hand it is now methodologically important to approach geography with a love of detail and exactness, yet on the other hand it is essential that general principles be brought out through further examples. Simple and clear examples can be found in the river valleys that brought forth the first great civilizations (Euphrates, Tigris, Nile, Huangho); coastal lands, where the requirements of life stimulated navigation (Greece, Portugal, England, the Netherlands, Norway); and perhaps also the deserts out of which conquering nomadic tribes burst. Quite soon the students will begin to pose questions for which the teacher must be prepared: What about the culture of the Incas, Mayas, and Aztecs? Why did Japan not become a seafaring nation earlier? Only if the teacher can enter into these questions do the students get the feeling that they are really dealing with objective matters.

A second important element here is working style. The students must now learn to reconstruct history by themselves, too. The teacher can give assignments by referring to documents, archeological finds, or facts. He might ask what statements certain structures — the Pyramids or Stonehenge — make about the society that built them. Texts from the *Odyssey*, from Aeschylus' Persian drama, or from Plato's Dialogue on the founding of a city (*Republic*, book 2, chap. 11-14), along with pointed questions, can stimulate the students to original thinking. For the students these documents also mean a confrontation with objectivity. They see that by coming to grips with objectivity, they themselves are able to form a picture of the past.

On the whole, thematically and methodologically, instruction in the tenth grade has a strong rational streak. This stands out particularly when themes that were viewed idealistically in the ninth grade — the origin of the democratic state, for example — are now thought through from geographic and socio-structural viewpoints, perhaps with the task of seeing what milieu makes a Socrates possible. Through this sober approach, which must be totally reasonable and comprehensible, the awakening subjectivity and rebellious feeling can become clarified. A feeling approach, in contrast, or a one-sidedly idealistic approach would be of no help to the young person's growth at this age.

When the instruction of the ninth and tenth grades has gone well, and the students have gained a first general orientation and relationship to objectivity, an eleventh grade class makes quite a different impression.

The turmoil has subsided. By their behavior, questions, and interests the students show that they have reached a new level. Their inquiries become more personal; easily or uneasily, they bring their own inner experiences into the lesson. Many of the questions and problems that have made an impression upon them are answered for them by the general cultural environment. They discuss how genes and environment affect them personally. Somewhere they have adopted popular psychologisms in their vocabulary, and speak of aggression and sublimation, of inferiority complexes and mother ties. This terminology is mostly used in an off-hand way, without any more precise notions, but it shows where their interests lie.

The German class seeks to meet this interest by taking up *Parzival* by Wolfram von Eschenbach. This epic is, among other things, an *entwicklungroman*, a novel of development. Through its images it lifts into perspective various stages and stations, crises and conflicts of the growing human being. While an uneducated person only bandies words about without as a rule understanding them properly, the reader of a finely and precisely drawn novel such as *Parzival* can learn to see and understand psychologically. One need only think of the scene with the three drops of blood in the snow: they so fascinate Parzival that he is completely entranced and cannot be distracted even by attacks from the outside — until Gawan hides the drops of blood from his view. Gawan knew what to make of such situations; he was a practical psychologist.

The history instructor who wants to enter into the students' latent questions has a more difficult task than the German teacher, because history is not primarily an image of personal inner development. Nevertheless, the history teacher must try to find aspects of history that will personally interest the students at this age. The facts of the Migration of the Peoples, the figures of the German kings and medieval monks do not at first glance appear interesting in this sense. It is another matter, however, if one makes the attempt to examine the individual cultures that were of significance for the Middle Ages, developing them out of their soul-spiritual background. When Islam, for example, is examined in this way — its strict monotheism, its fatalism, its prohibition against making images — so that its physiognomy within Arabic culture comes out, then the culture of Baghdad or the world of the Alhambra can be understood in its full grandeur and finesse. At the same time, it can be sensed that this culture is the end of a short development, that there is no continuation. In the same sense, Irish-Scottish Christianity, striving into form out of an amorphous but deeply felt experience of nature, can be seen as the seed of a culture capable of development — a culture that flowed into the early Middle Ages, fertilizing France and central Europe. In just this sense one can go into the aging process of the ancient world and the force of Christianity, out of which the old tradition was to be completely reshaped by the Germanic peoples.

However, such attempts at cultural physiognomy become fully understandable only when they are imbued with a more encompassing idea, a leading thought. Such an idea is that of development — development characterized by decline and rebirth, by change and individualization, by origin and aim. For the students of the eleventh grade, who themselves are passing through hidden doubts and crises, it is important to recognize that not just their individual development, but history as well goes through declines and can renew itself. Medieval culture has origins in the antique world; but this world and its traditions shatter. The ancient spiritual heritage disappears as into an underground stream. But it is recreated, transformed, and reshaped in the spirit of Christianity. The history of the Middle Ages lives upon goals that it reaches only in rare moments. From the simple germs of Frankish culture, in a course of development leading through repeated divisions and crises, individual cultures gradually articulate themselves and create their own organs: churches and monasteries, cathedral schools and universities, orders of knights, towns with craft guilds and merchants. All of these, however, are united in the idea of Christianity, as beneath a dome embellished with many figures. In this way the culture- and soul-forming power of the spirit becomes tangible to the student.

Students of the twelfth-grade have the ability to ask questions about the origin and goal of history per se. Important as detail may be to them, their actual interest is in fundamental questions: what shapes history, and where does it aim? And these questions are not meant in an abstract way. The students want to orientate themselves in life, to draw out their own plan for life, and history should help them here. The most oppressive problem of our time — and the eighteen-year-old experiences it with elemental impact — is the future, which appears bleak and hopeless. Certainly the prospect of the future is oppressive to the teacher as well; but it is not his task to greaten the fear or augment the visions of terror. A teacher must recognize that the materialistic visions of doom are one-sided and fail to take into account what is in fact also evident: the struggle for a new consciousness.

A healthy and helpful orientation can be found for the students only in an all-encompassing, precise overview, which raises them over the moment. Ideas linked with fashionable diagnoses of the times will be obsolete tomorrow. Nor can the ideas they need be gained from socio-logical analyses that observe only the symptoms of decline without see-ing the deeper, motivating forces. The decisive task of our time is a product of the very situation of freedom. But if one understands this freedom only as subjective freedom of opinion and choice, then one does not see the task at all. Only a comparison with earlier times shows us what freedom is. It is true that the high civilizations of ancient times were able to create small spaces of man-made culture, namely their cities (Ur and Uruk, Memphis, Harappa, etc.), but these were entirely embed-ded in the rhythms of nature (e.g. that of the Nile). In their thinking as well they scarcely rose above the world of life that carried them. In this sense they were quite unfree, dependent on the cooperation of nature. The Greeks freed themselves from their immediate location, moving around the regions of the Mediterranean and Black Seas, exploring Egypt and Persia, and finally pressing into India. This free mobility parallels their thinking. Their way of thinking was descriptive or speculative; it roved freely over and in the world, taking hold of its forms. And wher-ever it lighted with exactness, it understood the world. Such was the position of Aristotle. Our conception of freedom today still corresponds to the free-ranging thought of the Greeks. But when one pursues this free thinking of the Greeks to its historical end in Scholasticism, one sees it congeal and crystallize into a system. Neither the free-ranging thinking of the Greeks nor the systematics of Scholasticism go beyond contempla-tion of the world. The free, Apollonian contemplation of the Greeks develops into the ever more precisely-honed thinking of Scholasticism, with its clear and correct intellectual concepts. This rational thinking, this viewing of the world with the head, and the corresponding concep-tion of freedom as freedom-of-thought, rule our consciousness still.

Yet the reality of modern freedom is characterized by an active, experimental, transforming interference with nature. What is remarkable, however, is this: the experimenter, like the technologist, forgets that he is acting, that he is affecting nature. In his thinking he retains the Greek atti-tude of contemplation, believing that he is only describing the way things are, but forgetting his own doing, which creates the new phenomena and techniques. He stands before the results of his actions without quite realizing that it is the results of his actions that he is facing: he fails to recognize himself in his actions. What is happening today is that people are beginning in a small way to be aware of their own doing. But in the future there will develop a new way of thinking, which will accompany one's own action. Human beings will then think less "with their heads." They will try to sense consciously in their will what they are doing, experiencing, and perceiving. Culture as a whole will be set from its head onto its feet. What we are experiencing are the pains and crises of this transition.

The perspective on history outlined here represents one possible answer to the question that troubles the upper school students, particularly in the twelfth grade: the question of the meaning of the events in which they stand. The crisis and disintegration apparent today become understandable in this way. What is crucial in the twelfth grade is that the students do not get the feeling: there is no point to it all; we grow up in an absurd world; all we know is "no future." The outline sketched here also contains a goal: a goal that is not contrived, but can be found in the facts, if one has an eye for what is concealed in the facts.

For the students of the twelfth grade it is a necessity of life to discuss such questions. The teacher faces two challenges here. First of all he must be competent in his field, and he must concern himself with the questions that concern his students, which are the questions of the future. For example, he will reflect: what would a new way of thinking be like in social, human contexts? He will observe the phenomena of the times in order not to miss signs of the new. On the other hand he faces a quite personal challenge. Something of the new can be alive in the style of his teaching and the way he conducts class conversation, if the teacher finds his own actions and speech reflected in what meets him in the life of the class. The teacher's inner, spiritual difficulties — abstractness, lack of imagination, pessimism, rigidity of thought, overattachment to the wealth of material (it would be easy to find more) — all come back to meet him, directly or transformed, and give him the best incentive for continual work on himself. They give him the opportunity to renew his teaching — in keeping with the questions from the class and the tasks posed by the times — in such a way that the students will be able to take hold of their future.

5

THEME SELECTION FOR GRADES FIVE TO TWELVE FOLLOWING RUDOLF STEINER'S CURRICULUM

Rudolf Steiner's indications for the curricula of the individual grades are distinguished by their extreme terseness — and not without reason. He did not want to dictate to the teachers what they were to do in each particular. In the last conference of September 3, 1924, he speaks of this to the teachers of the Waldorf School in Stuttgart: "As a principle, the teachers have full freedom in everything having to do with instruction, but not in the way the school is administered." The suggestions he went on to give were also limited to pointers; they show certain possibilities, but they have no intention of representing a fully elaborated curriculum. The experience of the author has shown him that most colleagues have no major difficulty with the instruction in grades five, six, and seven. Therefore he has kept his recommendations short here. The task before the eighth grade teacher, however, clearly presents greater difficulties. Hence the attempt has been made to give a more thorough treatment to the themes in question, since they are unfamiliar to most colleagues. Still, enough room is left for the individual work of the teacher. This is important because it is what the teacher has worked through on his own that is pedagogically most effective. Should he even succeed in making discoveries or finding paths of his own, then he can hope that the spark of enthusiasm will jump over to his class.

In preparing for teaching history, it is well for the teacher to rely as little as possible on material tailored for school teaching. The ancient sources, Herodotus and Plutarch, as well as certain medieval chronicles (should the teacher wish to use them) are truer and more pedagogical in their content than the abstractions of textbooks. However, all depends on the teacher's success in creating a vivid picture of the events in his own imagination. In the training seminar for the first Waldorf teachers, Rudolf Steiner appealed to the teachers: "Try to portray history in a vivid way and it will be truer history." One gradually learns to appreciate the significance of this advice in the course of time. The usual history textbooks place great emphasis on certain concepts: the Greek polis, theocratic rule, feudalism, and so on. These concepts are by all means useful when they remain flexible and are nourished on a concrete view of particulars. Generally, however, they only serve to cover up many problems when they are used in the abstract. For this reason it is good advice for the class teacher — who is not always an historian — to concentrate heavily on individual figures and the circumstances of their life. Each day let him picture what he is going to present in the next lesson, visualizing exactly the houses and towns, clothing and streets, etc. In this way those elements that make for a concrete inner picture of time and space will be able to flow into the teaching process almost as an afterthought. The particular way in which these images can be connected and imbued with thoughts has been discussed in the previous chapter on the age levels.

For grades nine to twelve, my aim has been to work out a basic outline of Rudolf Steiner's suggestions in regard to content. Here — even more than before — it is only a matter of suggestions. Especially in the eleventh and twelfth grades not only will each teacher go his own way, but the classes too will help shape the lessons through their questions and suggestions. Certain of Steiner's suggestions I have not specially mentioned — the "growing younger of humanity," for example — because I believe that a fact of this kind can be best mentioned on occasion in a brief *apercu* illustrated with examples, but is unsuitable for systematic attention in the twelfth grade. If my deliberations on grades nine to twelve have turned out to be more extensive than those for grades five to seven, still I ask that they be regarded merely as working material, of which my colleagues are free to avail themselves as they see fit.

6

FIFTH GRADE

In his first curriculum lecture (September 6, 1919), Rudolf Steiner formulates the teacher's task for the first history lessons in this way: "In the fifth school year one will make every effort to see to it that the child is exposed to real historical concepts. One should not be in the least afraid of teaching children of that age concepts about the culture of the Eastern peoples and the Greeks." And Steiner adds: "Especially if one appeals to their feeling, ten- to eleven-year-old children are quite capable of being interested in everything that can give them an understanding of the Eastern peoples and the Greeks."

What sort of historical concepts can these be, however, for children before the age of twelve? In any case we will not be dealing with a consistent causal depiction of historical development or with a conceptual grasp of the inner impulses of history. The fact that the *culture* of the Eastern peoples is referred to makes it clear that the emphasis is on the differences of these ancient cultures; and in this difference, the decisive historical concept is actually already contained. For the fifth grader this difference of culture becomes visible through human characters, through their works and deeds. In point of fact, quite different moods and attitudes toward life reign in the various Eastern cultures, setting their stamp on them.

A difficult task confronts us right at the start: the portrayal of the ancient Indian culture. What has been retained of this culture in historical times is barely a reflection of the culture of which Indian legend is speaking when it tells of the great Manu and the seven Rishis. It may be possible to portray this primeval Indian culture in a vivid way if we begin with the reflection it has left in later times. Starting from the Vedic texts, the Upanishads or the Bhagavad Gita, the teacher can try to form a picture of this ancient consciousness that was open to a heaven filled with an infinitude of gods and divine figures. This divine world was so powerful that against it the earthly world was experienced as maya, as

74

mere semblance. Thus the interest of the ancient Indian — like that of the modern Indian sage — was directed not towards agriculture, not towards industry and livelihood, but towards the experience and apprehension of the divine world. Furthermore, the vegetation of the Indian subcontinent, originally rich, lush, and diverse, at that time made for a life in which little energy had to be spent on work. Thus it also permitted a life of the spirit little hampered by earthly constraints, free to immerse itself in the mysteries of the cosmos. The value placed on this spiritual life was mirrored in the caste system, which accorded the highest position to the priests. It makes no sense, however, to examine the caste system unless one can make it clear to the students that in early Indian culture, this social order was felt and perceived in a totally different way than it is today.

For the fifth graders to get a really distinct impression of this culture, however, they must experience it in some detail through a particular figure. This figure is the Buddha. Fortunately, the Buddha legend has preserved the life of Buddha for us in a typically Indian manner — with a wealth of imagery and figures. Moreover, it has been excellently depicted in the book by Hermann Beckh. Thus one is in a position to tell the students: "Now we shall see how the Indians themselves describe the life of one of their greatest human beings." Having pointed to the authenticity of this description, one can begin to tell about the descent of the Bodhisattva from the gods. One will describe the palace of King Suddhodana and the entry of the Bodhisattva into the womb, going into some detail on these and the other elements of the legend; for this wealth of images is characteristic of Indian spirituality. Of itself, this legend will communicate something of the special flavor of early Indian culture. In fact, the palace of Suddhodana still mirrors something of the original Indian culture, which was India's golden age.

At the same time, it is essential for the the student to grasp that the legend of Buddha is not a fairy tale — that the last offshoots of ancient Indian culture are still living, transformed, in India today. The India of today can be viewed as a sort of archeological remnant of an ancient culture, a culture much purer and grander than that which finds its way from India to the West today. When the students experience this, it becomes unnecessary to point out that the most ancient cultures were by no means "primitive."

An entirely different mood pervades the old Iranian culture, the world of Zarathustra. This culture revolves around taking hold of earthly tasks — cattle breeding, cultivation of grains, housebuilding, construction of canals, and irrigation of fields — in an area much less inviting than the Indian subcontinent. For we are dealing with the regions between the Pamirs and the Caspian Sea, south of the Oxus. It was the will of the ancient Persian culture to make this world into an image of divine will and divine order.

First of all the teacher himself will have to realize what it signified for the human beings of those times to take on a settled way of life. It meant to sacrifice a life of free mobility, as yet not bound to the earth. We who live today know the results of this process of settlement. We can hardly imagine life otherwise than living in houses and regularly enjoying the bread and other fruits of agriculture. We know that grain cultivation and settlement are possible. It was not so in the time before settlement; none of these experiences or concepts existed then. Furthermore, the adoption of a sedentary way of life also meant a complete change in the life of the human soul: from a mere consumer and enjoyer of the fruits of nature, the human being now became the producer of food and dwellings; from the hunter he now became the keeper and nurturer of animals. It happens that this process finds a reflection in the legend of Zarathustra. It is fortunate for the teacher that this legend, along with a great number of Zarathustrian texts, has now been collected in the book *Zarathustra* by D. J. van Bemmelen. The question, however, is how to proceed in the fifth grade. As with the Greek legends of the battle of Troy and others, the correct approach seems to me first to tell the legend, the life of Zarathustra, in brief episodes and then, using the archeological evidence, to show that these legends point back to a reality. In this way the student learns the value of such legends. He learns that in "olden times" people kept great events alive in their memory over many centuries, and that the memory, linked to rhythmic texts, preserves things of the greatest antiquity.

When contrasted with Indian culture and with the Buddha, the totally different character of the Iranian culture becomes plain. Here, human beings find themselves placed in a battle between light and darkness, between good and evil; and it is in this battle that they gradually find their footing on earth. Agriculture for them is worship: service of the divine. They are at battle with the demon worshippers, and they sidewith spirit of the sun, Ahura Mazda:

I scorn to be a dev-worshipper. I profess myself a worshipper
of Mazda, a Zarathustrian, an enemy of the devas (demons), a
believer in the Lord, a praiser of the immortal holy angels, a worhip-
per of the immortals. I promise all good things to the wise Lord, to
Him who is good, kind, just; to Him, the Splendid, the Magnificent,
I promise the best — to Him, from Whom come the cow, the law,
the heavenly lights! I choose for myself holy humility. I disavow
thievery and stealing of cattle, plunder and laying waste of villages.
To the housedwellers I grant free coming and going, free dwelling,
and also to the domestic animals with whom they share the earth.
With reverence, upon the holy water, I pledge this: henceforth I will
not commit plunder and ravage in the villages of the Mazda worshippers, nor covet their body or life. I profess myself as a worshipper of Mazda, a Zarathustrian by vow and confession. I pledge
thinking well-thought, word well-spoken, and deed well-done.
(Yasna 12, 1-3, 8).

This battle and the choice for the good also characterizes Zarathustra's life, threatened as it was from the very beginning. Zarathustra
continually had to fight against enemies in order to safeguard the new
way of life and preserve the cult of the good.

The fifth grade teacher is faced with especially difficult choices
when it comes to describing the culture of Mesopotamia. This land
"between the two rivers" — Tigris and Euphrates — is without doubt of
great importance: it is where humanity founded its first cities, where the
first writing system developed, and where the cultures of Ur, Assur, and
Babylon arose. But to fifth graders, one is hardly going to describe all
these cultures with their rises and declines. What, then, should be
selected? The Gilgamesh epic offers itself as a story — but is it possible to
describe the culture of Sumer on the basis of this epic? Or should one
rather describe a city like Babylon, using the reports of Herodotus? When
the development of writing is illustrated, should one look at cuneiform, or
does the development of the hieroglyphs in Egypt seem a more vivid
example? Perhaps the most reasonable approach is to decide right from
the start which elements of ancient civilization one will describe in connection with the ancient Mesopotamian cultures, and which ones in connection with Egypt. Certainly Egypt will illustrate the use of stone for
building (temples and pyramids), the rule of the pharaohs, and the cult

of the dead. Mesopotamia will show the founding of cities proper and the division of labor. Furthermore, the Gilgamesh epic can be used to portray early urban culture with its temple economy, while it additionally gives us the story of an unsuccessful initiation. As for writing, one could attach its development, along with education, to Mesopotamia, and later go into the hieroglyphs as an illustration of the deciphering of a script.

The Gilgamesh epic begins with a short description of the city of Uruk: its wall, which is decorated with facing stones, its temple to Ishtar. The teacher is in a position to add to this description from the archeological findings. He can tell of the hall of justice, the craftsmen, and the living quarters, and describe the life of the city, ruled by the temple. It is the temple that administers all economic goods; it is in the temple that the archive of clay tablets rests. Near it is the school, where some children press the stylus into moist clay tablets and so learn to write. Fertile lands irrigated by canals stretch round the city. It is in this setting that Gilgamesh appears, of whom the epic says: "This is the man who knew everything. He is the king who knew the lands of the world. He was wise. He beheld the mysteries and knew hidden things. He brought news from before the time of the great storm-flood — he built the wall of Uruk, the bulwark and the temple." Thus a description of the city and its life can easily be woven into the situation at the beginning of the epic.

The teacher who would like to look at a larger city at the peak of its culture has two excellent choices. One is offered by Walter Andrae's stimulating description of Assur; the other is the description of Babylon by Herodotus in his first book of *Histories*. To go into detail on the culture and religion of Sumer or Babylon seems difficult to me, but one might point out certain things: that observation of the heavens was particularly cultivated here, that the division of the zodiac is of Babylonian origin, and that sun, moon, and planets were considered forms in which the gods appeared: sun = Shamash, moon = Sin, Mercury = Nabu, Venus = Ishtar, Mars = Nergal, Jupiter = Marduk, Saturn = Ninurta. For the Babylonians, however, the whole universe was a spiritual state, a world of gods who worked in various ways: Anu was the sky that stretched over all; Enlil was "Lord Storm"; Enki the lord of the earth; and the earth, in another form, is also Nin-tu, the birth-giving queen. Thus the spiritual, divine world was experienced in a multitude of effects and deeds. Doubtless the most vivid way for the students to experience this way of apprehending the cosmos is through the Gilgamesh epic.

In our country the culture of Egypt is much better known, at least on the surface, than that of Mesopotamia. From the external viewpoint, this has to do with the fact that the Egyptian culture has remained in a much better state of preservation than that of — shall we say — Uruk or Assur. For one thing, stone — and not sun-dried brick — was used to a much larger extent in Egypt; and for another, the dry desert sand had the effect of keeping many objects intact. Still, when looking at a pyramid today, we have constantly to remind ourselves that everything we see is only the ruins of a glorious culture. Therefore in history teaching it is important not to introduce this culture by looking at the ruins first. Before the teacher begins describing anything, let him take the opportunity first to recreate this world in his imagination. We are in the fortunate position of being able to exactly reconstruct the plan of Egypt's first stone structure and determine its significance. This is the pyramid precinct of King Djoser at Saqqarah. The structures, built of stone around the pyramid, are a replica of the royal precinct of Memphis. Except for the step-pyramid in its center, the precinct of Saqqarah is a permanent stone copy of the royal residence in Memphis, which was made of sun-dried brick, wood, and wattle. In another but similar way, the images decorating the graves give us a picture of Egyptian daily life.

In order to bring out the achievements of the Egyptian culture, it is helpful to begin by giving the students a picture of the fertile Nile Valley with its lush vegetation and rich animal world. In the midst of this world we see human habitations, villages on hills rimming the fruitful valley, a few larger settlements ruled by chieftains, perhaps the seat of a prince as well — but all buildings are of sun-dried brick, wood, and bundles of reeds. In this world, within a very short time, kings create a state. The first king to have really reigned — after a number of precursors — was probably Djoser. Under this king and his wise counselor Imhotep, stone construction came into being practically without any earlier stages: immediately, in all perfection and on a grand scale, there rises the pyramid precinct of Saqqarah. The surrounding wall itself is an impressive 10 meters high and 277 x 544 meters long. Within this domain the first great free-standing sculpture of a pharaoh was found, as well as many bas-reliefs and the original form of the Egyptian script. It was also Djoser and Imhotep who gave form to the Egyptian state, essentially organizing it for the first time and giving Egyptian culture the basic form that it retained for over two thousand years — all in all an unimaginable process.

The construction of the Great Pyramids could also be discussed along these lines. Just the levelling of the rock base on which the Pyramids stand and the precise orientation of its sides almost exceed our imagination. And then to organize the construction! For the Great Pyramid of Gizeh, about 2,600,000 stone blocks with an average weight of 2.5 tons each had to be brought in. How many people worked here over a period of twenty years? How were they fed? Here the teacher is put to the task of slowly forming a picture of these circumstances for himself and then for the class, until he can really imagine a pyramid with completely smooth outer sides, 146 meters high and 230 meters long at the base.

Along with this first step in the presentation, a further one should be taken at the same time: to view these structures and the grounds surrounding them from the perspective of human experience. To imagine, for example, what an Egyptian must have felt when he walked up through the covered corridor from the Valley Temple of the Great Pyramid to the Temple of the Dead at its foot and suddenly had the shining pyramid before his eyes. In view of these tasks, it is gratifying to have available a very stimulating and factually authenticated book that is also useful for the teacher: *Der Mensch und sein Tempel, vol. 1: Aegypten*, by Frank Teichmann. Especially in regard to the Egyptian culture, the layman is inclined to interpret in an off-the-cuff manner without a great deal of actual knowledge. Teichmann has now opened up perspectives that are based on exact knowledge of ancient Egyptian statements — perspectives authenticated as to their content and giving interpretations derived as far as possible from the thinking of the Egyptians themselves.

It makes little sense to treat Egyptian history in separate periods: Old Kingdom, Decline, Middle Kingdom, invasion of the Hyksos and New Kingdom. It is enough to limit oneself to two elements of the Old Kingdom: the foundation of the culture and the building of the Pyramid of Cheops. Those who would like to spend more time here might go into the calender, the reckoning of time and year, the calculation of harvest quantity according to the flooding of the Nile, etc. Treatment of a figure such as Akhnaton, however, is best left to art class in the ninth grade, because this pharaoh's most visible achievements for us are in the area of the arts. If the subject of Tutankhamen comes up, one should not forget to point out that he was a most insignificant pharaoh whose grave was the smallest of the series of graves in the Valley of Kings. The essential character of Egyptian culture, however, will become quite clear from a very few phenomena of the Old Kingdom, and hardly requires reference to such an ephemeral figure as Tutankhamen.

With the transition to the Greek culture, an entirely different atmosphere should pervade the class. The grandeur of the Egyptian achievements, the strictness of Zarathustrian religion, and the otherworldly quality of Indian culture have something awe-inspiring, even perhaps oppressive, about them. Speaking of these cultures the teacher, too, will notice time and again that his understanding comes up against limits, that he is overpowered by such sublimity, such majesty. With the Greeks, however, our own way of understanding begins. Something of the transition necessary here is intimated in an account by Plato, contained in his dialogue *Timaeus*. Here, Critias reports on a trip taken by Solon to Egypt. An aged Egyptian priest tells Solon, who was visiting the city of Sais: "Solon, oh Solon! You Hellenes remain children always; no Hellene manages to reach old age." "What? How do you mean that?," Solon is supposed to have asked. "You are all young in your souls, for you do not keep within you any ancient understanding based on the oldest accounts, no knowledge grown grey with time... Whatever has happened among you, and in other regions of which report has come to us, has been written down and preserved here in our temples since olden times." It is with these words that the old Egyptian priest introduces his account of sunken Atlantis. This account makes it clear that in Egypt there still lived a wisdom and memory not bound to the individual. It is out of this superindividual wisdom that such creators of culture as Imhotep and Djoser were capable of acting.

In Greece, the culture stands under the sign of development and of thought. While the peak of Egyptian culture lies at its beginning, between 2700 and 2400 B.C., Greek culture develops from simple beginnings to a climax in the fifth and fourth centuries B.C. For the fifth grade it is important now to illustrate this evolutionary process through the most living, vivid figures and events. First, the teacher can use a number of legends to portray the heroes of earlier days: Perseus, Theseus, and Heracles, for example. So many archetypes of our thinking live in these legends that one can hardly leave them out. It is an open question, of course, whether these archetypal legends of European culture should be treated in the history block or whether they should be told to the students as stories on another occasion. As the beginning of history proper one could take the Trojan war. In conjunction with this one has the option of presenting the biography and researches of Heinrich Schliemann, which show in a memorable way how the legend of Troy was verified to the satisfaction of our own times. Next it is essential to present the figure of Odysseus; for this figure gives a living picture of the power of intellect that later pervades Greek culture. At the same time, the *Odyssey* reports with great exactness on the life of the Greeks at the time of Homer, one example being the description of Odysseus' arrival in the realm of the Phaeacians. Here one can take an incidental look at the life and social forms of the Greeks. A second phase of the teaching deals with Sparta. One will refrain from speaking in abstract terms of the Dorian wanderings; but this event can be touched on when the conquering of Laconia by the Spartans is discussed. At the center of the theme of Sparta should stand the figure of Lycurgus. Here, the students must be able to sense that the laws of Lycurgus are the product of a human mind, that all of his measures were highly artificial and designed to stop the natural course of things. One need only think of the iron currency or of Spartan education. A third motif can be the Olympic Games, which are representative of the many other games put on by the Greeks in honor of their gods.

With Solon, the history of Athens begins. Here we have a process similar to the one demonstrated by Lycurgus: one man makes laws for all. To examine the entire development of Attic democracy from Solon to Cleisthenes and on to the age of Pericles makes little sense. Hence one should place the greatest emphasis on the figure of Solon: his function as mediator and his various measures — to the extent they can be made understandable to the students. Further, one must emphasize the spirit, the kind of attitude that we see documented in Solon. When he had completed his work of lawmaking, he declared to the Athenians that he would now go on travels, and they were to swear to keep his laws until his return. Solon went on his travels, but he never returned to Athens: he wished laws, not a man, to rule.

It is unnecessary for students of the fifth grade to learn about the events following Solon: the tyranny of Pisistratus and such matters. The Persian wars, on the other hand, can be readily discussed, with emphasis upon the cultural history revealed in this battle between two world views. When one follows the accounts of Herodotus beginning in the fifth book of his *Histories*, one notices that the Greeks put their intelligence to use as a tool in war and in politics. The leader of the Ionian rebellion, Aristagoras, made use of a map of the world cast in bronze in order to convince the Greeks of the mother country to aid the Ionian Greeks. Themistocles had a play, *The Fall of Miletus*, written and performed in order to warn the Athenians of the Persian danger, and also used a subterfuge to force the Greeks into the battle of Salamis. To the Greeks, the Persians simply appeared as a sheer mass and their king as a tyrant who, absurdly, had the Hellespont whipped because the storm destroyed the bridge formed by his ships across the channel. One may regard Themistocles and Aristides as the central figures of this time. The tragic fate of Themistocles after the victory over the Persians also most decidedly belongs to Greek history: his ostracism, his flight through Greece, and his death as a tyrant in a region under the power of the Persian king.

A particularly difficult task from the pedagogical point of view is the portrayal of Athens at the time of Pericles; for this time period lacks easily conveyable dramatic events. Yet this period was the high point of antique drama; it is the time when the Acropolis was rebuilt, the time of the great sculptors, the time during which Socrates grew up, and furthermore the time of vital democracy, when the Attic people discussed every issue in the marketplace. One way of finding access to this period with the students is through drawing and painting. One might, for example, paint a picture of the Acropolis or the Parthenon. One could attempt to copy an Attic vase or a Greek sculpture — perhaps a metope from the Parthenon — to sketch the battle of the Lapithae with the centaurs or design a map of Athens and its connections to the Mediterranean world. Other avenues could also be followed: one could try to develop the Parthenon from the perspective of Phidias, or describe Attic education and life in Athens from the viewpoint of a growing youth. As a starting point one could also take the figure of Herodotus, who hailed from Halicarnassus, exploring his journeys, his investigations, his curiosity, and finally taking him to Athens — just as it happened in reality.

To conclude Greek history it is advisable to proceed directly to the figure of Alexander the Great and his teacher Aristotle, leaving out the Peloponnesian War and the period of Theban domination. The figure of Alexander is easy to describe, there being biographies in plenty. The difficulty here lies in two things: First, the tendency is to treat his youth in too great detail while acquitting oneself of the great campaigns with a few marks on the wall-map. Many of his campaigns, however, offer an opportunity to retrace and summarize the material of the fifth grade. Hence it would make sense to take up the theme: Alexander in Egypt, in Mesopotamia, in Iran, and in India. The second problem lies in the evaluation of Alexander. The murders of Philotas, Parmenion, and Cleitos put such an onus on Alexander's character that many researchers assert, not without reason, that the murder of Philip as well was arranged by Alexander. One might approach this problem by describing Aristotle's disappointment over the excesses of his pupil. The question of Alexander's role as a Greek colonizer in Asia also touches on the issue of evaluation. The teacher should be aware that the issue is controversial in the scholarly literature of our day: there are those who see the some thirty cities founded by Alexander as nothing but military bases, while others see him as the apostle of Greek culture to the barbarians. Whatever his motives, however, Alexander's significance in world history lies in his having opened up the Orient to Greek culture.

Bibliography for Grade Five

The following list has purposely been kept short. Wherever possible, easily obtainable literature is given. Several pocket books are listed that contain useful material, even if the author does not approve of their materialistic orientation.

Andrae, Walter. *Das wiedererstandene Assur.* München, 1977. (2nd edition)

Arnold, Sir Edwin. *The Light of Asia.* (The Life of Buddha).

Beckh, Hermann. *Buddha und seine Lehre,* 5th edition. Stuttgart, 1980.

Ceram, C.W. *Götter, Gräber und Gelehrte.* Hamburg, 1949.

Herodotus. *Histories.*

Jacobsen, Wilson Frankfort. *Dawning of the Giant.*

Kitto, H.D.F. *The Greeks.*

Kramer, Samuel Noah. *Cradle of Civilization.* Time-Life Books.

Lauer, Jean-Philippe. *Saqqara.* Bergisch Gladbach, 1977.

Leonard, Jonathan N. *The First Farmers.* Time-Life Books (Emergence of Man Series).

Plutarch. *Lives.*

Schliemann, Heinrich. *Autobiography*.

Schmökel, Hartmut. *Ur, Assur und Babylon*. Stuttgart o.J.

Teichmann, Frank. *Der Mensch und sein Tempel*. Bd. 1 Ägypten, Stuttgart, 1978.

Thucydides. *History of the Peloponnesian War.*

van Bemmelen, D.J. *Zarathustra*. Vrij Geestesleven. Zeist, 1968 (English), 2 Vols.

von Glasenapp, Helmut. *Die nichtchristlichen Religonen*. Fischer-Lexikon 1. Frankfurt, 1957.

Wilson, John A. "Agypten." *Propyläen Weltgeschichte Band 1.*

Wilson, John A. *The Culture of Ancient Egypt*. University of Chicago Press, 1957.

---- *Epic of Gilgamesh*. Various editions.

7

SIXTH GRADE

Just its thematic focus alone gives history in the sixth grade an entirely different character than in the fifth grade. The leading historical personalities now stand out much more as members of a group, as exponents of social associations. Hence very often a duality is found: two persons, two groups, two attitudes towards life confront each other, and between the two history is enacted:

At the beginning of Roman history: Romulus and Remus.
During the struggles between the orders: patricians and plebeians.
In the struggle for world domination: Rome and Carthage.
In the Middle Ages: Arabs and Franks,
emperor and pope,
monks and knights.

In this way history leaves the high regions in which human culture is founded, and enters the dimension of human confrontation. Naturally this principle is not absolute. Nonetheless, one can see that even the newly arising religion of Christianity was drawn into these conflicts: the Book of Acts itself already reports the differences of opinion that later were to be continued in quarrels over dogma and the conflict between Rome and Byzantium. In all these phenomena one can see the dialectical principle of the intellectual-soul.

In view of the abundance of material, the teacher himself must also make good use of his intellectual-soul and make decisions: from this overabundance, what is to be treated and what left out? More than in many other grades, the thematic focus of the sixth grade requires a plan that must be strictly followed; for by the end of the second history block of sixth grade the year 1400 must have been reached. Under no circumstances may the subject matter of the sixth grade be carried over into the seventh. At the beginning of a new grade, just as at the beginning of a

86

new block, the danger is always that one begins by expounding on things with epic latitude, only to notice later with astonishment that one has managed to cover but half of the material. As to dividing up the two blocks, it seems a good idea to limit the first block to the history of the Roman Empire, early Christianity, and the Migration of Peoples — an enormously comprehensive program. The second block would then start out with Islam and the world of the Arabs, go on to Charlemagne and the German Empire, and finally to the high Middle Ages. For once, I will suggest a possible chronology as an orientation aid in these two blocks.

Block I

Week 1: First three days: the foundation of Rome and the seven kings to 510 B.C. Next three days: the fights between patricians and plebeians and the resulting birth of law and the constitution.

Week 2: The battle between Rome and Carthage (Hannibal and Scipio); the Gracchi and the battle for social reform; Caesar as an example of the beginning of a new form of government.

Week 3: The spreading of Christianity in the Roman Empire, illustrated through the figure of Paul; Paul in Rome. The last three days: Huns and Goths during the Migration of Peoples; fall of the Roman Empire.

Block II

Week 1: First half of the week: Mohammed and Islam up to the conquest of Spain by Tarik. Second half: Charles Martel and the Franks. Charlemagne and the revival of the Roman Empire.

Week 2: Birth of the German Empire: Henry I and Otto I; the culture of the monasteries; the Cluny reform and the beginning of the conflict between emperor and pope.

Week 3: The Crusades, chivalry, knightly orders; the encounter of Orient and Occident; Frederick II ("the Great") and the beginning of urban culture. Attempt at summary: the shifting of history from the Mediterranean to northwest and central Europe.

Once again, this is merely a proposal and should not be taken as a binding canon. It may be that one teacher will rightly decide: I will leave out the battle between Rome and Carthage, the Gracchi and their social reforms. It seems more important to me to devote time in the Middle Ages to the Franciscan Order and the Hanseatic League. This decision, which is practically unavoidable in Bremen, Hamburg, and Lübeck, can only be welcomed. It matters alone that the teacher have a real plan before beginning his history blocks and does his utmost to teach in such an effective manner that the plan is carried through.

At the beginning of the sixth grade, the prehistory of the foundation of Rome leads us once more into the realm of legend. Rome's history appears upon the background of myth, a hint of which is seen in the legend of the divine origin of the twins, their abandonment, and the figure of the she-wolf. The murder of Remus, who mocked the law of the sacred wall, is significant. The newly founded city became a refuge for the homeless of the vicinity. This city could become great only through battle and pillage. The legend of the seven kings — particularly in the figure of Numa Pompilius, but also that of Ancus Martius — shows by what means the life of this community was regulated. So it is that the "ordering of legal relations" becomes the theme of the history of the early Roman Republic. The single king was replaced by two consuls, who conferred together and who each had the right of veto. The battles between the orders can now be used to illustrate the regulation of simple social conditions, since here the problems, positions, and solutions remain clear and simple: the formation of the plebs into a confederation (coniuratio = league by oath), the exodus to the Sacred Mountain, the mission of Menenius Agrippa and his famous fable of the limbs that refuse to serve the stomach, and finally the compromise in the establishment of the ten people's tribunes, which were also endowed with the right to veto. And on it goes in a similar vein up to the Twelve Tables: publication of a code of laws now makes equality before the law possible; from the year 376 on, plebeians can become consuls, from 300 on they can become priests; and starting in 287 people's decisions (plebiscita) are binding for the entire people.

The regulations of the Roman constitution will seem equally reasonable and comprehensible to the sixth graders. These are realized in the succession of offices (*cursus honorum*), in the principles of collegiality (friendly relations among colleagues) and annuity (one year term of office), as well as in the institution of the censor. Similarly, the fact the highest office of state was open only to one who had proven himself in the offices of quaestor, aedile, and praetor; that a censor inspected the conduct of offices; that every office — except that of the dictator, whose term lasted half a year (one summer's campaign) — was limited to one year; and that each office was occupied by at least two citizens to prevent concentration of power: all of these things make such sense that students find them deeply satisfying.

The theme of the second section might be the following: the Roman virtues create a world empire, and the world empire destroys the Roman virtues. The emphasis would fall strongly on cultural history here: The Romans, a farming people, allow themselves to become involved in a fight with Carthage, the commercial power. Once victorious, Rome is transformed. The clay huts give way to bigger houses; the streets are paved; Greek culture — with Greek slaves — enters the city; peasant culture disappears, and with it the Roman warrior who had defended house and farmstead. In his place comes the mercenary, dependent on soldier's pay and plunder. In the tenements dwell people who live on alms of oil and grain, people with a taste for exhibition fights at the circus. The cultural and political scene in Rome, the world metropolis, can now be illustrated through the figure of Caesar. Rome had become the center of a well-organized world empire. A two hundred-year period of peace and prosperity was beginning. The inner city was paved with marble; its walkways were covered; aqueducts brought fresh water into the city from the mountains. The rich bathed in thermal baths, while the poor were kept content with gladiator fights. Rome had perished.

The spread of Christianity is of incomparable significance for the entire subsequent course of history, hence it also belongs in the history lesson. The figure of the Apostle Paul unites in a unique way three elements that defined the world of that time: the Jewish, the Greek, and the Roman. In him, these three elements enter the service of the Christian impulse. By birth and religious background Paul was a strict adherent to

Judaism; by education — he had grown up in Tarsus — he had been touched by the Greek spirit; and finally he was a Roman citizen, a legal status that by no means all inhabitants of the Roman Empire enjoyed. Paul's journeys take him from Asia to Europe: through his preaching, we see him take infant Christianity out of the small Jewish world into the culture of antiquity, founding communities in Ephesus, Philippi, Thessalonica, Athens, Corinth, and probably also in Rome. The essential thing to make clear here is how, in the midst of an old culture, in the very smallest human circles, the germ of something new is planted; a single human, filled with the spirit and with his mission, forms communities that endure despite persecution and scorn, outlasting the fall of the outer civilization around them.

It is uncommonly difficult to give students a clear idea of the Migration of the Peoples, which is connected with the fall of the Roman Empire. This extraordinarily complex happening, involving various Germanic peoples as well as the Huns, Byzantium and Rome, is perhaps best illustrated through the story of the West Goths (Visigoths). Following their fate during the time of the Peoples' Migration, we are led out of the fertile areas north of the Danube up to the gates of Byzantium (387), to the conquest and pillage of Rome (410), to Gaul and the battle on the Catalaunian fields, and finally to Spain, where the empire of the West Goths was established. Their way of life provides perhaps the best illustration of the character of the Germanic peoples: the small village settlements, the farmstead, the retainers (or "following") of the lord, and the manner of justice. Each of their life-forms expresses the individual's claim to freedom. In freedom the retainer joined a leader, whom he could leave again; questions of justice and common undertakings were decided in free discussion. The woman was respected among the Germanic peoples and, as a priestess, was able to develop significant influence.

To the extent that it had not already become dysfunctional before the Peoples' Migration, the organization of the Roman Empire now collapsed. Traffic routes were endangered, trade broke down, cities became depopulated, hardly any state administration worthy of the name still existed; the urban world of antiquity had given way to the agrarian society of the early Middle Ages.

Mohammed and Islam cannot be left out of the curriculum. We begin with Mohammed's biography, his visions, his call to prophecy, his battles. Next it is important to show that Islam represents an entirely different type of religious life from Christianity. Islam knows no sacraments or ordained clergy. Greatest emphasis is placed on fulfilling the five religious duties: profession of belief in one God and his human prophet Mohammed, prayer five times daily, the giving of alms, fasting from dawn to dusk in the month of Ramadan, and pilgrimage to Mecca. The concept of Holy War (Jihad) results in Islam's conquest of wide areas. A second point of emphasis could be to study the cultural achievements of the caliphate under Harun al Rashid, for which one might examine a hospital in Bagdad, for example. A look at Islamic art is both important and impressive: an art without images, as exemplified by the Alhambra, for example, or by the Mosque of Abbas the Great in Isfahan. In this way a picture takes form of a magnificent culture founded on a very simple religion, a culture that towers above the Western world of that time and yet, strangely, shows little further development after its great blossoming.

Unlike the Goths, Vandals, or Burgundians, the Franks did not settle down as a thin upper stratum of rulers, but spread out as a people. Hence the kingdom of the Franks, in contrast to the other Germanic kingdoms founded in the course of the Migration of Peoples, survived the following centuries. Consequently, it was upon the Franks that the Arab assault shattered in the battle of Tours and Poitiers. In the sixth grade, however, these events are best only mentioned on the side, in order to gain time for Charlemagne. Charlemagne laid the foundation on which the western European world was to build henceforth. It was his work, the Carolingian renaissance, that began the process of interpenetration of Germanic, Christian, and antique worlds that developed in later centuries into Western culture. This is a most remarkable phenomenon: under the sign of Christianity, the Germanic tribes of western and central Europe assimilate, step by step, the culture of antiquity. Here, the task of instruction is to make this renewal of culture really visible. Certainly, the securing and extending of the empire cannot be belittled, but without a time-enduring cultural core, its vital significance would be lost. The image of the emperor should emerge: an emperor who gathered around him eminent scholars of his time — Petrus of Pisa, Paulus Diaconus, Theodulf of Orleans, and Alcuin; an emperor who promoted education and pastoral care, who founded and protected monasteries. These monasteries became a model to their rural environment through such things as their vineyards, orchards, and herb gardens. In the Capitulare de Vilis, Charlemagne decreed that every crown domain must plant a small herb garden with mugwort, mandrake, lovage, iris, carrots, sage, rosemary, garden mint, and many other plants. Thus, Charlemagne's concerns went beyond education and theology, monastic discipline and architecture: his cultural renewal also entailed a practical model for the rural population.

The beginning of German history, with King Henry I and Emperor Otto I, could also be discussed within this framework: the process of assimilating culture continues now in those areas that had entered the Frankish Empire the latest. The conflict between emperor and pope should perhaps not be made a special theme in the sixth grade; but the process underlying it — social differentiation — should. We are dealing with a process in which first the monasteries and then the clergy become more independent and remember the spiritual nature of their office. Celibacy is introduced for the priests so that they can devote themselves exclusively to their calling. In the monasteries, free election of abbots is instituted and worldly influence on the occupancy of this office is eliminated. In the same period, agriculture gets a fresh impetus: gradually, the wheeled plow takes hold in west and central Europe; the use of iron increases; now the horse joins the ox as a draft animal before the plow. What made this all possible is that since the middle of the eleventh century, the Truce of God (Treuga Dei, continuing the older Peace of God movement) had gained ever wider influence. In the Middle Ages, the customary form in the fight for justice was the feud, which followed definite rules. Now, by a peace decree, all those days of the week on which the Lord suffered — Thursday, Friday, Saturday, and Sunday — were declared days of peace, when the feud must rest. This gave much greater security to life, particularly for the peasant farmers, the tradesmen, and craftsmen. The safety of the traffic routes in turn affected the monastic movement, which now did not remain limited to a few monasteries. Supported by the emperor, it asserted itself in west and central Europe, finally taking hold of Rome as well. Out of this, the conflict between emperor and pope eventually developed.

Due to the separation of the spiritual and the worldly, a new spirit of asceticism spread through western Europe — not only in the monasteries, but also in large parts of the population. Out of this spirit the Crusades were born. Originally, the idea was to help the Greeks in Byzantium against the Seljuks and to create a new empire in the holy places of the East. The Crusaders, setting out with great enthusiasm and high earnestness, could not live up to their aims. The farther they pushed towards the East, the more dubious their behavior became. The conquest of Jerusalem in 1099 and the course of the Fourth Crusade appear as gruesome perversions of the original high goals. The cultural significance of the Crusades is disputed by modern research. Earlier, the cultural influence of the Orient on the West was generally credited to the Crusaders' encounter with the Orient, but recent investigators point out that the adoptions from Arabic culture likely took place through more peaceful contacts in Sicily and in Spain. In any case, in Italy the new acquaintance with Oriental products and techniques of production led to a great blossoming of its cities. Familiar words borrowed from Arabic or Persian point to the kind of products and the new knowledge involved: damask, cotton, muslin, gauze, coffee, marzipan, sugar, syrup, orange, spinach, apricot, nutmeg, cinnamon, caraway, *tasse* (cup), carafe, *pantoufles* (slippers), divan, sofa, mattress, magazine, check mate, algebra, and cipher.

In order to summarize this all, one could recount the life of Frederick II of Hohenstaufen: how he grew up in Sicily and encountered Arabic culture there; how he was then sent to Germany by Pope Innocent III as a rival king; the decisions he made in regard to the conflict between the princes and the cities, which were now growing independent; and his coronation as emperor in 1220. Other especially revealing deeds: the foundation of the University of Naples in 1224 and Frederick's interest in nature, evident in the book he wrote on falconry. On his crusade in 1228/29, the emperor negotiated personally, in Arabic, with the Sultan's representative, thus obtaining the return of the holy places to the Christians and an assured access to the coast. There are quite a number of other important and revealing situations in the life of this Hohenstaufen Emperor. To conclude a portrayal of the Middle Ages with this one figure, however, would leave too one-sided a picture. A person who stood, as it were, at the opposite pole from this glorious and tragic emperor is Francis of Assisi. He and his order represent a new type of piety. Because of the absolute poverty not only of their monks, but also of their monasteries, this order had credibility with the urban proletariat of upper Italy, and with the poor. This aspect of the works of the Franciscans can round off the picture of society, making visible not just the actions of the high and mighty, but also the fate of the ordinary man, the poor woman.

Up to now we have been dealing with a chronological approach oriented to themes of German history. The possibility exists, however, to let this approach recede into the background in favor of themes weighted more heavily towards cultural history. For the early Middle Ages, it would in fact be quite fortunate if the students first learned to comprehend the significance of the forest in the Middle Ages. The forest was the wilderness, into which hermits and outlaws retreated; it was wild and menacing. In many areas of Europe wolf hunting was among the duties of the peasants and knights. At first, the forest was common property. Acorns fattened the pigs; honey-hunters ventured deep into the forest to harvest the coveted sweetness. In the course of time the forest was pushed back more and more by clearings; the hunt became the right of the lords, and the common land became the lords' property. In the forest, small settlements grew into villages. The peasants worked the land under two- or three-field crop rotation. The unfree peasants were bound to corvée labor for their master, and many a one gazed grimly up towards the walls of the castle, for which he had carted the rocks. Again and again one hears of popular revolts in the Middle Ages: of peasants rising up against their lord — against Henry IV, for example. Many a farmer, especially in southern Germany and in France, was glad if he could come under the protection and sovereignty of a reformed monastery, for here there was no overseer demanding service for himself above and beyond the service to the monastery. The monks in the monasteries not only offered the farmers protection and encouragement for their agriculture, but also addressed their sermons directly to the people — something that had not happened before the reforms of Cluny and Hirsau — so that the farmer learned not only matters of faith, but also what was taking place in the wide world.

The ground plans of medieval monasteries — that of St. Gall, for example — show that the monasteries were a closed-off world to themselves and at the same time a world for others. In the interior of the cathedral one recognizes fifteen altars where the priest-monks sang or read mass several times a day and where they prayed day and night for the deceased and for the living. Besides the library and scriptorium, the abbot's house and the cloister, many other buildings belonged to this monastery: the pilgrims' hostel, the guest house, the hospital, the school, and the house for craftsmen. Then there were all the buildings of the monastic economy, from the stables to the mills and baking house. There was a doctor's house and an apothecary and a garden of curative herbs. Thus, following the commandment of St. Benedict, work was joined to prayer.

Just as peace reigned in the monastery, so did peace principally reign in the medieval city. Peace meant protection and law. The town wall protected the burghers; the gates were guarded. Within, the law, the regulations of market and measurement, gave protection. The city air had a liberating effect, and in many cities this freedom led to self-government. In Cologne, the municipality split itself into twenty-two branches or guilds; these, together with the departing town council, selected the new councilmen, who in turn elected the two mayors (*bürgermeister*) for a term of one year. The council decided upon expenditures and revenues, on taxes and alliances, and about war and peace. The mayors represented the town to the outside world. Within the town, the guilds controlled the quality of the merchandise, the weights and measures. Through this capacity for self-government, this awareness of freedom, such cities as Cologne, Strassburg, Basel, and others as well, were able to free themselves from the rule of the bishops and became the cradle of a new legal, artistic, and intellectual life.

Bibliography for Grade Six

Rome: The best basic source is still Livy and Plutarch (see Fifth Grade). For teachers and students:

Brooks, Polly Schoyer and Walworth, Nancy Zinsser. *When the World was Rome.* J. B. Lippincott Co. New York.
Niederhäuser, Hans R. *Römische Sagen und Geschichten.* Stuttgart, 1980.
Oppermann, Heinz. *Caesar.* rororo Monographie 135.
Bleiken, Jochen. "Rom und Italien." *Propyläen Weltgeschichte,* Band 4 Berlin, 1963.
Hoffman, Wilhelm. "Roms Aufstieg zur Weltherrschaft." Ebenda
Heuss, Alfred. "Das Zeitalter der Revolutionen." Ebenda
Heyer, Karl. *Von der Atlantis bis Rom.* Breslau, 1939.
Häusler, Friedrich. *Weltenwille und Menschenziele in der Geschichte.* Dornach, 1961. Kapitel: "Historische Metamorphosen."

Christianity:

Die Apostelgeschichte (The Acts According to the Apostles).
Bock, Emil. *Caesaren und Apostel.* 5 überarbeitete Auflage, Stuttgart, 1978.
Bock, Emil. *Paulus.* Stuttgart, 1981.

The Middle Ages:

Brooks, Polly Schoyer and Walworth, Nancy Zinsser. *The World of Walls.*
    J. B. Lippincott Co., New York.
Nitschke, August. "Frühe Christliche Reiche." In: *Propyläen
    Weltgeschichte* Band 5.
Braunfels, Wolfgang. *Karl der Grosse.*
Le Goff, Jacques. "Das Hochmittelalter." Band 11 der *Fischer
    Weltgeschichte,* Frankfurt, 1965.
Nette, Herbert. *Friedrich II von Hohenstaufen.* Reinbeck, 1975. rororo-
    mon. 222.

8

SEVENTH GRADE

Rudolf Steiner's curriculum lectures of 1919 contain his only direct statement on the thematic focus of seventh grade history: "In the seventh grade the object is to make it so that the child really can understand the life that begins to arise in humanity with the advent of the fifteenth century, and then to describe the circumstances in Europe etc., up to about the beginning of the seventeenth century. This period of time is of the utmost importance, and it must be treated with great care. It is even more important than what follows it." In accordance with this judgment, while the sixth grade is allotted two blocks to cover two millennia, the seventh devotes the same amount of time to two or three centuries. Now the question is what topics to discuss. Should we deal with the emperors and kings — Sigismund, Frederick III, or Maximilian and Charles V? With the reform of the empire and councils? Or are other themes more important? The character of the modern age will certainly not be brought out by looking at the further development of medieval problems and forms of life. What is essentially new in the modern age first appears in the discoveries — with Vasco da Gama, Columbus, and Magellan — and in the inventions, particularly with Gutenberg and his printing press, the development of clocks, the invention of gunpowder, and in the mills and turbines. It appears in the new form of commerce, i.e. in figures such as Jacque Coeur, Jakob Fugger, the Welser family, and others. It further appears — though with a certain limitation — in the German Reformation, while politically it becomes visible in the Netherlands' fight for freedom and in the English victory over the Spanish Armada.

One new element of the greatest importance can be seen in the changing relationship of human beings to the experience of their senses. In the Middle Ages it was usual to regard the sensory appearance of things symbolically. The educated theologian, for example, knew what was said in the Bible about the various animals and in which prophecies they occurred. Therefore a wild ass was not just a wild ass. And so when Luidprandt of Cremona saw wild asses in Byzantium, he was reminded of the saying of Hyppolytus: "The lion and his cub together shall chase away the wild ass," and the issue was how to interpret this saying. It was similar with the phenomena of the heavens: they were revelations of God, meant to be read and understood. This certainly does not mean that the people of the Middle Ages did not see wild asses and lions quite soberly as well, or that at the cattle market they did not know how to judge an animal as to its age, strength, weight, and value. But the way people thought about things was not yet determined by their sensory appearance alone.

It is precisely this which changed. Looking at the first modern navigation charts, we see that exact surveying of the coastline and exact determination of the degrees of latitude have now made it possible to render purely physical forms. The earth is covered with a network of exact measurements. Similarly, anatomy now dissects the corpse, furnishing an exact description of the physical body: each organ is described as to its form and position. The manipulation of forces and mechanisms goes hand in hand with such understanding: people learn to harness wind and water in mills, to measure the speed of a ship, and to measure time with the sundial, hourglass, and finally with the mechanical clock. Whoever wishes to gain insight into this new way of looking at things will find it most beautifully and impressively embodied in Leonardo da Vinci. The change in consciousness visible in Leonardo is the change that is taking place quite generally: the sense for the practical, mechanical, and technical is growing, the sense for the wondrous and sacred is fading.

This brings us to a factor that formerly did not play such a significant role, and even now, in the seventh grade, should not be overly emphasized: the economic aspect of human action. Rudolf Steiner has pointed out that the effective forces of history are not the same at all times. There are times that are moved primarily by spiritual impulses. In other times the legal relations among human beings are dominant. But in the early modern age, economy plays a special role in human activities. This is by no means to assert that economic life takes on complete independence — that pure economic processes are independently effective — but it does mean that the motivation of human beings may be guided by economic ideas, or that the people who set the tenor of life are those who think economically. Rudolf Steiner illustrates this at one point:

If we investigate events in the light of truth and not of illusion, if we investigate all that underwent a metamorphosis through the Reformation at the beginning of the more recent historical development, we must say: A powerful upheaval has indeed taken place in the population, and at the beginning of the modern age the different strata of the population have undergone a rather quick change. It arose through the fact that before the Reformation, people who, for example, owned land chiefly in Western Europe, were not identical with those who owned land after the Reformation. The leading men who counted most, as it were, in the social structure before the Reformation, lost their power through the Reformation. To a far greater extent than one generally supposes, the tenure of lands and estates was, before the Reformation, dependent on the rule of priests. The rule of priests was in general a very strong factor in the economic conditions before the Reformation. Those who owned land, owned it to a large extent because they held it in tenure, as it were, for authorities somehow connected with the Church.

If we investigate things less idealistically perhaps, but more in keeping with the historical course of events, we find that almost throughout Europe the Reformation tore away from the Church its old property and transferred it to secular rulers. This was to a high extent the case in England and later on, also in Germany. You see, later on, in Germany, many of the territorial rulers were in favour of the Reformation. But not everywhere was enthusiasm for Luther or the other reformers the guiding motive, but — to express it mildly — the hunger for the property of the Church, the longing to secularize ecclesiastical property. An immense ecclesiastical property of the Middle Ages passed over to secular rulers, to the territorial rulers. In England a large majority of the landowners was expropriated and emigrated to America. The great majority of those who emigrated to America — yesterday we saw from another standpoint what really lay at its foundation — consisted of the expropriated landowners. Economic conditions were therefore to a high degree responsible for the transformations in the modern historical development which is generally designated as Reformation. From a superficial aspect, matters present themselves as follows: People declare that a new spirit must enter the human souls, that the old church-rule connects the secular element too strongly with the spiritual one, that a more spiritual way to Christ must be found, etc. etc. But viewed more deeply and less superficially, an economic metamorphosis takes place by transferring ecclesiastical property to secular owners.[1]

Certainly the idea is not to make these formulations of Rudolf Steiner the content of seventh grade instruction in this form. Still there is a difference whether, when discussing the discoveries, we take the mythical figure of Prester John as our starting point or whether we discuss the fact that since the beginning of the fourteenth century the overland caravan route to the Far East (Mongol route) and Oriental trade were to a great extent blocked if not altogether extinguished by the power of the Turks and other developments in the Orient; or whether we mention the flowing out of Europe's gold reserves to the Orient. Thus, in the seventh grade such economic connections are given a factual basis, and they are comprehensible to this age level.

Similarly, the style of instruction can also change for such themes. Certain topics can now be worked through in class. For instance, the question might be asked: think of all the preconditions you can that were necessary for the discovery of America. From this point of departure it is possible to treat shipbuilding, astronomically oriented navigation, the compass, geographical knowledge, and the development of maps in such a way that the students themselves come upon these preconditions. The task of the teacher is then to show the particular form these preconditions actually took in history. And in the process, it may well be found that there are students in the class who already know something about the development of cogs, the Jacob's staff, or the quadrant — knowledge they can share with the class. The same approach can be used for the invention of printing or clocks.

Thus it is very good to begin with the discoveries, so that right at the beginning of the seventh grade the students can experience what is new about the modern age. Despite all scholarly objections and despite the fact that the achievements of the Portuguese do not represent a totally new beginning of the discoveries, we may begin with Henry the Navigator. The importance of this man is that he was the driving force behind the discoveries. As treasurer of the Order of Christ, which was

---

[1] Rudolf Steiner: Lecture of October 12, 1919, from: "Soziales Verständnis aus geisteswissenschaftlicher Erkenntnis," Dornach, 1972, p. 102-3.

the continuation of the Knights Templar in Portugal, he was able to employ their financial means to promote the especially difficult phase of discoveries along the Sahara coast. At the same time, these voyages, which were to stretch as far as the equator and finally to the Cape of Good Hope and all the way to India, shattered medieval notions of the uninhabited regions and boiling seas in the South.

In treating Columbus' discovery of America, for which the ship's log should prove a useful resource, one should not forget to go into the further — and tragic — fate of Columbus. This might be followed by the conquest of Mexico or Peru. As a counterweight to these topics, which really anticipate the problems of colonialism, one should also take up the activities of Bartholomè de las Casas, who took a stand for humane treatment, education, and instruction of the Indians. A focal point in the battle of this Dominican is his audience with Charles V. Further, it would make for more economical teaching if one could touch on ocean currents when speaking of Columbus' voyages, or develop a picture of the Inca Empire, the Andes, and the geographical conditions of western South America and the eastern Pacific when speaking of the conquest of Peru.

When we look over the fifteenth century, the question arises whether or not to discuss Joan of Arc — and if so, how. When we consider that after the intervention of Joan of Arc the English were permanently driven from France, and that England and France now began to develop into more and more distinct national states, we see that this is an event of such significance that it cannot be bypassed. At the same time, for the seventh grade it is a good idea to treat the life of Joan of Arc quite soberly and to bring in contemporary sources. The childhood of the Maid of Orleans is also a good way to illustrate peasant and village life in the late Middle Ages, while the trial against Joan of Arc could be an opportunity to speak of medieval justice or the treatment of heretics. In conclusion one could examine the Peace of Picquigny, in which Louis XI of France bought from King Edward of England his claim to the French throne.

After this intermezzo of political history, the invention of printing takes us back to cultural history. Symptomatic of this invention is that — like the discoveries — it did not happen by chance, but was the result of long and systematic efforts. For it is not solely a matter of printing being invented. The idea of movable type that can be cast in series with a matrix is more than mere printing, and this invention in particular had demanding prerequisites. The letters could be neither too soft nor too hard, requiring development of an appropriate alloy of lead, tin, and bismuth; a printer's ink had to be found that would stick to the letters and quickly dry on paper; and absorbent paper had to be available. The significance and effects of the invention are in accordance with these preparatory efforts. The fate of the inventor is akin to that of Columbus: neither of them reaped the benefits of his achievements.

The teacher is faced with the task of making visible the effects of this invention. The course of the German Reformation is well suited to showing this. It was once said that the word of the Reformation spread as though the angels were its messengers. Perhaps it was not the angels, but the 95 theses came out in Wittenberg at the end of October 1517, and in November they had already been reprinted in Leipzig; they then appeared in German translation in Nuremberg and in book form in Basel. After Gutenberg's invention, the art of printing spread with the greatest speed. Around 1500 there were 20 print shops in Augsburg, 21 in Cologne, 151 in Venice, and a total of about 1120 print shops in 250 cities in Europe. The Reformation considerably heightened the hunger for reading and also the need for discussion. Significantly, writings were now also printed in German: in 1518 there were 150 such, in 1521 already 620, and in 1624 around 990 publications appeared in German.

A much more prosaic topic is the development of early German capitalism. Jakob Fugger is the outstanding figure here. Originally engaged in the textile business, in 1487 the Fuggers went into the mining industry when, as security for a loan to Prince Sigismund of Tyrol, they were granted the right to buy at a special price all silver and copper produced in Schwaz until the debt was paid. Ever increasing areas of the coal, iron, and steel industry of that time were soon in the hands of the Fugger family, who extended their business into Hungary. The collateral which the princes put up was effectively managed, and thus the Fugger family became the biggest banking house in Europe. Through their capital they decided the occupancy of bishop's seats and the choice of the Holy Roman Emperor.

With printing and early capitalism, two important factors of the Reformation period have been singled out. Even if the complex conflicts and religious problems of the Reformation are not fully accessible to the seventh grade students, a short sketch of the deeds and effects of Luther's life should be given. It would be best to limit this to the time up to 1525, ignoring as much as possible the ensuing complications: e.g., the League of Schmalkalden, the Holy League. One can depict how Luther grew up in the pious religiosity of the late Middle Ages, how "in a stroke of lightning" he decided to become a monk, how he devoted himself with great seriousness to his penance; his journey to Rome, and then the familiar great events: posting of the theses, controversy with Eck, appearance before emperor and empire at the Reichstag in Worms; Wartburg; translation of the Bible; return to Wittenberg to confront the zealots there; and finally, Luther's stand against the peasants in the Peasants' War. In all of this it is important to stress what C. F. Meyer* formulated so beautifully: "His spirit is the battlefield of two ages." That is, Luther is not a "modern man" in our sense: both old and new, the Middle Ages and the Modern Age live within him. Luther's position in this respect is clearly manifested in his religious conversation with Zwingli at Marburg.

A customary presentation of history would go on now to the Counter-Reformation, the foundation of the Jesuit Order, the Peace of Augsburg, perhaps to Calvin as well, and the Huguenot Wars. First of all, however, these religious conflicts are hardly "digestible" for a seventh grader, and secondly, these questions have receded far into the distance today. On the other hand, there are many themes that would be most desirable to treat, but are difficult to present. One of these is Paracelsus, who fought for a medicine based on experience and observation. Another is the battle over the Copernican view of the world, from Copernicus to Giordano Bruno to Kepler and Galileo. However, these subjects should be taken up only if the teacher feels able to make them completely vivid. Particularly the life of Paracelsus, with his dramatic battle against tradition and booklearning and his famous cures, can be of great interest. It is necessary, however, to develop an understanding of this man's way of thinking, and therein lies the difficulty. The life of Galileo is similarly significant, dramatic, and vivid. In contrast to Paracelsus, however, this life seems more ambivalent; and it would be essential here not to moralize about it, but simply to make it really comprehensible.

The great battles in the second half of the sixteenth century, the battles that decide the future, take place in western Europe. On the one

---

*Conrad Ferdinand Meyer (1825-1898): Swiss poet and historical writer. [transl. note]

side is the Spain of Philip II, on the other are the Netherlands with
William of Orange and Elizabethan England. Here it would be worth-
while, before entering into the military conflicts, to paint a picture of
Spain under Philip II: the strict protocol of the Spanish court, the
Escorial, a session of the city council, the personal bearing of Philip, and
to complete the picture, a look at the internal situation of the country,
emphasizing the question of the Moriscos of Granada. This province, the
most flourishing of the kingdom, had an exceptionally large Moorish
population, to whom Christianity still remained alien sixty years after
their "conversion," and who had more in common with the Moors on
the other side of the Strait than with the Spaniards of the peninsula.
When Philip forbade the Arabic language, Arabic books, and Moorish
customs, rebellion broke out — a battle that was fought with relentless-
ness on both sides. The result was that the entire province of Granada
was swept clean of Moors (Moriscos). In this way one of the richest
regions of Europe was transformed into a desert, but the problem of the
Moors was not solved by the deportation. Between 1609 and 1614 they
were completely driven from Spain. With the loss of the Moors, Spain
had lost the section of its population most skilled in the crafts. Despite all
the silver and gold in its colonies, Spain now slowly became a poor and
backward land; for the money did not remain in Spain, but was used up
for the religious wars in other parts of Europe. The decline of the
knightly class that ruled in Spain has been described in a well-known
piece of world literature: *Don Quixote* by Miguel de Cervantes.

We come into a totally different world when we set foot in the
southern Netherlands. In Ghent, Bruges, Antwerp, Brussels, and many
others towns lived a rich class of burghers: merchants, craftsmen, and
manufacturers. Leadership lay with aristocrats, of whom the best known
were Counts Egmont and Hoorn. When the Inquisition was first introduced into the southern Netherlands, the aristocracy soon mounted a
mass petition asking for the withdrawal of the Spanish troops and the
recall of the Inquisition Edict. In their own way, craftsmen, peasants,
sailors, and folk of the lower classes joined in their effort, leading to the
infamous desecration of Churches.* Hereupon the duke of Alba was
entrusted with the command in the Netherlands, and the well-known

---

* When Calvinist mobs ravaged Catholic churches, destroying images and
furnishings. [trans. note]

developments followed. The symptomatic feature of this is that in the end the rich, southern Netherlands are defeated, while the much poorer and less hospitable land of Holland asserts its will in a protracted battle for freedom — at first under the leadership of William of Orange. It is here that the new culture arises. Leyden becomes the leading university of Europe. The religious tolerance reigning in Holland attracts numerous important scholars to the land. The life that evolves here represents the true spirit of the age. It is the world we know from the paintings of Rembrandt.

Spain's other opponent was England. In England, too, a commonwealth was coming into being, giving the individual greater opportunities. Both the English gentry and the aspiring English towns were represented in the House of Commons. Elizabeth understood how to rule with the Parliament. She ruled sparingly, furthered the undertakings of her subjects, and kept no standing army in England. The English fleet, which conquered the Armada, was built only in the last ten years before the battle broke out with Spain: it consisted of no more than forty relatively small but agile warships, but these were manned by seasoned seamen, pirates, and warriors. The Spanish Armada with its 130 cumbersome vessels still presented the picture of battle tactics reminiscent of the Middle Ages: the warriors on the Spanish ships — actually land soldiers under the command of a knight — were trained to fight aboard ship. While the Spaniards massed their ships into blocks that impaired their mobility, the English relied on their artillery and their art of maneuvering. They avoided any near approach that might expose them to the danger of being boarded. To the Spanish this was a sign of cowardice: it meant that the English could do nothing but shoot and then flee when endangered.

Just as the golden century begins in Holland after its victorious battle for freedom, so in England the victory over the Armada ushers in the age of Shakespeare. Perhaps this phenomenon of the theater enjoyed only a short period of flowering, but unlike other amusements it fascinated all levels of society: each week around twenty thousand people visited the theater productions in Southwark.

Bibliography for Grade Seven

Bitterli, Urs. *Die Entdeckung und die Eroberung der Welt.* Dokumente
und Berichte. Band 1: Amerika, Afrika. München, 1980. Band 2: Asien,
Australien, Pazifik. München, 1981.

Brooks, Polly Schoyer and Walworth, Nancy Zinsser. *The World Awakes.*
J. P. Lippincott. New York, 1962.

de Madariaga, Salvador. *Kolumbus.* München, 1978.

Hale, John R. *The Age of Exploration.* 1966.

Kolumbus, Christoph. *Bordbuch.* Frankfurt, 1981.

Konetzke, Richard. "Uberseeische Entdeckungen und Eroberungen."
Propyläen Weltgeschichte. Band 6.

Peschel, O. *Geschichte des Zeitalters der Entedeckungen.* Neudruck
Berlin, 1968.

With limitations, and often useful only in a few chapters, the following
books pertaining to the voyages of discovery:

Brion, M. *Die Medici.* Wiesbaden, 1970.

Harrer, Heinrich and Pleticha, Heinrich. *Entedeckungsgeschichte aus erster
Hand.* Würzburg, 1968.

Herrmann, Paul. *7 Vorbei und 8 Verweht.* 10. Aufl. Hamburn, 1978.

Herrmann, Paul. *Das Grosse Buch der Entdeckungen.* Reutlingen, 1958.

Kaiser, Ernst. *Paracelsus.* Reinbeck, 1969.

Moeller, Bernd. *Deutschland im Zeitalter der Reformation.* Göttingen,
1977.

Nette, Herbert. *Jeanne d'Arc.* Reinbeck, 1977.

Presser, Helmut. *Johanes Gutenberg.* Reinbeck, 1968.

van Roosbroak, Robert. *Wilhelm van Oranien, der Rebell.* Göttingen,
1959.

von Pölnitz, G. Frhr. *Die Fugger.* 3. Aufl. Tübingen, 1970.

von Poturzyn, M. J. Krück. *Die Sendung des Mädchens Jeanne d'Arc.*
Stuttgart, 1961.

9

EIGHTH GRADE

"In the eighth school year the attempt is to bring history up to the present, but it is really cultural history that one must be considering all the way through. Most of what makes up the content of history instruction today should only be mentioned as an aside if at all. It is much more important for the student to learn how the steam engine, the mechanical loom, and such things have transformed the earth than to know of such curiosities as the amendment of the Ems telegram." (First curriculum lecture, Sept. 6, 1919.)

In order to make it clear how the industrial revolution changed the face of the earth, the preindustrial world must first be described. The preindustrial world hardly knew what we call growth today. Periods of population increase were followed by epidemics, wars, or famines, which reduced the number of people again. In the towns, the craftsmen were organized into guilds, and the guild saw to it that there were never too many workshops of one kind in the town: each master craftsman was to have his livelihood. For example, in 1714 Tübingen had 73 butchers, 54 shoemakers, 46 tailors, 36 baker-confectioners, 26 ryebread bakers, 21 linen weavers, 20 coopers, 19 cloth and fabric makers, 18 carters, 14 tanners, 14 cabinet makers, 12 barbers, 9 locksmiths, 8 potters, 8 carpenters, 7 masons, 7 tawers [= dressers of white leather], 7 cartwrights, 6 blacksmiths, and about 130 artisans of other kinds, among them button makers, nail smiths, sieve makers, dyers, saddlers, and braidmakers. Altogether, 64 different crafts are listed. Naturally there were also farmers, winegrowers, gardeners, hunters, as well as — in Tübingen — the students and professors, town soldiers, police, judges, scribes, and so forth. The work of the craftsmen was largely done to order; there was as yet no production for an anonymous market.

Up to around the year 1800 and even after, the dwelling area of the burghers lay within the walls of the city, which presented a visible barrier to growth. Besides these visible barriers there were also invisible ones.

107

The towns, unless situated on great, navigable rivers, had to draw their provisions from the immediate environs. Land transport was so costly that it did not pay to haul grain great distances except in times of extreme famine. Moreover, newspapers were few, and very few burghers learned what happened in the outside world.

Tübingen's register of craftsmen does not yet mention a single watchmaker. There were doubtless clocks in Tübingen at the time, but evidently only a few. Life in the preindustrial world — this must be emphasized again and again — was hardly idyllic, but it was not yet run by the clock. Life still followed the daylight, the farmer's day; for as a rule the craftsmen too had a field and a garden. Each season had its labors; life had its rhythm.

The industrial revolution is a process that is suited to the need for a causal approach. The fact that this revolution of our living conditions had its starting point in England is no accident. The first prerequisite to mention here is England's mineral resources, most importantly its coal deposits so close to the surface. Then there are the many small watercourses, as on the slopes of the Pennines, which were able to turn mills and did turn them, too, thanks to relatively frequent rainfall. A second condition was met by the patent right in England. In 1624, the English Parliament had already passed a law regulating the issue of patents and preventing the misuse of the patent right by order of the Crown. The Crown could grant the real inventors and producers exclusive right of use for twenty-one years. A further precondition was the improvement of agricultural methods, which made it possible to nourish greater numbers of people with less manpower. Numerous small holdings failed because of the enclosures, releasing the manpower that was later utilized in the industrial revolution. Finally the Puritan work ethic doubtless also played a role here; the value that the Puritans placed on time later gives rise to the slogan "time is money." In the eighth grade, there is no need to go into all of these factors in detail, but one can certainly refer to one or another of them.

The history of the actual inventions has been falsified in many legends. Thus, James Watt did not get the idea for his steam engine by watching his mother's cooking pot. The process was quite different. Already in 1711 Newcomen had constructed a steam engine which was used in the coal mines for pumping water from the excavations. This machine swallowed incredible amounts of coal, for every stroke of the pump was brought about by the cooling of the cylinder. At the age of twenty-one, James Watt had gone to the University of Edinburgh as a university mechanic. There he was commissioned to repair a model of the Newcomen machine. After long deliberation, during a Sunday walk the idea came to him to have the cooling process take place in a condenser separate from the cylinder. This was in May 1765, but a patent was not granted him until January 1769. It took until 1776, the year of the American Declaration of Independence, before two new steam engines built by Watt were finally in operation. It was not for lack of demand that only these two existed, but rather because Watt, as a simple and practically destitute mechanic, required a partner who could undertake the actual production of the machine. This was not easy, as we see from the fact that the first attempt at collaboration with John Roebuck, owner of the Carron ironworks, foundered. Then there arose the classic cooperation between Watt and Boulton, a leading manufacturer in Soho near Birmingham. But here, too, there were difficulties: very precise and stable cylinders and pistons were needed for the cylinders of the condensers. It was only when John Wilkinson had developed a new boring machine (1774) — originally intended for the production of cannons — that the production of the actual steam engines could begin. The machines that were now built — Watt and Boulton manufactured a total of 496 engines — were true models of precision, some of them remaining in operation for 120 years. I have sketched the development of this invention in some detail because, in my view, this reality is much truer than the legends. The real story shows us that inventions are set in a great social context, that great inventions are based on a vast amount of preparatory work and cooperation on the part of many human beings.

A second aspect of this theme focuses on the social consequences of each invention. The textile industry is an especially good example here. In 1733 John Kay had invented the fly shuttle. This device made it possible to weave broader cloth at twice the speed. At the same time, the demand for textiles was increasing, so there was no unemployment as had been feared. But the spinners could barely keep up with the demand for yarn; therefore the working day in the spinneries had to be lengthened to as much as fifteen hours. It took eight to ten spinners to spin the yarn needed by one weaver. Therefore in 1751 the Royal Society of London offered a prize for "the best invention of a machine capable of spinning six threads of cotton, flax, or hemp and serviced by one person only." But it was not until 1764 that James Hargreaves was able to produce such a machine, one actually equipped with eight spindles. Soon after, Arkwright produced an improved spinning machine that could twine yarn substantially more firmly. Pure cotton cloth could now be manufactured in England. Later, in Cromford, Arkwrite also founded the first spinnery that could be given the name of a factory. The spinning machines were further improved within a very short time, so that one machine could spin twenty to fifty threads. It was Arkwright, again, who first used steam engines to replace the customary means of driving the machines by a mill, thus making the operation independent of unevenly flowing water-power.

The introduction of machines — spinning machine, steam engine, and mechanical loom — now led to the development of actual factories where machines replaced or supported human skill and labor, though it was not until 1805 that the mechanical loom broke the hold of the hand-loom. The development of factories proper had momentous social consequences. Until factories were built, all work — if we disregard manufacturing workshops, mining, and hauling — was done at home. The home was the place of living, working, and bringing up children; a home for the old, and a warehouse all in one. Following Otto Brunner, we can speak of the "old European house" as the place of undivided life. This can be pictured quite vividly. Just as the farmhouse also sheltered the cattle and stored the feed, grain, and other supplies, so the house of every craftsman had its workshop, and usually some livestock and a garden as well. The provisions were stored in the cellar. On the ground floor were the kitchen, a living room, and the workshop. Behind the house, in the yard or in an outbuilding were chickens, perhaps some pigs or a few goats. The upper story was where the grandparents lived and children and parents slept. Hay and straw were stored under the roof. Every household also had a garden outside the town, and often a small meadow or field. The children grew up in a world where work was a necessity, and they quickly learned to help their parents by doing all kinds of chores. Education took place not verbally, but by model and by work. The grandparents, if they were still alive, were also fully involved in the work of the house. They minded the little ones, advised and helped the mother during childbirth and lying in. Thus, the whole of life was within view: birth and death, work and consumption lay open before everyone's eyes. Yet this was certainly no idyll. One must be aware that around

1750, 60-70 percent of all children still died before their fifth birthday; that in the springtime there was almost no fresh food; that all water had to be pumped and often fetched from a well; that fuel had to be gathered in the woods; and that lighting was a luxury.

The factory, however, now divided home and workplace. Near the factories the first workers' settlements were soon built, housing workers at the closest quarters. Often the whole family lived together in one room. There was a stove, one or two beds, a table, and some benches. Everyone able to work went to the factory: men, women, and children. But this mechanical work no longer offered the picture of full life. It was not until the second half of the nineteenth century that the misery of early industrialization was significantly alleviated. Slowly, school attendance replaced child labor. In Germany, insurance was created in the 1880's to relieve the worst straits of old age, illness, and disability.

A totally different kind of consequence resulted from the increased demand for cotton. At that time cotton was cultivated chiefly in the southern states of the United States. This work required extremely intensive labor since the cotton had to be deseeded. It took a female worker a whole day to clean one pound of cotton. Since not enough Negro slaves were available, the cleaning process led to a bottleneck in the supply of cotton until 1793, when Eli Whitney succeeded in inventing a well-functioning cotton gin. Manually operated, this machine produced 50 lbs of cotton per day. Cotton production rose from 190,000 bales in 1791 to 41,000,000 bales in 1803. The escalation of cotton cultivation required more Negro slaves, who — until 1807 — were mass-transported from Africa.

Due to the Napoleonic Wars, after the year 1800 England could not export cotton products to Europe and began to search for new markets. Not only was cheap calico shipped to Africa, but exporting also now began to India, which was already an English colony and could not defend itself against British imports. The result was the destruction of India's own cotton-weaving industry. From now on Indian cotton-processing was limited to home industry for the rural population. After the end of the Napoleonic Wars, English textiles also found a market on the continent. The English production and the budding German textile industry then led to such situations as the misery of the Silesian weavers, which Gerhart Hauptmann depicted in his drama *Die Weber*.

From these examples out of the history of industrialization, we can recognize that the process of the transformation of the world by machines was as rich in preconditions as it was laden with consequences. The processes are very complex and not at all suited to a linear way of thinking. For example, our discussion did not mention the repercussions of the rapidly growing textile industry on transportation and machine building. The latter in turn gave a new impetus to the production of iron and steel, all of which together was a strong incentive for coal mining.

In the eighth grade as well the selection of subject matter is an issue. One reasonable criterion might be the social significance and effects of an invention complex. Thus, once the initial phase of the industrial revolution has been dealt with, the following choices would be available:

> Revolutions in transportation
> Electricity and its applications
> Chemistry or medicine

With all these complexes of inventions and innovations, it is important that their incisive effects on human social life really come clear. Thus it would be rather banal to say, as an effect of the invention of railroads, that before their invention it took a man thirty days to walk from Basel to Hamburg, if he walked thirty kilometers a day and took three days of rest, while today that distance can be covered in eight hours on the intercity train. Rather, it should be shown that railroad building was the greatest pacemaker of the industrial revolution. Between 1860 and 1900, forty thousand kilometers of rails were laid in the German Empire. Initially, this meant that production of iron and steel and the mining of coal experienced an unprecedented boom (coal production rising from 12.3 mill. tons in 1860 to 109 mill. tons in 1900). The construction of railway routes elicited new skills: tunnel building, bridge building, and dam building; expansion of the signalling system; application of the morse telegraph; and construction of a great variety of railway cars besides locomotives. This work gave millions of laborers their bread for decades. A few examples, such as the building of the Gotthard railway and tunnel, can illustrate the kind of achievements that were made during those years. To finance these giant undertakings was beyond the means of any one individual. Thus, joint-stock companies were founded, and banks that issued the stock. Stock exchanges began to grow in importance.

Another decisive factor is the effect of the modern means of transportation collectively. With steamboats and railroads together, merchandise which formerly was transportable only under favorable conditions could now be shipped in great quantities. Canadian and Argentinian wheat could be brought by rail to the big harbors and from there to Europe. Besides wheat and feeds, now tobacco, cacao, sugar, and rubber, oil-bearing fruits and seeds, ores and precious woods could be cheaply transported and delivered to the storage centers of the industrial nations. These in turn delivered industrial equipment and products to distant countries. World trade was born, and areas that otherwise would perhaps never have been opened up now became accessible: Siberia, central Canada, parts of the American Midwest.

This development too has its heroes: the entrepreneurs. As a teacher one should not allow oneself to be influenced by wrongly understood socialism; for even a Karl Marx knew that bourgeois entrepreneurs have their world-historical role in developing the forces of productivity. In Germany, the names of Brosig, Krupp, and Harkort — among others — can be mentioned here. Their biographies became the biographies of the enterprises; their success the success of industry. But it is too easily forgotten how many similar undertakings came to naught in the early period of industrialization. Success was by no means only a result of capitalist unscrupulousness. It also resulted from personal hard work, efficiency, prudence, and initiative. With this in mind, it is quite good to go into the biographies of Borsig or Harkort here and at first to present this development in a positive light. A critique of social conditions will be appropriate when the working and living conditions in this early period are described.

Thus, technical progress in the nineteenth century enlaced the whole of Germany in a well-functioning traffic network, and this network became the foundation of what is called urbanization. This is easy to see from the numbers of inhabitants: In 1850, Berlin had 419,000 inhabitants; in 1900 it had 1,889,000. In 1850, Hanover had 29,000 inhabitants (it is not on a major river); in 1900, it had 263,000.

The industrial revolution created entirely new conditions of life in these cities. Masses of human beings lived together in a limited space. Tenements and workers' housing developments are just as characteristic of this conglomeration as the luxurious residential districts. But in contrast to the twentieth century, technology had not yet penetrated into the houses and households of the nineteenth century. Before 1890 or 1900, there was hardly any electric lighting. Well-equipped apartments had running water, fireplace, and stove. Household machines, however — refrigerators, electric stoves, washing machines, central heating, and telephones — were completely absent. Bathing facilities were rare. The household chemicals so common today — washing powder, cleansers, and cosmetics — were also rare or missing altogether in many households. In short, the industrial revolution affected mainly larger spheres. It created cities, factories, piers, canals, railroads and railway stations, mines and blast furnaces, but it did not yet provide the individual with the many conveniences available today: the range of machines for household work and entertainment, or the automobile. Like the households, the farms and villages were as yet largely untouched by technology and industry. Certainly, somewhere within a ten mile radius was a railroad station. In many places there were threshing and mowing machines, better plows and hay tedders. In the United States there were even harvester combines, although these, like the relatively uncommon steam plow, could only be used in very large fields. Thus, life and work on a farm around 1900 was closer to that of around 1820 than that of 1980. It is useful to set up this kind of "balance sheet" in order to throw into relief the changes that have come with the inventions in electrotechonology, chemistry and physics, with the building revolution, and with petroleum and natural gas.

   With all inventions it is important to distinguish between the invention itself, the following development phase that brings it to the production stage, and finally its application. The application of electricity started with the telegraph. The telegraphic process used low voltage current which was obtained from galvanic elements by chemical means. It was Michael Faraday's discovery of electromagnetic induction (1831) that first laid the foundation for production of economically and technically suitable generators. In Germany, the Siemens Concern took the lead in this technology. As early as 1847 Werner Siemens, at that time still an artillery officer, had built a telegraph line from Berlin to Potsdam. In 1849 he left the army and together with Halske, a mechanic, established the company Siemens and Halske, a telegraph-building concern. Siemens' first important invention was the seamless insulation of telegraph wires by means of a coating of gutta-percha. Soon the firm received large orders, among them the laying of the St. Petersburg-Moscow-Crimea telegraph line, which was installed before 1860. The crucial development, however, was that of machines capable of transforming mechanical energy into electricity: In 1856, the shuttle armature was built, followed in 1866 by a direct current machine based on the dynamo principle. It was only now that Faraday's discovery could be applied.

Thomas A. Edison was now able to build upon Siemens' invention. He was the first to use the steam engine to generate electricity, building the first power station on this principle. Edison also invented the carbon filament lamp (incandescent light bulb), the light switch, and the fuse; he also brought the electric meter up to production standards. After the problem of power transmission had been solved by Oskar von Miller (in 1891 he built the first power line between Lauffen on the Neckar and Frankfurt — 179 km) the electric motor could now begin its triumphal march. The power network now supplied a cheap and economically convenient form of energy — and not just to large-scale concerns: soon electric motors could be found in small businesses and in the workshops of craftsmen for whom a steam engine would not have been profitable. Many more examples could be given to show how electricity furthered the application of technology. At first these applications were distributed rather sparsely through the country, but after 1900 they began to penetrate more finely, in the most variegated branches of life and in the most varied applications.

The biography of Thomas Edison is an especially rewarding study for the eighth grade. His life not only illustrates the rise of a self-made man, but also the process of systematic research and invention — as far as this had come by 1880 — as well as the way in which the very same invention was often worked on simultaneously in different places (e.g. Swan and Edison on the incandescent lamp). It should always be made clear that the inventions of Faraday, Siemens, Edison, and others were based on goal-oriented methodical work and careful consideration, not on some haphazard circumstances.

There are good reasons for taking up a few figures out of the development of medicine in the nineteenth century. For one thing, we are indebted to medicine for combatting epidemics, for the lowering of infant mortality, and the lengthening of human life — demographic factors of inestimable significance. For another thing, it is important to learn about an aspect of progress that from the start had a humanitarian intent. Far too often there is a tendency today to vilify modern technology in favor of a romantic glorification of the stagecoach era. Precisely this mentality must be avoided in the eighth grade. At the same time, the development of medicine in the nineteenth century is particularly difficult to portray in a way that the eighth grade students can understand fully. In these circumstances, one might wish to pick out one or two figures significant in the development of modern medicine or hospitals. Perhaps Robert Koch could serve as a paradigm of these researches. If he is chosen, however, the work of Pasteur should at least be referred to, in order not to overlook the social context of these developments. Knowledge of the role played by microbes led to a new conception of hygiene. And out of the old hospitals developed modern ones whose hygienic methods, x-ray machines, operation rooms, and various forms of anesthesia are often taken for granted today.

Modern medicine and especially pharmacy are inconceivable without modern chemistry. In the early nineteenth century, chemistry was first developed as a supplier for the textile industry. Soda was produced — following the Leblanc method — chiefly for washing cotton textiles; chlorine was produced as a bleaching agent; and the dye industry too at first served the textile trade. A name like BASF (Badische Anilin und Soda Fabrik) is typical of this early period. Quite soon agricultural chemistry, which largely goes back to Justus von Liebig, took its place alongside the dye industry. Products such as ammonium sulfate, saltpeter, calcium nitrate, and potassium salts were mass-produced and put at the disposal of agriculture. The twentieth century, finally, became the era of synthetic materials. Starting with bakelite and cellophane, this development went on through nylon, perlon, and other synthetic fibers to the untold thousands of products such as artificial flavors, varnishes, and plastics. For such a topic, it may not seem necessary to work with biographies. Here, for once, the class might work together to survey the chemically produced materials in their everyday life and understand their origin.

Among the topics mentioned in relation to the industrial revolution, quite a number of popular or less popular inventions are missing: the automobile, the airplane, radio and television, not to speak of the cement industry, the new printing techniques (rotary press, offset printing), the petroleum industry, and the computer. In addition, everything relating to arms technology has also been left out. In fact there are a number of areas with which the students generally become acquainted outside of school — in part from reading or from their home environment. Such missing elements can be filled in by the students during the summary at the end. Whatever inventions are chosen as examples, all that matters is that the students really learn something about their significance and their effects.

The Social Aspect of Technological Development

Earlier, while discussing the textile industry and the railway system, we referred to the social aspect of industrial development: the social distress associated with urbanization, the dissolution of the old European household with its extended family and self-sufficiency. In Germany, this phase of social misery lasted up to about 1900 or 1905 and reappeared with the world economic crisis of 1929. This misery is strikingly documented in *Deutsche Sozialgeschichte*, vols. I and II (cf. suggested lit.). With the passage of time, however, a significant improvement in social conditions became evident. The working day, which was often more than 12 hours long in the middle of the nineteenth century, could gradually be reduced. Around 1910 it was on average 9 hours; in 1918 is was limited to 8 hours, which made for a 48 hour work week. Today it is 40 hours, and since our vacation time must also be taken into account in a comparison with earlier periods, we could speak of a 36 hour work week today. This means that since 1850, when there was still a 72 hour work week, the amount of work time per week has been cut in half. From 1850 to 1910 weekly wages tripled or quadrupled, depending on the region and trade. Similarly, real wages doubled between 1950 and 1964. The comparison becomes particularly drastic when we compare the gross hourly wages of 1913/14 to those of 1976: setting 1970 wages at 100 percent, in 1913 they were 8.1 percent, in 1976 they were 168.8 percent — a twenty-fold rise in gross wages.

These figures reflect a mass affluence, an affluent society that now consumes not only groceries of high quality, but also clothing and shoes. The children of the poorer classes once wore wooden clogs in winter and went barefoot in summer. Even in 1936 children often owned only one pair of shoes. It was very much the same with clothes.

Even in petit bourgeois (lower middle class) circles, suits and clothes would be turned after a few years' wear. Of course, such long-lived goods as automobiles, television sets, and electrical appliances were absent before 1910. More important is the housing situation. In 1976, for example, in the Federal Republic of Germany there were almost exactly twenty-four million dwellings with an average of 4.2 rooms and 2.5 persons per dwelling unit. Finally, to get a picture of the general prosperity one must also reckon in the gamut of public services, such as social security. This kind of affluence begins with streets and roads, goes on to lighting and playgrounds and finally to such things as public baths and social welfare institutions.

Thus the poverty of the first phase of the industrial revolution, when the primary accumulation of capital took place, was succeeded already in 1910 by another phase, during which the material well-being of the people in the industrialized countries visibly increased. Starting in 1950 it is even possible to speak of general affluence. The question to what extent industrialism is responsible for the poverty and distress in the Third World is not so simple to answer. It is true that modern medicine has been a decisive factor in population growth, one of the main problems of the Third World. It is also true that the introduction of modern machinery has led to the destruction of old, traditional, ecologically sound methods of production. On the other hand where modern technology has been used sensibly, as for example in China, it has not only raised the general standard of living, but it could even be said that without such technology China would hardly be able to feed its exploding population. Often, political conditions are at the root of Third World problems. To be sure, the former colonial powers are not without guilt in regard to these conditions.

The crucial consequences of modern technology are of a different sort. From the social standpoint, we see a fading of the old division of society into definite levels and classes to which a human being belonged by birth. Today's society is increasingly divided according to its functional systems. Formerly society had an upper stratum that spoke Latin or French. Today there are groups in society who are knowledgeable in computer languages, others in problems of chemical production, still others in engineering, etc. And it is not just in technical occupations that we find such functionally specialized knowledge. The different areas of management also have their own: insurance, banking, the work of social offices, legal bodies, and so forth all involve their own ways of thinking. Certainly, earlier centuries also had "specialists," but today's specialized fields are each based on separate "sciences," bodies of knowledge that must be studied before they are known. In earlier centuries, it was quite possible to understand (though not to master) the work of most specialists simply by observing production processes.

This first result is linked with a second one. Today's technological implements and installations, factories and production processes actually conceal what goes on inside them and through them: the natural processes are withdrawn from our view. Thus, the technical processes are incomprehensible to the layman. Moreover, just as the technical process itself is hidden from our eyes, technology sees to it that we come less and less into contact with nature. When riding our car over the asphalt, walking the shopping district of a large city, taking our entertainment from the television, or being treated in a modern clinic, we find ourselves in a world in which we are very largely shielded from any natural impression. Fewer and fewer people know the world that actually carries and sustains them. Just as the merchandise in a store is prepackaged for the customer, leaving no clue as to its origin, we have light and heat, water and cooling placed at our disposal without our knowing where they come from.

This brings us to the third great change caused by the industrial revolution. Earlier, most households were to a certain degree economically self-sufficient. They provided for themselves from their own well, their own garden, their own fields and livestock. Provisions for the winter were stored in the cellar; firewood was stacked up in the yard. In any case, people were in a position to look after and support themselves for quite long periods of time. Today, should the electric current or motor fuel be suddenly cut off for only two weeks, we would be all but helpless. Catastrophes would be the result. And what is true of the household is also true of the entire working world. Industrial work not only provides more than half of all employment, but also provides for practically all people who are not active in industry.

These three aspects of the consequences of the industrial revolution should not at this point — in eighth grade history — be treated with an eye towards cultural critique. Still, both sides of the picture should be given: specialization, besides it creditable productive achievements, has also led to social differentiation; the convenience provided by technology requires the use of processes concealed from view; the rise in standard of living due to technology also means dependency on technology. Thus, both advantages and disadvantages should be clearly presented and balanced. The fashionable, one-sided criticism of technology is in most cases dishonest; for in most cases the critics themselves employ the achievements of technology and industry without any qualms. Even in reading a book, we are profiting from the technology of printing, from the manufacture of paper, and from the transportation system that delivered the book. That children and young people can go to school today until the age of eighteen is a result of the fact that they are no longer urgently needed as workhands.

Bibliography for Grade Eight

For a more thorough understanding of the problem of industrialization:

Hardmeyer, Jakob. *Die Gotthardbahn.* Zürich, 1979.
Häusler, Friedrich. *Brot und Wein - Stoff und Geist in der Wirtschaft.*
    2. Aufl. Stuttgart, 1972.
Josephson, Matthew. *Thomas Alva Edison.*
Kohl, Werner. *Die Feuermaschine.* Heusenstamm, 1973.
Peirson, Kurt. *Borsig - ein Name geht um die Welt.* Berlin.
Rübberdt, Rudolf. *Geschichte der Industrialisierung.* München, 1972.
Schröder, Ernst. *Krupp.* Göttingen, 1957.
von Weiher, Sigfrid. *Werner von Siemens.* Göttingen, 1970.

Having to do with inventions:

Gaebert, Hans W. *Der Grosse Augenblick in der Technik.* Bayreuth, 1971.

Useful collections of source-material:

Pöls, Werner. *Deutsche Sozialgeschichte.* Dokumente und Skizzen, Band 1
    1815-70. München, 1973.
Ritter, G. A. and Kocka, J. *Deutsche Sozialgeschichte.* Band 2, 1870-1914.
    München, 1977.
Treue, W., Pönike, H., and Manegold, K. H. *Quellen zur Geschichte der*
    industriellen Revolution. Göttingen, 1966.

10

NINTH GRADE

It is the task of the ninth grade to study recent history up to the present once again, but this time it is the ideas, the inner motives, and the larger trends of these periods that are to be looked at. Steiner suggests comprehensive themes for the separate centuries in order to give the students a broad view over these greater trends:

Fifteenth and sixteenth centuries: humanity's expanding horizon and the significance of this expansion.

Seventeenth century: the dissolution of the old social associations and the development of the new political ones.

Eighteenth century: the effects of the Enlightenment on history.

Nineteenth century: the "flowing together of the history of the peoples."

Today the history teacher has the added task of summarizing the twentieth century in this sense, and so bringing history up to the present. Accordingly, it will be necessary to keep the review of the earlier centuries quite short.

The expansion of humanity's horizons in the fifteenth and sixteenth centuries is connected with an entirely new feeling about the world. The medieval picture of the world had a religious, mythical character. The flat earth was the center of the world, and everything revolved about it. The center of this center was Jerusalem, while the boundaries of the world were somewhere in the unknown and inaccessible: the sea boiled in the south, ice threatened from the north, and in the west the world was closed off by the ocean. Not only did discoveries demonstrate the spherical shape of the earth, and the theory of Copernicus reveal the earth as a small planet revolving around the sun, but maps, too, made it possible to view the world as a whole; anatomy opened the view to the inside of the human being, and printing rapidly disseminated all of this knowledge. Thus a secularized picture of the world took form, and human beings found themselves set into a space where free movement was possible. This free movement in space — a space no longer occupied by qualities — was the forerunner of later freedoms.

The position in which human beings find themselves in relation to the world at the end of this epoch is clearly shown to us in Cervantes (*Don Quixote*), Shakespeare (*Hamlet*), Giordano Bruno, and Bacon. The spiritual world of the Middle Ages, the old order, and the rule of chivalry have all perished. Man faces a new world, a world stage on which the old figures have become ridiculous. Along with Hamlet, however, people sense that the world is "out of joint," that it needs a new kind of order. Bacon recommends the empirical method to explore this world. Through Galileo, Kepler, and Newton, the next century creates a new order and shows how people can understand the world in which they find themselves. In the political sphere, the question arises how the state and society should be organized. It is characteristic that first utopias are now written by Thomas More, Thomas Campanella, and Bacon, and that Jean Bodin draws up his theory of state: everywhere there is a consciousness that the old order has perished and that a new order must be created — an order that can be planned, shaped, or thought by human beings.

Accordingly, in the next century there are rudimentary attempts everywhere to create a new political system. Upon seeing Cape Cod, the emigrants who had left the Old World in 1620 on the Mayflower made the famous "Mayflower Compact," deliberately uniting into a "body politick" that was intended to make its own laws and manage its own affairs. This new spirit becomes clearer in the foundation of Pennsylvania. In his letter to the first settlers of Pennsylvania, William Penn writes: "You shall be ruled by laws that you have given yourselves, and shall live as a free and, if you will, as an industrious people." This spirit makes itself felt right into the planning of the town of Philadelphia.

The foundation of a new political system proved more problematic where old feudal orders still existed. Thus it is not surprising that in France it was only after the battles of Richelieu and Mazarin and the Fronde uprising that Louis XIV finally was able to establish his absolutist state with its mercantilism and bureaucratic administration. The process was similar in England, where it also took many battles before the modern state finally came into being, although the form of the state itself was quite different, indeed opposite to that in France. Both states, England after 1688 and France under Louis XIV, had a form of rationality peculiarly their own: in England it was the rationality of parliamentary control of royal power and the idea of rule by law; in France it was the rationality of centralization, of a mercantile economy with manufactories, streets and canals, and a uniformed, trained, standing army.

In Germany, this development was retarded considerably by the Thirty Years' War, which threw the country back more than a century. In addition, the country's state of splintering into three hundred different sovereignties was unfavorable to a progressive development. And finally, the empire was threatened and weakened by the Turks in the East and the predatory wars of Louis XIV in the West. So it was not until the eighteenth century that the renewal of state organization in Germany assumed significant form and proportions. In Russia, however, Peter the Great broke with tradition and made St. Petersburg the new capital of the empire. In its planning, layout, and institutions, and especially as a window opening Russia to the West, this city manifests the will to express a new spirit.

As the theme of the eighteenth century, Steiner proposes the "effects of the Enlightenment on life in history." The formulation itself seems significant: if one takes it exactly, it is not speaking of the Enlightenment in the abstract. In other words, it is not a matter of a pure history of ideas, but of making the spirit of the Enlightenment visible in concrete historical developments. One development well-suited for this is the the battle against witch trials and the methods of torture connected with them. Belief in witches is a typical symptom of an unenlightened belief in spirits. In the sixteenth and seventeenth centuries witch hunts periodically swept over entire regions like a plague, claiming thousands of victims. It was the efforts of Friedrich Spee, Balthasar Bekker, and Christian Thomas — and later those of Maria Thersia as well — that brought these witch trials to an end, while Frederick II (the Great) of Prussia completely abolished torture in the punitive process with his edict of June 3, 1740.

For another concrete example of the effects of the Enlightenment on life in the course of history, one may look at how the ideas of human rights and the separation of powers were realized in the United States and in the French Revolution. Here we are fortunate to be able to give a vivid account of the life and travels of Montesquieu: how, while in England, he seized upon the idea of separation of powers (an idea conceived earlier, but differently, by Locke), exactly how he understood it, and how he then spread this idea in France. One can take the opportunity here to glance at the dissemination of books: in the space of eighteen months, Montesquieu's *L'Esprit des lois* went through twenty-two editions with a total of thirty-five thousand copies. What is of central importance here, however, is to show how the fathers of the U.S. Constitution actually took up this idea and realized it in their document, and how later it was also the guiding idea of the French revolutionaries in the first phase of the Revolution.

Human rights are the other important and fundamental expression of the Enlightenment. These rights have been formulated in quite different ways. One way lays the emphasis on high principles, according the human being a whole series of comprehensive rights that have been continually extended to our day. Thus, the rights to freedom, life, and equal treatment before the law have been joined by the right to work, to education, to decent living quarters, to leisure time, etc. In contrast, when we look at the oldest formulation of human rights, the Virginia Bill of Rights of June 12th, 1776, we notice that it treats basic principles quite sparingly, while giving much more attention to measures and institutions intended to protect the individual from the abuse of governmental power. These rules embody the spirit of practical Englightenment: regulated criminal process before twelve jurors; limited term of office for delegates or governments; free elections; protection against arbitrary arrest and house search. The students should learn to appreciate the value of these social inventions in particular, because they have really shaped life in the course of recent history, while the "right to work" and the "right to leisure time" remain problematic declarations.

Finally, the Enlightenment represents a particular attitude towards life. Kant defines the Enlightenment as man's growth out of his self-incurred state of minority, and gives of the Age of Enlightenment the motto *sapere aude*: have the courage to use your own mind. There are indeed a great number of figures whose lives seem determined by this saying. Benjamin Franklin is an excellent example: not only because he worked his way up from printer to author and newspaper publisher to inventor of the lightning rod and ambassador of the United States to the French royal court, but above all because he also applied his reason to himself, submitting himself to a rigorous self-education. In his memoirs, he describes how he set up a catalogue of thirteen virtues and undertook to pay especial heed to one particular virtue each week and note down exactly any transgressions against it. This practical procedure makes it clear what the inner foundations of the human rights are: the proclaimed freedom requires a basis of self-control and self-education.

For the nineteenth century, Steiner suggests the theme: "Confluence of the history of the peoples." At first glance this theme may appear somewhat odd — it is difficult to picture just what is meant. However, when we look at the whole nineteenth century, beginning with the French Revolution, it becomes evident that the time of isolated national development was coming to an end. Even before the turn of the century, the French Revolution appears as an event of European dimensions. Within a very few years it had seized Italy, the Netherlands, Switzerland, and western Germany. It enthused great minds throughout Europe: in Germany, Fichte, Hölderlin, Hegel, and Schiller, to name but a few. The events in Paris reverberated throughout Europe; and in the final analysis the political, legal, and social transformation which Europe experienced from 1789 to 1815 was, directly or indirectly, the work of the French Revolution. Nationalistically-minded writers of German history have never made it sufficiently clear that for the Rhine regions, the period of French rule meant a liberation for large groups of people, that the law reforms effected by the Napoleonic Code were a blessing, or that in many areas of life the Revolution set standards which only the further history of the nineteenth century managed to live up to.

The subsequent course of history in the nineteenth century also shows that in many ways Europe had now become a whole. The Revolution of 1848 was a European event. From Paris, the spark of revolution jumped to Vienna, Prague, Frankfurt, Berlin, Milan, and Rome. Everywhere the bourgeoisie rose up, demanding a constitution, trial by jury, and freedom of the press. The later collapse of the revolutionary movement as well was an event that took place across Europe.

Despite the "failure" of this revolution, the political development of Europe continued along the lines laid out by these ideas. By the First World War, government by law had prevailed in almost all important countries of Europe, as had universal suffrage and constitutional monarchy, albeit in different degrees. By 1914 liberalism was victorious in most European states.

This is not all. It is perfectly natural that the industrial revolution took hold of all Europe as it moved from West to East. It is also well-known that the traffic network made rapid communication possible. Nor it is surprising that under these circumstances work on technological innovations began simultaneously in many places, and that within the year of their invention, new technologies were known and applied in Europe and the United States. Yet ideas as well spread quickly through Europe: the doctrines of Darwin and Haeckel, the insights of Pasteur and Koch did not remain national events. The first edition of Darwin's chief work appeared in 1859; a German translation was ready by 1860. Even the improved English editions came out in new German translations after a short interval. The dissemination of Darwin's ideas, however, was only part of a larger process: after 1850, natural science and scientific thinking began their victory march. This way of thinking may not have the tendency to unite nations, but at least it does not know national differences of the kind that national literatures show.

Another common theme that began to occupy the European mind was the social issue emerging in the course of the industrial revolution. In the industrialized regions of Europe, legal measures were now taken against child labor; in some places working hours were regulated, and the state appointed factory inspectors. Even before 1848 the discussion of solutions to the social question was in full swing. The cooperative movement had begun, as had international cooperation among the socialists, which was very often carried by emigrants. In 1864, the International Workers' Association was founded, and a lively international communication arose through a network of personal acquaintances made in travel and stays abroad.

A special theme in social development — though it does not concern Europe in chief — is the abolition of the slave trade and slavery in the nineteenth century. The first important figure here is William Wilberforce in England, who stood up in Parliament for the abolition of the slave trade. In 1807 Parliament prohibited slave trade with English ships. In 1833 slavery was abolished in the English colonies. English pressure put an end to the transatlantic slave trade. And now began the conflict over slavery in the United States, which led to the Civil War and finally, on January 1, 1863, to the Abolition. To be sure, problems regarding the Black population remain in our own times. A noteworthy aspect of this process is that it drew the attention of the interested world. Here, for the first time we are able to see a kind of human rights movement that stands up for the rights of other peoples across continents.

The end of the nineteenth century, finally, is characterized by a process of colonial acquisition that is customarily treated under the heading of imperialism. This is not the place to broach the imperialism debate, but it might still be mentioned that the uniquely economic interpretation of this phenomenon is extremely vulnerable to attack. In Germany, colonial acquisition was neither demanded nor promoted by enterprises or cartels. Until 1914 the German colonies were not regions in which appreciable capital was invested, nor were they important to the German economy as suppliers of raw materials. Schumpeter's argument seems likely to be closer to the truth: imperialism was an atavistic movement carried on by adventurers, military men, problematic characters, and missionaries looking for a field of activity.

Another way to look at the process of colonial acquisition, the opening up of Africa, certain areas of Asia, and the Pacific island world, is in terms of the confluence of the history of the various peoples — as a Europeanization of the world. First of all, it is striking that colonial acquisition was preceded by a phase of intense activity on the part of discoverers and explorers. In 1849, Livingston began his African journeys, which took him to the Zambesi, the Victoria Falls, and through the Congo. In 1850 Heinrich Barth explored the Sahara. In 1858 Burton and Speke reached Lake Victoria and Lake Tanganyika. In 1861 Heuglin travelled through Abyssinia. In 1864 Schweinfurth began his exploration of the eastern Sudan. From 1865 to 1867 Gerhard Rohlfs traversed North Africa. In 1868 Richthofen penetrated the interior of China. Nachtigal explored the Sahara and the Sudan in 1869; Stanley, the Congo in 1874; and Cameron, central Africa in 1875. After colonization, the activity of the explorers was usually followed at first by quite peripheral European trade settlements and a very thin European population. Everywhere, however, whether slowly or quickly, European technology, medicine, and administration took hold. This process occurred most quickly in Japan, but it took place in India and South America as well. In our century, oddly, the process of decolonization actually brings with it an intensification of European influence through technology, trade, the introduction of European science, etc. Even the great revolutions, the

Russian and the Chinese, serve to facilitate the acceptance of a particular variety of modern thinking, administration, and working that originated in Europe.

At the beginning of the twentieth century, the world was in the process of becoming a unity in various areas. World trade was beginning to span the globe; a telegraph network made worldwide communication possible; wireless telegraphy had begun. Events taking place in one country began to affect all other countries. It became impossible to speak of clashes in Turkey as happening somewhere far off on the other side of the earth.

The 20th Century

It would be rash to formulate a general theme for the history of a century that has not yet run its course; nevertheless, a number of important traits can be distinguished with clarity. When the situation in 1900 is compared with that in 1980, the first thing that becomes clear is that Europe then still appeared as center of the world. The significant political events played in an arena between London, Paris, Vienna, Berlin, and St. Petersburg. It is true that Japan and the United States had begun their ascendency as new states in the power structure, but they did not yet play a leading role. Today, Europe is divided in two. The old Europe has perished. Berlin and Vienna have become insignificant. Washington is more important than London. It is not without meaning that we now speak of the Soviet Union instead of Russia, and that its capital, symptomatically, is in Moscow. Peking and Tokyo are at least as important as Paris. African, Asian, and South American issues occupy the world public more than the conflicts of the EEC (European Common Market).

A second distinct characteristic of the twentieth century, one clearly connected with the first, is the reshifting of social classes. In previous centuries the leadership of most nations — with the exception of the United States and a few others — was in the hands of a thin upper layer of society; often it was the aristocracy or patricians who set the tone in public affairs. This altered fundamentally in the twentieth century. Not only did skilled workers and laborers rise to high government offices, but now labor unions and workers' parties also took on a leading position in society alongside of the governments. After World War II African and Asian leaders, many of whom had come to power as freedom-fighters or revolutionaries, now appeared on the world stage bringing different attitudes and ways of thinking to bear. Superficially perhaps, when such leaders speak at the United Nations or at world economic conferences, the world view of the Arabs, Chinese, Japanese, Black Africans, Indians, and Malaysians cannot readily be distinguished from that of the Europeans. The nations behind these representatives, however, are moved by other emotions and motives than those familiar to us. Hence we are sometimes exposed to shocking experiences, as occurred recently with Iran. The problem that poses itself today stems from the fact that nations and individuals still know each other far too little in this respect. Here, by the way, it is the task of the history teacher to give a few examples that will help the students experience the essential character of other peoples, as this will prove important for the future.

A third sign of the times can be read in the development of art in the twentieth century. Until 1900 the art of Europe, dominant since Renaissance times, had tried to grasp visible reality in one way or another: the Renaissance grasped it as a spatial reality, the Baroque period as form in movement, the Romantic period as an expression of the soul, and Impressionism as an optical impression. With Expressionism, interest in the outer form fades; figures are broken or recreated out of inner experience. This impulse, however, lasts only a short time, and what for centuries had been art finally disappears altogether. This is an important symptom — not because the disappearance of the old art is to be lamented as a "loss of the middle," but because it reveals that a "Weltanschauung," a way of viewing the world, is quite literally no longer present. In place of art-works come exhibits that confront the viewer with banalities. This technique of confrontation produces a shock, and that is its aim, too.

The common denominator of these three basic traits is that a world familiar to the European for centuries had fallen apart — a world that had seemed surveyable, understandable. Now there is no unified orientation, no set form of behavior, no center to the world any more. There is no common way of looking at things. Thus in many respects one can speak of a Europeanization of history.

With the loss of a center comes a corresponding lack of real insight or ability to create new social forms. The twentieth century requires new social forms, but strangely, the old forms assert themselves again and again. Thus, the Russian Revolution may have swept away Tsarist rule with its secret police and the rule of a minority; yet a new tsar arose in Stalin, another minority seized power, and the secret police — changed in name only — once again became the instrument of oppression. The old power structures were soon back again, only now they had become more effective, more bureaucratic. In Germany, too, it was the creation of new forms that was really needed after the November Revolution of 1919 and after 1945 again. All the attempts made in this direction — certainly with much too feeble powers — brought no success. Thus the old power structures, societal structures, and party structures prevailed again, since mere improvements in the constitution alone were powerless in the long run. There is not a country the world over that has succeeded in leaving behind the governmental forms that were conceived in the Enlightenment and put into practice in the American and French Revolutions. Indeed, no one has even fully achieved the separation of powers conceived by Montesquieu. The political system of the Federal Republic of Germany, for example, has no effective parliamentary control of government, not to speak of control of the bureaucracy or the economic power complexes entwined with it.

All these symptoms point to a lack of creative shaping power, the lack of a kind of vision that can pierce through symptoms, grasp phenomena as a whole, and stimulate deeds. Lacking also are new ideas that are more than mere attempts to cure the symptoms. Where such things are lacking, a new experience meets us which can also be illustrated with a few symptoms:

Until the end of the nineteenth century the history of modern times was determined, as we have said, by the expansion of Europe. European nations reached out into the world, subjugated it, and exploited gold and silver deposits wherever they found them. They exported their goods, their kind of Christianity, and also the people who were not satisfied with conditions in Europe. Many a domestic European problem was defused because of this possibility for expansion and emigration, so that conflicts in Europe itself could be avoided. Today the nations of the Third World make their demands heard in Europe. OPEC sets the oil prices. People of once subjugated colonies and other members of underprivileged nations immigrate to Europe: Indians, Blacks, Turks. Like the Christian missionaries who once swarmed out across the world, now Oriental gurus find their devotees in Europe. The consequences of European expansion and United States hegemony have struck home in the lands of their origin.

It is similar with our relation to nature. Far into this century, nature seemed to have been placed without limits at our disposal. Man could expand into nature, into his environment. In colonial areas or in the Midwest he could ruthlessly exploit it, polluting lakes, seas, and air, dumping his waste wherever he pleased. As early as the thirties, however, devastating consequences (erosion) became evident; and today it is known — at least in the more densely populated regions of the world — that this kind of behavior is no longer permissible. We are approaching a time when people will have consciously to care for nature, otherwise the life-threatening consequences of their own behavior will strike back at them. The same is true of the way we deal with raw materials and energy resources. Earlier, we simply made use of the gifts of nature, the fossil fuels. Today, it is being discovered that we must derive energies from forces that will not be used up forever by our need for energy.

A third symptom concerns human beings themselves in their relation to technology and industry. In this century technology has reached into every household, and the process of industrializing all work processes is far advanced. At the same time, people have become more and more dependent on technological systems, and individuals are less and less in control of their fate. We feel a threat to life from economic crises, possible natural catastrophes or wars, and we know that a war today would be more destructive and inhuman than any war before. This knowledge, these anxieties, this uncertainty about the future have weakened human beings both psychically and physically. Around the turn of the century workers worked sixty to seventy hours a week, while today's workers suffer under their forty-hour work week (really only thirty-six-hour, counting vacations and holidays). It is evident that people living in a mechanized environment can tolerate less and less. Helplessness, dissatisfaction, protest, and disease are on the rise. As a result, increasingly expensive systems are created to serve health, welfare, and nursing care needs. Technology has expanded to the point where it has become a burden instead of a boon.

When these three symptoms are taken together, it becomes clear that certain expansive tendencies in our way of life have reached a limit, and that beyond this limit they fall back upon humanity in the form of problems and difficulties. Man is being confronted with the consequences of his own actions. In many cases, however, there is no inclination to observe these limits or to recognize these consequences for what they are.

With these two groups of symptoms in mind, it becomes possible to summarize much of the history of our century quite clearly.

In the first place, the two world wars were an expression of conflicts resulting from an expansive urge that was no longer suited to the times. World War I was a conflict of imperialistic powers all acting in terms of expansive power politics. Their interests collided in areas outside of Europe, while in Europe they engaged in an arms race that intensified the mutual distrust and fear. World War II was triggered by powers (Germany and Japan) who, believing themselves to have been shortchanged by history, renewed this will towards expansion and once more took up the battle for world dominance. Both wars did a great deal to accelerate the collapse of European supremacy. After 1945, for twenty years, two empires faced each other, both highly armed and set on expansion. After 1965, although these two empires did not vanish, other powers independent of them now appeared on the world political scene: China, the Arabs, and the nations of Black Africa. The expansive strivings of the powerful states continued to poison world politics. The United States sought to assert its claims to hegemony in Vietnam, South and Central America, and to install a ruler in Iran who was agreeable to it. The Soviet Union suppressed the nations of Eastern Europe and drew Afghanistan into its sphere of power. Most important, however, was an arms race that went beyond all bounds of reason and prevented a sensible use of economic resources.

States that practice politics of expansion or aggression experience tensions and conflicts within, and these become manifest in social oppression. There are always minorities or groups that are stigmatized as enemies of state, society, and progress. Some groups appear as enemies of this policy because they do not want to participate in such nonsense. In the German Empire it was the Social Democrats; under the Nazis it was the Jews and others; in the Soviet Union it was the different varieties of "class enemy": all became victims of the "purges." The United States, during the McCarthy era, experienced the communist "witch hunts"; in addition, there were and still are other oppressed minorities. Comparable conditions have been witnessed under all dictatorships — in Argentina, Brazil, and Spain, for example. In China many groups have been persecuted not only during, but also before and after the Cultural Revolution. Oftener still, the problem of oppression assumes different forms: certain population groups have lived in dire misery, characterized by permanent unemployment and other deprivations. In this connection, it must be remembered that mass unemployment was unknown before the industrial revolution; it is the product of an unbalanced economy that desires constant expansion.

These are all symptoms of social illness: the urge to expand, destruction of nature, oppression, mistreatment of minorities. Such symptoms occur because the timely tasks of society are not grasped. And it is this failure to grasp them, this failure to renew society that has led to a worsening of the symptoms in the last decade: an increase in crime, drug addiction, and youth protests. What our society quite clearly misses is a spiritual knowledge of the human being, out of which goals might take form for a re-creation of society. The conception of the human being that remains dominant to this day is clearly oriented to economic and materialistic aspects alone. There is a belief that systems to increase material welfare, rising wages, growing affluence, and economic growth should be able to solve the social questions. What this brings forth unnoticed, however, is giant apparatuses in industry, bureaucracy, the social services, and clinics, which gradually become ends in themselves, make processes opaque, rob the individual of his voice and sovereignty, and force new growth in order to maintain themselves.

In this sense the history of the twentieth century is a history of social illness, and this illness can be explained from the failure to grasp new spiritual goals due to a deficient image of the human being and of nature. The difficulty that this problem poses to the teacher is of the highest order. Should students of the ninth grade, who want to grow into this world, be confronted with such a negative description of their century? Would such an analysis not prove too much for a fifteen-year-old? Questions of this kind by no means concern history teaching alone. They are life questions: How do young people today grow into their times? How do they learn to interpret and understand them? History instruction cannot solve the questions that have not been solved in outer reality, but it can contribute to an understanding of our times.

Such understanding, however, does not come about by focussing solely on what is negative. It is quite possible to direct attention to what is now in the process of coming into being, even if this manifests itself much less plainly. Structures that have long since taken form — state, economy, science — naturally press into the foreground of our view. In the background, however, something can be sensed that has vaguer contours — it is still in the domain of will and longing only. One can observe, for example, how the attitude towards war has changed since the year 1900. Until 1914, war was still considered a political tool. In 1914, millions went off to war filled with enthusiasm. Pacifism was looked upon as madness. Today, these aggressive attitudes have completely disappeared in large parts of the world, and war is unequivocally looked upon as the direst evil. In a similar fashion, basic social attitudes have changed as well. The old forms of class pride and rigid class consciousness have disappeared. Not only are workers protected by law, in many places they also have the right to a real say in the decision-making process. There now also lives a will to overcome racial prejudices and stand up for the rights of all human beings. In private relations as well, the will is growing towards tolerance and mutual understanding of other ways of being and thinking. Here we are referring not so much to the ecumenical strivings of our century as to forms of interaction in everyday life, to the will to listen, to a new capacity for understanding the thoughts of another human being.

This new mood becomes especially obvious in the sphere of education. Outwardly it appears in the changed attitude towards corporal punishment, now outlawed, which was general practice at the beginning of the century. There is a desire to see and meet the needs of the child as a child. It now seems absurd to speak of children as little adults or consider them only in the light of their future occupation. One can notice a general desire in people to understand children, to enter into their world and questions, and create a world for them. Of course it is easy to object that this desire often leads in wrong directions, but it simply cannot be ignored how widespread and serious these efforts remain to this day, despite all shortcomings. It must be recalled that such developments and learning processes take time. The ideas of the Enlightenment did not prevail in a few years, and neither will the development of a pedagogical spirit. It is also important to see that this tendency has its origin not in universities or state institutions, but in a wide variety of private initiatives on the part of individuals and groups.

In a similar way, a new understanding for nature seems to be awakening. In the areas of environmental protection and conservation, groups are arising who not only have a selfless love of nature but are also really willing to learn from it. There is concern for species of animals threatened by extinction: research is being done on their living conditions, and the damage caused by a one-sided technological and chemical understanding and treatment of nature is recognized. In this way new questions and new ways of thinking emerge out of the negative experiences.

These positive tendencies in our century can be illustrated through a great number of figures in history class: Count Bernadotte or Dag Hammerskjöld in the fight for peace; Gandhi and Martin Luther King in the liberation of the underprivileged; Rachel Carson for the new willingness to listen to nature. Particular movements belong to the history of the new way of thinking and feeling: the youth movement of the beginning of the century, the student movement that began in 1966, the Prague Spring and the Polish workers' movement. Everywhere we see a will to reshape life, to create new social forms. To be sure, the great majority of these movements and efforts have foundered, often already starting off with problematic foundations in their ideal orientation. One of the reasons that the student protest movement failed, for example, was that it took up the old doctrines of Marxism again. The idea of a free cultural/spiritual life as an independent element of the social organism was lacking. And so was the necessary content for such a cultural and spiritual life: an insight into the human being and a knowledge of the spirituality of nature and the cosmos. The situation in the "alternative" movements and in environmental protection today clearly shows that everything depends on how these questions are understood.

Thus, two worlds are found in our century. One world, the old, has turned into form, into concrete. Clearly defined as a powerful apparatus, as science, industry, and trade, it is easily recognized — what is old and developed is always easy to recognize. Yet the beginnings of something new, something that is still full of contradictions and hides behind many — sometimes foolish — figures, can also be sensed. The new world lives as an inner mood, as a wish, in the young. Again and again it founders, however, because it lacks the spiritual element, the ideal orientation that really corresponds to this new world felt in the soul.

Here, the teaching of history can accomplish one important thing. It can sketch the tasks of the future by looking at the problems at hand. It can show that the new inner life wanting to blaze itself a trail falters because of a state-run, over-administered school and university system that hinders the development of free thinking, that steers research and training onto prescribed, sterile paths, and thus suppresses the free development of the individual. An individuality that is suppressed in this way, that finds no space for a real and free meeting with the world, becomes a rebel. Further, not only does the proliferative growth of state administration require an exorbitant, truly injurious, financial expenditure, but such an administrative system cuts off communication among citizens and prevents democratic self-determination of society. Finally, its entanglement with economic interests makes this state into a promoter of giant projects that make no economic sense or one-sidedly favor certain economic interests.

Over against these pathogenic tendencies still active in the social organism, the idea of a threefold social organism can be developed.

In the ninth grade, this idea can be taken up in connection with the idea of the separation of powers. This idea of Montesquieu's is aimed at controlling power. The three powers of the state are intended to hold each other in check. The idea of a threefold social organism is comparable to the idea of separation of powers in that neither of them presents a plan for an ideal, utopian state or says how everything ought to be. Thus, the idea of a threefold social organism also limits itself to practical recommendations — that is, to instrumental measures — which overcome power in certain areas of human life, if power means making decisions for other people. Neither a free cultural life nor an economic life organized associatively by the human beings involved in it — neither of these know power in this sense. And the role of the state is to regulate legal relationships among people in keeping with the principle of reciprocity, which can also be called equality.

Only with such a perspective on the future is an understanding of the present possible. A purely objective present, depicted without its future-oriented tendencies and necessities, is nothing but brute facticity. With an eye for the coming into being and the passing away of things, with an insight into what makes society sick (dysfunctional) and what makes it healthy, we gain an orientation. Out of an involvement in contemporary issues, each teacher has the ability to bring in his personal concern and commitment. What is crucial is that the teacher really manage to grasp the emerging impulses of the future where they reveal themselves, and convey them to the students. Compared with this, negative cultural criticism and rigidly-conceived utopian constructions are not very fruitful, because they do not help the students grow into their times.

Bibliography for Grade Nine

Reference to a few lesser known works for the themes of the ninth grade. An extensive bibliography is beyond the scope of this work.

Baschwitz, Kurt. *Hexen und Hexenprozesse*. München, 1963.

Bouman, Pieter Jan. *Kultur und Gessellschaft der Neuzeit*. Olten, 1962.

Bouman, Pieter Jan. *Verschwörung der Einsamen - Weltgeschichte unseres Jahrhunderts*. München, 1964.

Ellert, Gerhart. *Richelieu*. Wien, 1973.

Franklin, Benjamin. *Autobiography*.

Huch, Ricarda. *1848 Die Revolution des 19. Jahrhunderts in Deutschland, früher:* "Alte und neue Götter." Zürich, 1944.

Klessman, Eckart, editor. *Deutschland unter Napoleon*. Düsseldorf, 1965. (Reihe: Augenzeugenberichte)

Rosenstocck-Huessy, Eugen. *Die europäische Revolution*. Stuttgart, 1951.

Rosenstocck-Huessy, Eugen. *Out of Revolution*. Argo Books, 1969.

11

HISTORY IN THE TENTH GRADE

The Adoption of a Settled Way of Life

In the ninth grade, the ideal element in history, art, and literature was cultivated in particular. Now, in the tenth grade, the earth becomes the general theme. As the aim in geography, for example, the Waldorf School curriculum gives "description of the earth as a morphological and physical whole." In physics, classical mechanics is studied; in chemistry the formation of salts is given special attention; and in surveying, finally, the earth is grasped by actually measuring and calculating. For history, the curriculum indicates: "History will begin by looking at the dependence of peoples upon the earth, upon the climates of the hot or temperate zones."

Tenth grade history also begins a second "run-through": history is taken up from the very beginning again. Thus the task in the tenth grade is to work particularly on the ancient civilizations and the history of Greece up to the appearance of Alexander — all from the viewpoint of "the dependence of the peoples upon the earth." This task gives history instruction a decidedly rational streak. The teacher must capture processes, events, and conditions in sharp outline and go into their bases in some detail. The students should be allowed to participate in reconstructing conditions and establishing reasons and bases for them, and the logic of the events themselves should be made accessible to them. They experience this as very beneficial and at home they might say: "Now we really have to think!" To the student, "really thinking" means, here, in this context, starting from the physical earth, from the geographical facts, and from them grasping the legal system, for example. It is not good for the students at this age to have the feeling that history class is really religion class.

The educational value of this way of proceeding might lie in avoiding any false estheticism, among other things. By looking at the empirically real, material conditions for human action, the students are educated to think concretely — and not only to experience in a feeling way, however sensitively. This gives them a certain assurance and realism. It might be objected here that today's students are realistic enough as it is — are they not far beyond their parents when it comes to a realistic frame of mind? Today's students undoubtedly are very strongly influenced by the idols of the rampant materialistic and technological fantasy world. The amount of business done in science fiction literature testifies to this, as does the fact that the books by von Däniken (*Back to the Stars*, etc.) stay on the bestseller lists and are devoured especially by students of this age group. The proper remedy against materialistic fantasms of this kind lies not in the beauty of idealism or in religious edification, but in laying hands on real material conditions and understanding them.

A decisive step in the early history of mankind was the adoption of a settled way of life. The change from nomad to farmer has rightly been designated as the first great revolution in human history after the end of the last Ice Age. Radiocarbon dating today sets the end of the Ice Age at around 10,000 B.C. The earliest traces of an incipient settlement process are found in about the eighth millennium before our era. Settlement is not easy to treat because of the constant danger of oversimplifying and falsifying this tremendous process. It may be thought that it could be traced back to a simple matter of food scarcity. ("When the nomads began to notice that game in their hunting regions had grown scarce and the fruits of the forest were no longer sufficient for their needs, their women had to plant grain in order to fend off starvation.") Whoever invents such tales fails to consider that in such cases nomads were accustomed to seek out new and richer hunting and gathering grounds. Even less thought is given to the nomads' basic attitude towards life. Ammianus Marcellinus, an historian of late antiquity, reports of the Huns: "They never come under the roof of a house, but shun it like the grave. Not even a hut covered with reeds can be found among them. Restlessly they move through mountains and forest, and from childhood on accustom themselves to endure frost, hunger, and thirst. Even outside of their homeland they never enter a house without urgent necessity, for due to their beliefs they cannot feel safe underneath a roof." If we wish to make the attempt to understand the process of settlement, we must put aside the primitive notion that hunger and love make the world go round.

The adoption of a settled way of life is a process that must be approached most carefully, and still only its broad outlines can be tentatively reconstructed. The question as to its cause is best left in peace for the moment. Faithful to the motto of the tenth grade, we go straight to the geographical conditions and ask: *Where* are the first traces of human settlement found? *Where* did human beings take on a sedentary way of life? The spade of archeological research points towards Asia Minor, to the areas of today's Palestine, Syria, and Iran. The first cultivation of grain has been shown to have occurred in regions on the edge of Mesopotamia. A place of especial archeological importance is Jarmo in present-day Kurdistan (a border area between Iran and Iraq), where researchers found two kinds of barley; the pig, sheep, and goat as domestic animals, as well as sculpture and ceramics. This settlement dates back to the fifth millennium. Such settlements are found in upland valleys, in basins, and also in plains, which at that time were lightly watered. Why, one wonders, did settlement not begin in the great river valleys of the Indus, the Nile, or Mesopotamia? The answer lies in the great floods that ravage these valleys each year with devastating force. The task of taming the waters would at first have been too great for any groups wishing to settle down there. In contrast, open valleys or plains fed by smaller, tamer rivers make it possible for even small groups of human beings to master the elemental power of water, irrigating the land with numerous small ditches led off from streams. The scope of this simple irrigation method is made visible by aerial photographs of the now desiccated Persian highlands. When the sun is low in the sky, the shadows cast by it reveal on some plains a systematic network of ditches and canals that once watered these regions. These irrigation ditches clearly had a great significance; they were covered with stone slabs and, according to the testimony of old Iranian religion, were kept meticulously clean.

Once the setting of these events has been clarified in this way — a way that we can but touch on here — one can turn to the process of settlement itself. The archeological finds make plain that this was a complex process, but that it revolved around three central elements: the house, the field, and the animals. The construction of a house, the establishment of whole settlements requires the manufacture of tools. Not only axes, hoes, and plows were made, but also jugs and woven material, clasps, needles, and sculptures. All of this, however, took place under the sign of the revolution that changed man from a mere user and consumer of nature to a producer who planned his own destiny, built his house, and stored his harvest; who had turned from nomad to farmer and thus to a caretaker of the earth.

Care of the earth involves not only working the land, irrigating or draining it, but also living with and caring for domestic animals. As living beings, the earth and the animals show the human being the results of his own deeds. The nomad, in contrast, could still turn his back to the consequences of his actions. The greatest wonder of the process of settlement, however, is the cultivation of seeds. Through cultivation, large grasses evolved into cereal. Here we stand before a riddle. According to today's standards and knowledge, the breeding of grain must have been a tediously long and drawn-out process. Did people, generation after generation, repeatedly sort out the biggest and best of the grass seeds and use only these as seed? If so, how did they know that this method would work? And did people then, for hundreds of years, save the best seed and refrain from eating it so that we would be able to reap the fruits of their labor today?

Such considerations, when worked through jointly with the students, begin to make clear that the settlement process is unthinkable without an accompanying deep moral change in the human beings who experienced it. Yet in the tenth grade it is not advisable to begin with this moral transformation. First must come a thorough consideration of the external conditions — as outlined above — and only then can one proceed, step by step, to examine the elements that speak of a human transformation. The first and most obvious element to discuss seems that of legal relationships, since these flow directly out of working the land. Property comes into being. Property results from work. The maker of a tool owns it. The one who develops the new field is its owner. Thus every house also has its owner. One can surmise that one family lived in each house, and that monogamy was the rule. As these legal relationships come into being through work, so does the possibility of breaking them. Once "mine" and "yours" exist, so does theft, so does good and evil. With the words "good and evil" we have left the legal sphere and entered the moral domain. Once morality exists, and moral evaluation of actions, there can now also be self-control in regard to one's own actions and attention towards the actions of others. This in turn leads to the development of sharp *boundaries*, both in outer reality and in human consciousness. There were many institutions that developed such a consciousness, one being the boundary stone. The placing of a boundary stone was a cultic act, for it meant cutting out a particular part of the earth which was common to all. Hence on the occasion of demarcating the boundaries, sacrifices were made and many witnesses summoned. To move such a marker secretly or without permission was a grave offense.

Early on in the settlement process, the contrast of good and evil developed altogether naturally into the historical contrast between the Iranians and the Turanians, the latter people having remained nomadic. To be good was to be Iranian, and to be an Iranian meant to follow the vital commandments of settled life. The horse-riding peoples who came storming down from Turan in the North, threatening the peaceful existence of the villagers, were experienced not merely as enemies, but as evil. Evil was the rider who did not touch the ground with his feet. Hence in ancient Persian religion there was a kind of confession of faith in which the man who was turning to agriculture promised: "I choose holy humility; may it be mine. I forswear theft and stealing of cattle, plundering and laying waste to the villages of the worshippers of Ormuzd. To the housedwellers I grant free coming and going, free dwelling, as to the domestic animals with whom they share the earth... I pledge thinking well-thought, I pledge word well-spoken, I pledge deed well-done." (Yasna 12, 3, 8.). Texts of the Vendidad show that agriculture here is a divine command. A man, so it is written, asks: "Creator! What gladdens this earth with the greatest gladness?" Ahura Mazda answers: "When a man truly develops the most grain and pasturelands and fruit-bearing plants; when a man irrigates the dry lands and drains the water from the wet lands. Not glad is the earth that has long lain barren, earth that should be cultivated by the plowman, that wishes this as a good work from her dwellers." The divinity then says further that the earth speaks when a man works it with the right arm and the left: "Man, who workest me with the left arm and the right, with the right arm and the left: Surely I shall reward the land for this, surely I shall become fertile; all fruits shall men bring home, more grain than they can carry!" (Vendidad 3, from verses 23-27.)

The discussion has now slowly arrived at a point where the significance of religion can be taken up. It has been seen that working the land, doing what is right, and keeping the peace were unequivocally divine commandments. In this phase of human development, morality is not the purposeful morality of reason or intelligence. Morality is a gift from above. Without religious sanction, no morality! The historical battles against the Turanians, too, are more than mere battles for self-preservation. From this perspective, the battle between Iran and Turan is a battle of world history, a battle between the good God Ormuzd and the evil

Ahriman, Servant of the Lie. Religion and agriculture, morality and history were all one at the time when human beings first bound themselves to the earth. The decision for humankind at that time was: agricultural life or nomadic life. The decision was seen against the background of a divine battle: "And in the beginning were these two spirits, the twins, who by their own words are called the good and the evil in thought, word, and deed. The doers of good have chosen rightly between them, but not the doers of evil." (Yasna 30,3.)

Looking back at this development, one can pose the question: How did the process of settlement come about? This question can be discussed at great length in the classroom. Perhaps this will result in the discovery that it was not "economic necessity" — the existence of which is highly questionable — which prompted human beings to adopt this new way of life. It seems more probable (as the old Persian legend itself reports) that a prophet — called Zarathustra[1] by the legend — founded this culture, or that together with companions and followers he at least exercised an extremely great influence on the direction this culture was to take. This legendary Zarathustra is not identical with the founder of the religion, who lived around 580 B.C.

The Foundation of Cities — Origin of the First Ancient Cultures[2]

Some details of the earliest foundings are still unclear in many ways. On other questions experts voice contradictory opinions. Yet in face of all these uncertainties, the essential features of human history around the turn from the fourth to the third millennium B.C. stand out all the more clearly. It is widely agreed that the first cities were founded in Mesopotamia, near the mouth of the Euphrates and Tigris rivers.

---

[1] Besides the references listed for the 5th grade, cf. also: Bernard Schlerath (ed.), *Zarathustra*, Darmstadt, 1970 (Wiss. Buchgesellschaft); and Werner Hinz, *Zarathustra*, Stuttgart, 1961.

[2] Cf. especially: Jacquetta Hawkes, *The First Great Civilizations*, Harmondsworth, 1977 (Penguin Books).

These first cities of mankind, Eridu, Uruk, and Ur, shall be taken here as ideal types to illustrate the essential nature and course of city foundation.

The Tigris and Euphrates have their source in the highlands of present-day Armenia. The short period of melting snow in the spring and the autumn rain cause great masses of water to rush violently down from the high mountains each year. The rivers race along in torrents, carrying mud, rocks, and debris, often seeking new channels. In the centuries before the period of city foundation, the rivers would soon recede into their riverbeds again, leaving behind fertile silt, ponds, and moisture. Within fourteen days of the inundation, the moistened land was transformed into a wilderness garden, but after four or five weeks the splendor faded away again as quickly as it had come, wherever no water pools supplied moisture. These river valleys posed a challenge to the settled farmers. They saw that the soil in the river valleys produced more abundantly than that of the upland valleys. The short period of wetness, however, made it necessary to dam up water in order to have reserves. Canals had to be built so that the fields could be irrigated later in the year as well. But all their efforts were in vain: the very next spring, flooding almost regularly destroyed their weirs and filled their canals with silt. Against the mighty river, the work of single farmers or small villages was powerless. Around the year 3,100 B.C., a decisive change entered in. In the tenth grade, this change can now be collectively worked through and reconstructed. Here it is more important for the students to grasp the various elements of the change in their function than it is for them to "learn" how this took place historically — a subject that is disputed in any case and can scarcely be judged by nonspecialists.

First the fundamental question is posed: How can human beings meet the challenge of the river? It is obvious that only a very large group of people would be able to defy its power. Then another problem appears: a mere mass of people collecting in the river valley cannot solve the task posed by the river either. In relatively short order the class reaches a consensus: such groups would be incapable of guiding themselves by a democratic, decision-making process. This group of perhaps eight thousand to ten thousand human beings must be led by one person or a few people who are endowed with special qualities. The qualifications of such a leader are: he must have an idea, a plan how to tame the Euphrates; he must know his companions and their particular abilities in order to put them to work effectively; and finally, he must be just, so that the others follow him willingly. After the students have gone through these considerations, they are prepared to read the first lines of the Gilgamesh epic: "He saw everything, the Lord of the Land. He came to know each one of his people and each one's skill and work, and he understood everything. He saw through people's lives and doings. He brought to light secret hidden things... One-third in Gilgamesh is human, two-thirds is god."

Now it is a matter of exercising the imagination and getting a clear picture of the tasks confronting a founder of cities. He must assign work among his people. The first great necessity is canal and dike construction. On the upper reaches of the river, a canal must be started, leading the water along the edge of the valley with the least possible incline. In this way after a few kilometers the canal, running parallel to the river, is several meters higher than it. Now the fields can be irrigated from this canal. The second thing that may be necessary is to protect the fields against high water with a dike. In any case the town itself will be erected on a hill or mounded earth, and it will be protected by a wall against water and enemies. The Gilgamesh epic remembers: "Gilgamesh the victorious hero built the wall around Uruk. High as a mountain rises the holy temple in the enclosed town. Hard as brass lies the banked-up ground."

The labors of canal, dike, and wall building are simple but strenuous. It can be surmised that at times up to a third of the population was occupied in this work. This third had to be fed by others. The necessary work on the land was accomplished by still another group. But how did the canal and dike workers actually get their bread, their food? Agricultural produce and all the bounties of hunting and fishing were delivered to the "temple": "Under the protection of the sublime house where the God of Heaven dwells, high above the narrow streets stretches wide the granary of the city." The temple distributed food, implements, and clothing to everyone — it was the center of life. As the house of God, it was plastered with facing stones; it gleamed in the light, high above the narrow lanes that separated the mass of tightly crowded houses made of sun-dried brick. From far away the people could see the hill of Uruk and the house of its god, in which priests and priestesses performed the duties of their office. In these ancient times, the activities of priests were concrete, like their wisdom. They gave instructions for cultivation and harvest, guidance in the building of houses and dikes. Yet it was not only work that they apportioned and divided, but also time: it is to them that we owe the calendar, the division of the year into the twelve signs of the zodiac, and the division of the day into twelve hours. (In those days hours were still flexible, however: the night hours were longer in winter and the daylight hours shorter, the opposite being true in the summer.) In the temple, crafts were plied and taught. Occupations came into being — potters, weavers, tanners, and carpenters. Such qualified "professionals" were not many, and their special skills set them above the crowd.

All activity had to regulated safely and justly. The task of distributing food, clothing, and other products equitably to thousands of people simply could not be done without a crutch to help the memory keep track of all the countless details. In the beginning it may be that simple seals, pressed into moist clay that immediately hardened, served as marks or reminders. In the period of city foundation, an ingenious invention — one of the first such — was also already known: a cylindrical seal that is rolled onto the clay. At this point writing was invented. Writing was not done to glorify rulers or praise the gods. It was not necessary to commit the holy word to clay; for ritual and praise lived in the rhythm of song and the life of the people. What *was* necessary, on the other hand, was to fix and record earthly, economic details that were not bound to any cosmic order. It was for the temple economy of Uruk (Uruk IVa, ca. 3,000/2,900 B.C.)[1] that humanity's earliest form of writing was developed. First arose an archaic, pictographic script with about two thousand symbols, as well as a number system based both on the decimal and sexagesimal systems. Soon the picture symbols developed into cuneiform characters that were no longer obviously related to the pictures. It was now, at the very latest, that writing had become the province of the select few. There were now those who could write and read and those who had not mastered these arts. With this, a deep cleft had opened: on one side those initiated into writing, the educated, and on the other side the common people — workers, farmers, and craftsmen. Once begun, this split deepened in the course of time. The day came when stories, legends, and cultic songs as well began to be recorded — in the Sumerian language. Around the turn from the third to the second millennium B.C., the Sumerian people perished. Their language, however, was preserved: it

---

[1] As in Troy, various layers have been found in Uruk, indicating various stages of development.

became the language of religion and religious services, of history and tradition. Since that time, the sphere of cultural/spiritual life began to detach itself from everyday life. It made use of a secret language. It was no longer a heightened and elevated element of life itself. Slowly and imperceptibly, it was tending towards a *world of form*. Pupils now had to be introduced, laboriously, to tradition. They had to learn to understand something that no longer had immediate life, something abstracted from life. Priest-teachers lived in another world that developed a power of its own.

Just as writing developed a world of its own, so the other occupations soon developed through the course of their practice. The canal worker learned to build canal locks and lifting devices. Artists became specialists, as did craftsmen: now there were bakers and brewers, blacksmiths and cartwrights. The warrior now became a special class: there were soldiers and even special troops — royal guards and chariot fighters. Commerce, too, must not be forgotten. Archeological finds indicate that trade relations existed with the cities of the Indus Valley: Mohenjo Daro and Harrappa. In this way the life of society became richer and more differentiated; at the same time, however, it lost its immediacy. A particularly telling sign of this is that from about the year 2,000 on, the state began to regulate the relations of human beings between each other. The first climax of such organizing of human interrelations is found in the law code of the Babylonian king Hammurabi (1690 B.C.). The Code of Hammurabi contains 282 paragraphs. Considering that these paragraphs regulate criminal law, property and possession, family affairs and monetary law, not to speak of physical injury, adoption, land tenure rights, and much more besides, then one must admit: compared with today's forest of paragraphs, 282 is not many. At the same time this is a clear sign of how complicated life of the city and the land had now become.

The contemporaries themselves soon became aware of the step that they had taken in humanity's development. Once again the Gilgamesh epic tells of this transformation. Gilgamesh, the Lord of Uruk, is a city-dweller. The epic now recounts the fateful meeting of Gilgamesh and Enkidu. One day the hunters of Uruk come to a watering place and find a strange figure there. "Now he stands there, his body covered with hair, alone in the grassy plain. The hair flows down from his head like a woman's. Like wheat his hair sticks out. He knows nothing of lands and people... He eats the herbs of the field along with the gazelles. He drinks with the cattle at their watering place. He sports and splashes in the swarming waters." Another verse explains: "He came from the wilderness, he knew neither scissor nor scraper." Enkidu, also called Eabani in other versions of the story, is successfully lured into the city, where he meets Gilgamesh in a wrestling bout (which appears here as the older, original form of handshaking). Gilgamesh leads him into his palace. "Enkidu enters the shining hall of the King. His heart is oppressed and flutters like a bird of the sky. He longs for the plains and the beasts of the field. Loudly he laments his pain and cannot be held. He hastens back to the wilderness, out of the city." In the prairies, however, Enkidu senses that he has become estranged from the animals.

With the figure of Enkidu, the legend gives a picture of the human being still wholly at one with the cosmic powers. To the city-dweller, he embodies the memory of the long-lost age when the Sumerian people came down from the mountains to the valley lowlands. Enkidu is a picture of what the city-dweller has lost. It is more than what we might sentimentally speak of as "oneness with nature." The city-dweller no longer understands the language of the animals. The singing of the bird is beautiful to him, but it no longer speaks a secret language.

Gilgamesh and Enkidu become friends. Enkidu dies. In this moment Gilgamesh awakens to the question: "Will I not also die, like Enkidu? My heart is seized with woe. I now fear death!" The thought of death shows that man has become lonely, that he is no longer sure of being in the hands of a divine cosmos. Novalis characterizes just this moment in world history in his first "Hymns to the Night":

> One thought alone it was
> That dreadful, stepped up to the merry tables,
> Enveloping every soul with wild terror...
> It was death that broke up this pleasure feast
> With fear, with sorrow, and with tears.

> Nur ein Gedanke war's,
> Der furchtbar zu den frohen Tischen trat
> Und das Gemüt in wilde Schrecken hüllte.
> Es war der Tod, der dieses Lustgelag
> Mit Angst und Schmerz und Tränen unterbrach.

The Gilgamesh epic shows us the fate of the city-dwellers as they begin to build a world of their own, a human world. The building of such a world — a world that begins to dominate nature, order the relations between men by laws, and create a separate sphere of learning and culture — is the preliminary stage of a consciousness that questions and seeks. The fate of this kind of consciousness — namely loneliness — is foreshadowed in the Gilgamesh epic in its thematization of the bitterest and most elemental form of loneliness: the experience of death.

When this much has been worked through with the students, one can summarize. The founding of cities has shown itself to be a many-layered phenomenon. We must assume that in the beginning there was a tribe led by a leader. In this leader — an individual of great stature (who need not be identified with Gilgamesh) — lived the impulse to take hold of the earth and become master of the valley. He led his people — perhaps out of the mountains of Iran — into the lowlands of Mesopotamia, where the soil was so fertile that it could nourish a great number of people in a small area. In this limited space, people learned to check and tame the elemental power of the water. The domain over which man had power could be easily kept in view. All necessities of life could be produced in the vicinity of the city and transported into it without great difficulty. The groups of people could also be kept in sight. They were divided and assigned to different work: division of labor had begun. Some groups worked "outside," others "inside" — in the temple. In this interior space of the temple a separate world developed. The first form of removed knowledge began. Outside there was now a productive world, a world of canals and drainage trenches, fields, gardens, and date groves, and farther off the cattle herds. Ever more powerfully, the urge toward specialization and hence also towards isolation grew in this world. No longer did life simply and directly regulate itself: now, emanating from the God-King, there arose the beginnings of a legal culture with detailed ordinances. Different levels and classes developed in the population. And, finally, directed by priests, there arose a spiritual life that ordered and encompassed the whole, but at the same time separated — abstracted — itself from the common life. As yet there were no abstract ideas, however: people still thought in pictures and myths. But the spiritual/cultural sphere as a whole had abstracted itself from the life of the people. The price that had to be paid for these accomplishments on the physical plane is expressed in a new consciousness: "The friend whom I loved has turned to earth. Enkidu, my friend, has become as the clay of the land."

The initial impulse to develop the world had become reality in this way — the earth had been shaped and transformed. But the human being too, when he shapes the earth, experiences himself as "clay." He becomes conscious of death. Another insight also arises: without the great river valley with its fertile soil, no such early civilizations could have come into being. Yet they are born not out of the geographical conditions, but out of a battle with them. When we have gone through this portrayal, perhaps we have followed the suggestion that Rudolf Steiner makes for the tenth grade curriculum in the Waldorf School: "One can discuss, for example, how a people changes when it moves down from the mountains into the valley."

Egypt — a Unique Case

Probably no other culture so clearly shows the influence of land, river, and climate as that of Egypt. It provides us with an extreme example of the tenth grade theme.[1] The reason for this is that nowhere in the world is the landscape of a culture determined by so few factors: a river

---

[1] The actual history of Egypt can be treated in relatively short order. For the Old Kingdom, one can consider the working of stone and construction of the Pyramids; for the Middle Kingdom, the inner colonization (Fayum) and reorganization of the state; for the New Kingdom, the extension of Egyptian rule (Thutmosis III) and the figure of Akhnaton, atypical though it appears. *Literature:* J. H. Breasted, *Geschichte Ägyptens*, outdated but still very instructive; E. Otto, *Ägypten, Der Weg des Pharaonenreiches*, Stuttgart 1953; J.A. Wilson, *Ägypten*, in: *Propyläen Weltgeschichte*, vol. I, 1961; I. E. S. Edwards, *The Pyramids of Egypt*, Penguin Book, revised edition 1961; Kurt Lange, *König Echnaton*, Munich 1961; Manfred Lurker, *Symbole der alten Ägypter*, Weilheim 1964; also: Frankfort/Wilson/Jacobsen, *Frühlicht des Geistes*, Stuttgart 1954. Jacquetta Hawkes. *The First Civilizations*. Hammondsworth, 1977 (Penguin).

in a desert. The climate remains always the same. In Upper Egypt it rains once every hundred years. The desert always remains the same. The river swells and recedes always in the same rhythm — only sometimes more and sometimes less. Even the wind blows almost always upstream with the Nile. Such uniformity, such constancy cannot remain without consequences — and in fact, despite seven great invasions, despite the introduction of technology and modern political and military institutions, and despite modern ideologies, the most ancient ways of life have maintained themselves here to this very day.

It is the extremely plentiful and ever recurring tropical rainy seasons in the highlands of Abyssinia and the source areas of the White Nile that cause the river to swell each year in the summer. The swelling is tremendous, but calculable. In August, if the water had reached a level of 7½ - 8 meters at the first cataract of the Nile, a good, adequate harvest could be counted on. Everywhere after the inundation, the water was diverted into small canals; land was irrigated; fertile black silt covered the fields. If the Nile remained under the desired mark, correspondingly less land was irrigated. Since there was not a single other factor that could compensate for the missing water, famine threatened with certainty — but this as well was probably calculable. If, on the other hand, the Nile far exceeded the mean mark, the calamity was no less serious: dams and dikes would be destroyed, canals were in danger of silting up, and settlements could be endangered.

Even if the height of the inundation was unpredictable, as soon as it was known the rest followed by necessity — it could be calculated. The exact height of the Nile's flooding enabled the pharaoh to compute the volume of the harvest exactly. In this way the level of taxation could also be established, and no deception was possible because the land had been exactly surveyed. Such calculability of events was further favored by the fact the Nile Valley is flat and open to view. Under these circumstances the Egyptians developed a practical geometry. The Dutch, who in their flat Rhine delta are faced today with tasks not unlike those that faced the Egyptians five thousand years ago, have developed a strong sense for rationality and clarity. Scholars well-acquainted with Egypt assert that Egyptian religion as well has a distinctive trait of clarity and symmetry.

It is evident that only a people with intelligence and a will to shape the world could have mastered the task posed by the Nile. Later, the regularity, the eternal monotony of events necessarily led to a certain rigidity of spirit, to conservatism. An example is given by Egyptian art. With little variation (and one exception: Akhnaton) it maintained the same basic forms for two thousand years. An even more striking sign of rigidity, however, is found in the chronology of the Egyptians. The regularity of the flooding of the Nile led them to search for an astronomical occurrence that coincided with this event and could count as a signal of it. Such an occurrence was the moment when Sirius (Egyptian: Sothis) became visible again in the morning sky after having been invisible for some time because of proximity to the sun. Counting the days until this "bringer of the flood" reappeared, one arrived at the number 365, a number that seemed to be confirmed in succeeding years. In this way the calendar could be fixed, which meant that from then on the number 365 remained its basis. As we know, however, from an astronomical point of view the year is almost exactly one quarter of a day longer; and so, after continuing in this way for 730 years, the calendar had shifted so far "off" that yearly festivals were celebrated at exactly the opposite time of year ("Christmas" on "St. John's Day"). Conservative as they were, however, the Egyptians retained this calendar in its original form. After 1,460 years it reached a time of correctness once more, only to pass slowly out of synchrony again.

To explain the extremely conservative attitude of the Egyptians solely by the regularity of the Nile, however, is perhaps really to overstress the causal significance of a single factor. Other factors contributed as well. Until the incursion of the "Hyksos" (ca. 1715 B.C.), Egyptian culture developed without any detectible outer influence or contact with the rest of the world. To the west of Egypt stretched the Libyan desert, to the east the desert of the Sinai Peninsula and the Arabian desert. These deserts and the Red Sea initially formed an effective barrier against any attempt to penetrate Egypt; at the same time they also prevented the Egyptians from leaving the country and becoming acquainted with the world. Finally, the Mediterranean Sea was not, at that early date, a navigation route. Hence, Egyptian culture developed in complete isolation — a unique occurrence for a high civilization. This isolation made Egypt "incomparable" in the truest sense of the word, and under these circumstances it never occurred to anyone that anything could be different than it was.

Let a suggestion be made here about teaching procedure. It is a good thing to begin by working through the geographical facts together. Care should be taken, however, not to use the word Egypt in a totally unhistorical way. The Egypt of the ancient Egyptians was initially only the Nile Valley. No Egyptian would have called the desert surrounding his country "Egypt" or said that 96 percent of Egypt was desert. The territory of the modern state of Egypt lies, for the very most part, outside of what was then known as the "Two Lands" — Upper and Lower Egypt. Next, taking the characteristics of the Nile Valley as one's starting point, one can begin to reflect about the influence of this landscape on the mentality of its inhabitants. It seems reasonable to speak here of a natural conservatism — something which must of course be distinguished later from an anti-revolutionary conservatism like that of Edmund Burke.

The method followed here, which enables students themselves to derive the mentality of the people from the conditions of the land, must become fully conscious to them in time. After all, it is not a matter of a direct influence of the land upon people's mentality. The decisive, connecting link is their way of life. The environment makes possible one or more ways of life, and these in turn shape to an extent the thinking, feeling, and will of human beings. Let the students think about what it means to live in a land — as in central Europe — where a person never knows what the weather will bring next week. Or let them discuss what it means to live in a land where it is difficult to get an overall view — hilly or mountainous country that always presents a different aspect, having forest and pasture land, field and meadow. In contrast, it can now be made clear that Egypt knows only one kind of weather, apart from the sandstorms that can develop in April and May. One phenomenon rules the "weather" of Egypt: the sun. Now the discussion comes around to the significance of the sun in the life and religion of the Egyptians. Two factors are the givers of life: the Nile and the sun. In the night it gets cold very quickly, and in the morning the sun rises almost vertically, without a long period of twilight. In the poems of Akhnaton this contrast between day and night comes to expression as a most immediate and feeling-charged experience:

Night

When you sink on the western rim of the sky,
The world lies in darkness, as if it were dead.
They sleep in their chambers,
Their heads are veiled,
Their noses are stopped up and no one sees the other.
All their belongings are stolen from underneath their heads,
Without their knowing it.
Each lion comes forth from its den;
All serpents begin to sting.
Darkness prevails; the world is silent;
For he who created it has gone to rest on the rim of the sky.

The pure contrast between this poem and the following is obvious:

Day and Man

Bright is the earth
When you rise on the rim of the sky,
When by day you shine as Aton.
Darkness is banished
When you send out your rays;
Both lands (i.e. Egypt) daily celebrate a festival,
Awake and standing on their feet,
For you have raised them.
They wash themselves and take their clothes;
Their arms lift in worship when you appear.
All men do their work.

The bare simplicity, the utterly direct experience speaking from these lines can be explained only on the background of reality — a reality dominated by one eminent factor, the sun.

At the same time, it is good to give special consideration to the inner attitude reflected in this pure and simple apprehension of reality.

The Egyptians took the world as it was, and took the way it was as the norm. This becomes clear in their writing and language. The first significant aspect of this writing system is the very fact that it remains pictorial and does not advance to the abstraction of letters. To work with letters speaks of an ability to analyze the wholeness of the word and reduce it into elements; and this means an ability to picture the signified object in such an abstracted and generalized form. The Egyptian did not do this; he stayed, as far as possible, with the impression, the perception. Egypt, i.e. the Nile Valley, was as flat as a pancake; and so the hieroglyph for it looks like this: ⬤ The world surrounding Egypt — the desert and the other countries — showed mountains and valleys. The hieroglyph for "foreign parts" was ⌣⌣⌣ A similar sign meant "mountains" ⌣ and thus symbolized the mountain chains rimming Egypt on the west and east. The Egyptian language shows the imprint of the landscape in a similar fashion. South is simply called "upstream" and north "downstream." It was especially confusing to the Egyptians when, during the period of Egyptian imperialism in the New Kingdom, they experienced the Euphrates and the Tigris. They called these two rivers the backwards waters that flow downstream while flowing upstream. Rain, unknown in Egypt, presented a similar problem. In a poem to the sun god, Akhnaton says:

> Even to the foreign lands you give life,
> You have set a Nile in the sky for them,
> That it should fall down for them
> And make waves upon the mountains
> And water the fields...
> The Nile in the sky is for the foreigners,
> But the real Nile wells up out of the underworld
> For Egypt!

In other ways as well, it was obvious that the rest of the world differed from Egypt and hence from what was right. Egypt was flat and all open to view. The Nile was an excellent traffic route: to go down-stream, a ship drifted with the current; going upstream, the wind blowing up the valley helped, and so all ships heading south set their sails. How different was the world in Asia! An Egyptian scribe reported to his colleague at home: "You do not know the way to Meger, where the sky is dark in the day; it is overgrown with cypresses and cedars reaching right to the sky... Terror seizes you, the hair of your head stands on end, your soul lies on the palm of your hand. The road is full of boulders and rubble." Another such letter complains that the land in Asia is impassable because of its many trees and mountains.

Under these circumstances it is no surprise that to the Egyptians, the only real human being was an Egyptian. The word "Egyptian" meant "human being," and the Asians and Africans were distinct from "the human beings." This concept of man was not racial or ethnic, however: foreigners could become human beings too if only they lived in Egypt long enough and adopted the language, attire, and way of life. But the isolation and uniqueness of the Nile Valley were not the only reasons that the Egyptians accorded themselves this significance. The real reason for their pride and self-assurance lay in the culture of this land, and the culture begins with the uniting of Upper and Lower Egypt. This state — that is, the achievement of a political unity capable of continual self-renewal — was certainly a gift of the Nile, the uniting link between the "Two Lands." At the boundary between them stood Memphis, originally the *per-aa*, the great house, from which our language later derived the name of the ruler, the Pharaoh. This state was aligned towards one fundamental virtue which was called *ma'at* in Egypt. The word is untranslatable. There is no German* word that carries a comparable number of meanings or nuances with it. Sometimes ma'at is translated as "truth," "justice," "uprightness," or "order." Often ma'at relates to good ruling and administering, but the concept itself is of cosmic origin. It expresses what the Egyptians felt to be the essence and being of their land, what underlies the creative power that made Egypt. Ma'at was the cosmic force of harmony, order, stability, security; it was established already at the beginning of creation as the organizing quality of all created things, and it was ritually reaffirmed each time a new king took office. The king's service in the temple also reaffirmed each day that the king would rule in the spirit of the ma'at, by commission of the gods. Thus the king, son of the sun god Re, was himself a force of cosmic origin, and one of his functions was to see to it that his people were nourished. He com-

---

* and doubtless no English word either [trans.]

manded the water to make Egypt fruitful: "The Nile is at his service and he, the King, opens its caverns to give Egypt life."[2]

So we see that in Egypt, the marvellous order of nature was inextricably intertwined with the marvellous order of the state; for the two were one and the same: they were order and harmony, ma'at, the fundamental cosmic and human virtue. It goes without saying that this virtue also determined life in the kingdom of the dead, which, of course, also had a Nile and everything else that was known here on earth. Perhaps this great simplicity in which the order and harmony of the world were experienced can also cast light on the Pyramids. Are there anywhere on earth structures of such simplicity as the Pyramids, structures that do not symbolize, but *are* clarity and order? In ancient times the Pyramid, which was utterly smooth and even, appeared as a triangle shimmering white in the sunlight; indeed, it was light and purity themselves, a sunbeam on which the divine king ascended to the gods.[3]

Life, Sea, and Land of the Greeks

The territory of the modern Greek state includes both more and less than that of ancient Greece. In classical times, Macedonia was not counted part of Hellas, while the Hellenic cities on the coast of Asia Minor were — Miletus, Ephesus, Phocaea, and many others. The center of the Hellenic world was the Aegean, and approximately in the middle of this center lies Delos, the island on which Leto gave birth to Apollo beneath a palm tree. Since the eighth century B.C. the Greeks had migrated out from their Aegean center, settling the more hospitable coasts of the Black Sea and the more favorable points of the Mediterranean: Massilia (Marseille), Nicaea (Nice), and Mainake (near

---

[2] Cf. John Wilson, *Ägypten.* In: *Propyläen Weltgeschichte*, vol. 1, Berlin 1961, p. 352. And John Wilson: "Ägypten." In: *Frühlicht des Geistes*, Stuttgart 1954, p. 80.

[3] Cf. I. E. S. Edwards, *The Pyramids of Egypt.* Harmondworth, 1961, p. 288-292; and: Frank Teichmann, *Der Mensch und sein Tempel.* Stuttgart, 1978.

present-day Malaga) are Greek settlements, as are Syracuse, Taormina, Rhegion (Reggio), and Neapolis (Naples). Thus — in Plato's words — the Greeks sat around the edge of the Mediterranean like frogs around the edge of a pond. The sea was the very air the Greeks breathed, their element. Xenephon tells of this in his *Anabasis*, describing the joy of the ten thousand men when, after a long march through Asia Minor, they at long last behold *thalassa*, the sea. The sea smoothed the way home; it was almost "homeland" itself.

The land of the Greeks is full of splits and separations. Mountain ranges divide one region from the other. Between Laconia and Messenia the long, snow-covered Taygetus chain rises 2,400 meters into the air. Attica is separated from Boeotia by the Kithairon and the Parnes mountains. Near Themopylae the Kallidromos rises 1300 meters, barring the way to Phocis and Boeotia. One could continue describing landscapes and mountains of Greece in this way, but it would all only go to show clearly that the chief route of traffic and transport had to be the sea: the land separated, the sea connected. The many individual regions that take form in the plains or valleys between the mountains tend to foster landscapes with their own forms and tribes with their own peculiar qualities. The number of dialects alone is astonishing. The Attic Poseidon was called Poseides, Posides, or Posideon in Ionic, Poseidan in Aeolic, Poteidun in Thessalian, Poteidaon in Boeotian, Poteidan in Doric, Pohoidan in Spartan, and Posoidan in Achaean. This variety of dialects, however, only mirrored the differences of the individual tribal and regional characters, and these are as different as the wide plain of Thessalia, nourisher of horses, is from mountainous, stony Attica with its olive trees, and grapes, as well as roses, violets, and crocuses that spread its fame in antiquity.

Ancient Hellas connected two continents: Asia and Europe. Troy, Miletus (the city of Thales), Ephesus (where Heraclitus lived), and Halicarnassus (the home of Herodotus) were all in Asia. Athens, Sparta, and Thebes, on the other hand, were European cities. Between Europe and Asia, like stepping stones in the sea, were the islands north of the Cyclades and Sporades. They made it possible for the seafarer to cross the Aegean on sight alone, by trusting his eyes. Both coasts, that of Europe as well as that of Asia, lay open to the seafarer with an inviting gesture, offering him natural harbors and flat beaches. Thus by its situation and character, Greece formed a bridge between the ancient cultures of the Orient and the young peoples from the Northwest who thrust southward in waves. Out of the South and East came cultural impulses from Egypt and Assyria, transmitted by the seafaring Phoenicians. To the latter the Greeks owe their alphabet. Later came the Persian threat, through which, as they repelled it, the Greeks first awakened to their selfhood. Finally, out of the Southeast came Christianity, whose greatest advocate, Paul, travelled through Asia Minor to Troy. His path then led him by way of the island of Samothrace to Philippi, Thessalonica, and finally to Athens. From the North and Northeast, however, came migrating peoples, Indo-european tribes: the Ionians and, north of them, the Aeolians and Achaeans. Six hundred years later, around 1300 B.C., a second wave of migration began that culminated in the Dorian migration (ca. 1100-900 B.C.). The Macedonian conquest can be looked upon as a third great movement of peoples from the North. The variety of landscapes, the absence of wide rivers or large plains, and the high, impassable mountain ranges were responsible for the fact that the invasions — precisely those from the North — nowhere led to the formation of great states. The streams of peoples had to divide and scatter in the Greek landscape. To the seafarer, the most diverse regions of the land lay open to access, but to view — or rule — them as a whole was by no means equally easy. Thus the splintered nature of the peninsula protected its inhabitants from any effective, large-scale domination, creating the conditions (much as in inner Switzerland) for free self-government of small regions. Nor could cultural influence from the Southeast be forced upon the Greeks: it remained their choice to which influence they would be open and to which they would mobilize forces of resistance. Thus, not only is the land a bridge between the Northwest and Southeast, but Greece itself lives in the balance between damped-down influences from North and South.

In keeping with this balance, we also find that the life of the Greeks was balanced. The people were neither oppressed by excessive poverty nor spoiled by riches. The meager soil yielded just enough to satisfy the needs of life. In classical times, the fare tended to be scanty: meat was scarce and considered a distinct luxury; fish was for Sundays. The normal fare was bread, olive oil, and wine, along with a bit of vegetables. The Greeks thrived on this fare, as one can tell from the longevity of the poets, philosophers, and statesmen. Desires that went beyond the produce of the soil were met by the crafts and trade. Quite early the Greeks became inventive, and soon every region had one or more specialties: Attica exported the great jugs filled with olive oil; Miletus, vases and textiles; Melos, the marble; the little island of Peparethos, the wine; Thessalia furnished chestnuts and oily almonds. What with all this and a great deal more, commerce flourished. Craftsmanship strengthens self-confidence; a man can see that he has accomplished something. *Commerce, however, develops the intelligence,* whether for evil or for good. As long as the crafts exist within a theocratic system as in Ur or in Egypt, they serve the whole; they are nothing but a little link in an all-powerful order. In Greece, however, the crafts did not serve religion or the priest-kings; they met human needs through trade. Trade encourages mobility, spreads knowledge, and liberates people from their background. Free trade was absent in the old theocracies.

The Greeks were interested chiefly in the human being — this becomes evident when we regard the gods of Olympus. They are no longer superhuman gods with animal heads and an unwavering, expressionless mien. The gods of Homer are human gods. One need only think of the countless legends telling of Ares and Aphrodite, of Hephaistos, Zeus, and Hera — all of them are distinguished by humanity. Zeus, father of the gods, is not a tyrant but a primus inter pares. It seems that the land of Greece itself favored a human mean and measure, for it did not bring forth too much of anything and the human being had a share in everything. Therefore Protagoras could formulate the philosophical statement: "Man is the measure of all things — of how they are, for the things that are; and of how they are not, for the things that are not." Also significant in this connection is the second aphorism with which a person was greeted upon entering Delphi: "Nothing in excess!" Once again, it is the motif of equilibrium that we encounter here.

The Greeks themselves gave thought to the influence of the land on the way of life and character of the people. When one considers that hardly any Greek settlement is more than fifty to seventy kilometers distant from the sea, its overwhelming influence immediately becomes apparent once more. The fourth book of Plato's *Laws* contains this passage: "For though the sea that washes a region may well be agreeable for the daily needs, in fact it is surely a bitter and harsh neighbor. For by promoting commerce and retail trading and thus the acquisition of money, by breeding fickle and untrustworthy ways in men's souls, it makes the citizens faithless and loveless to one another." In these words one hears Plato the severe moralist, who, like other Greek authors, puts strong emphasis on the negative.[1] One will have to agree with Plato that egotism is necessarily an occupational illness of all traders and merchants. At the same time, one will have to add that, inevitably, only intelligent egotism will be successful in the long run. Commerce forces people to be calculating and watchful: one must observe the situation of the market as well as the needs of the people. As a seafaring trader one must be on guard; for pirates and storms might threaten, and not every coast offers equally good landing. In time, however, the trader becomes acquainted with the world; he sees the great variety of ways of life and livelihood. In Carthage he sees how carpets are knotted, in Egypt he becomes familiar with the processing of papyrus, elsewhere he encounters mining. At home in Athens he has dealings with a great range of industries: there is one smith who forges armor, another helmets, and a third scythes; there is even one who makes trumpets. Contact with these various worlds makes him mobile in spirit: he must adjust to each customer and supplier, at the same time keeping his own advantage in mind. Intelligence is developed in this way. Legend reports of Thales of Miletus that he, too, developed this mercantile intelligence: While walking among the olive groves he noticed that the impending olive harvest would be especially abundant. He secured all the oil-presses in the city, and with this monopoly in hand he could dictate the price for their use.

Behind this image of the skilled and cunning merchant emerges the figure of his spiritual ancestor, wily Odysseus — not a merchant, to be sure, but in any case a seafarer. The virtue of craftiness also counts upon the dullness of the other: the wooden horse outwits the Trojans, who — characteristically — take this fabrication for a divine image. The name "no man" dupes Polyphemus. And finally, it is with a ruse that Themistocles twice deceives the Persians and so wins the victory at Salamis and the withdrawal of the Great King.

Cunning and intelligence, sprung from the merchant's way of life, then prove themselves in the inventiveness of the craftsman. The place where trade and the crafts come together is the market. Modern, economic thinking has abbreviated the concept of market to the place where prices are set in relation to supply and demand. The market in Athens,

---

[1] Cf. Hippocrates: Of Airs, Waters, and Places. In: *Hippocrates, Schriften.* Rowohlts Klassiker, Hamburg, 1962, p. 105.

the *agora*, was more. It was the place where people assembled, the place of the great political speeches and battles. Yet how could the fate of the nation be negotiated in the marketplace? The answer is that the market was also the place where not only goods, but experiences too were exchanged. It was through the exchange of experiences, through conversation and report, that ideas were developed and then freely discussed. The market as the place of discussion is the basis of learning, and it is doubtless no accident that it was in this very market that Socrates appeared — the man who through his discourse won the day for human insight and wisdom (Greek: *anthropine sophia*[2]). That Socrates had listeners and partners in conversation, however, is something he owed to that talkative atmosphere of the marketplace that is also reported in the Acts of the Apostles: "Therefore disputed he ... in the market daily with them that met with him" (Acts 17, 17). "For all the Athenians and strangers which were there spent their time in nothing else, but either to tell, or to hear some new thing" (Acts 17, 21). It is said that logical, intellectual thought was born in Greece out of pictorial thinking that clings to the appearances of phenomena. The place where this birth took place is the market, the assembly place where a man like Pericles spoke to the people and sought to convince them by reasoning.

It has been shown above that the situation and nature of the land was such as to provoke and promote industriousness, mercantile spirit, resourcefulness and enterprise, as well as knowledge of the world. Further, it was said that the market was the place in which the human spirit could appear publically in the form of thoughts. These statements, however, must not be confused with the assertion that commerce arose *out of* the nature and situation of the land or that philosophy arose *because of* the market. Land and location, commerce and market are not the *cause* of the spirit. Land and location challenge human beings to take a certain attitude. Their actions are an independent answer to such a challenge. The land or the sea may favor and encourage some things, but land and sea do not create trade. The market of Athens, indeed the whole city, was without doubt the foundation for Socrates — for his life's work and for his death as well. And this is why he refused — as the dialogue reports — to leave the city that threatened him with death. Doubtless the teachings of Socrates and Plato, the form of the artistic creations of

---

[2] Plato, *Apology of Socrates.*

Phidias or Sophocles could have arisen only in Greece under the balanced conditions we have described. But the content of the ideas, the beauty of the artworks have their cause in the inner laws of the spirit. Greece provided the arena for their manifestation.

The following summary may serve to illustrate the immense significance of the geographic element:

Egypt

The Nile, as a unifying element, promotes the great unitary state (theocracy).

The isolation of the country by the desert promotes cultural stability for two thousand years and hinders understanding for foreign peoples and things.

The uniformity and richness of the Nile Valley, the regularity of its flooding tie thought to definite phenomena and make it rigid. Writing remains bound to appearances (pictographic script, hieroglyphs).

The chief source of livelihood, agriculture, is at the mercy of the omnipotent Nile. No other factor determines life. Promotes resignation to fate, submissiveness, since there is no escape from the Nile Valley (exception: Israel!). Conservative mentality and mythical consciousness of the peasant.

State economy under control of the pharaoh regulates relationships. Rulership of priests with fixed modes of thought relates to mental life.

Greece

The diversity of the land encourages the development of many relatively small cities (polis-democracy).

The openness of the land, the necessity of seafaring, leads to the encounter with different cultures and peoples, promoting understanding for, and interest in the outside world, which is carefully described (Herodotus et al.).

The land, in its meagerness, elicits inventiveness and a spirit of enterprise. The seafarer learns to compare the most diverse things and to see the common concept within them. Analytic thinking, analytic writing system (letters).

Crafts and free trade arise as other sources of livelihood. Each man is the architect of his own fortune. Many Greeks emigrate (Sicily). No coercion is possible. Awareness of own achievements occurs. Mobility of thought develops.

Significance of logical argument in the daily political fight.

Market economy leads to exchange of experiences. Men regulate their relationships by themselves. Dialogic thinking develops argument (Socrates).

In conclusion, a short reference may be permitted to the political-historical relevance of the new Greek mentality. Within Greece itself, the contrast between Egypt and Greece is repeated in miniature in Sparta and Athens. Sparta appears as the conservative land-power lying in a narrow valley ringed by high mountains. In the land of the Spartans proper, the sea is blocked from view by a high ridge that runs eastwards from the Taygetus, thus closing off the valley towards the south. Athens is quite the opposite: it stretches out into the sea on its peninsula. From the Acropolis one sees the sea, one sees Salamis and Aegina. The poverty of the soil condemns the Athenians to become craftsmen and seafarers.

The polarity of Sparta and Athens, however, is by no means based on nature alone. Through insight and conscious will this contrast was intensified. Both states chose lawgivers who shaped the life of the community through goals and plans of their own free construction. It is this that raises the Sparta-Athens contrast onto a higher, peculiarly Greek level. In Sparta it was Lycurgus who acted as lawgiver, and one of his most incisive measures was the introduction of iron money, which made all trade with non-Spartan regions impossible. In this way Lycurgus heightened the natural isolation of Sparta and succeeded in making agriculture its only means of livelihood. Thus, the conservatism of the Spartans was reinforced. Another element in the measures of Lycurgus was the equal distribution of the land among the Spartans, which smothered any economic ambition. And a third element was the totally uniform education of the children. In this way Lycurgus created an Egypt in Greece — an Egypt on a higher, Greek octave, for it was willed in thought. In this regard it is interesting to note that the Spartan constitution remained stable for five hundred years, while experimental Athens went through about seven different constitutions in the same time. In 594 B.C. Solon, following Draco, became the lawgiver and conciliator (*diallaktes*)³. Only one measure of Solon's will be mentioned, namely the "currency reform" he implemented, which replaced the Aeginetan standard used in Athens with the Euboeic-Milesian. Because of this division of money into smaller units, Athens gained entry into the Milesian sphere of trade and entered into competition with Corinth. In this way Solon promoted commerce and crafts, desiring and achieving exactly the opposite of what Lycurgus wished for Sparta: Solon opened Athens even more to the world, and laid the foundation stone of its future power at sea. Education in Athens, though it included gymnastic and musical training, took place primarily through the theater. As Aristotle tells us, theater is a school of compassion. By compassion, i.e. by suffering with another being, one learns understanding. And the Athenians raised this understanding far above the measure usual even today. In 470 B.C., Aeschylus composed a drama on the victory of the Greeks over the Persians. The greatness of this drama, to me, is that it completely renounces any desire to see the war from the standpoint of the Greeks. Not one of the Greek leaders is even mentioned by name. Aeschylus portrays the suffering of the Persians. He actually asks of his fellow Athenians to put themselves emotionally in the place of the Persian queen, Atossa, who resides in Susa. To describe the battle of Salamis from the Susan point of view — this is the apex of self-renunciation. Any trace of Egyptian self-centeredness is gone. Here, thinking consciousness has extended itself to the limits of the known world.

³ Of the abundant literature on Greek history and culture, one example is given here as a reference: H.D. F. Kitto, *The Greeks*. Pelican, Harmondsworth (numerous editions).

12

ASPECTS OF HISTORY FOR THE ELEVENTH GRADE

In the Waldorf School curriculum for the eleventh grade, history is closely connected with German class, which takes up (among other things) Wolfram von Eschenbach's *Parzival* and Hartmann von Aue's *Poor Henry*. In reading these two epics, our attention is drawn to the peculiar fact that both poets describe a medieval world of extraordinarily wide range. Poor Henry, a Swabian knight, knows the physicians in Montepellier and journeys to Salerno; the prelude and story of Parzival take place between Bagdad in the East, Capua, Seville, and Toledo in the South, and the legendary lands of Arthur in the West. The epic knows the world of the court and chivalry, it knows the Castle of Wonders (*Schastelmarveil*) and the Grail Castle, but oddly, it does not speak of the pope or of the emperor, of the great brotherhoods of monks or of archbishops and cardinals. Similarly absent are the theological concepts of Scholasticism that we usually meet in the Middle Ages. They are foreign to this epic; in their place is the tradition of the Grail. Indeed, *Poor Henry*, Wolfram's *Parzival*, the epics of Chretien de Troyes and Gottfried von Strassburg, the Christian *Song of Alexander*, and many other traditional narratives show that the spiritual life of the Middle Ages knew a now lost vision of history and the world that gives expanded meaning to the history familiar to us.

In his discourse with Parzival on Good Friday, Trevrizent says: "diu menscheit hât wilden art." "Mankind has a strange and wild nature" (489,5). This "wildness" was characteristic of the Germanic tribes in the eighth, ninth, and tenth centuries, and it is also characteristic of the young Parzival, who kills Ither. Step by step Parzival is led to a new nature. His path takes him from his instruction by Gurnemanz through his failure at the Grail Castle, into *zwîvel* — doubt, inconstancy — and to renewed seeking. The history of the Middle Ages goes

166

through this path as well. One can make the attempt to describe this path in the development of medieval society as well: one can try to show how impulses drawn from Christianity transformed this society, but how it too was led into *zwîvel* or near the sphere of the Castle of Wonders. With this inner theme in view, one can ask oneself where to begin and how to proceed.

The Three Legacies

The history of antiquity, as taught in the tenth grade, ends with the fall of Greek freedom in the battle of Chaeronea in 338 B.C. The theme of the eleventh grade — as we know — is the history of the Middle Ages. The first question facing the history teacher is whether the birth of Christianity, the Migration of the Peoples, and Islam can be left out altogether, in order to begin medieval history with the Merovingians or Carolingians, for example. In my opinion this is a possible way of proceeding: it offers the advantage of allowing one to treat medieval history thoroughly. Personally, however, I have always chosen another way, because I believe that the history of the Middle Ages is difficult to understand without reference to antiquity. It is not, of course, a matter of making a rapid run-through of the whole of Roman history, the Peoples' Migrations, etc., but of focussing attention on those elements of antiquity that were significant for the evolving Occident. Thus, the history blocks could be introduced with a survey illustrating the three-fold legacy of antiquity: Greek thought, Judaic conception of history, and Roman state. In the Middle Ages, these three streams flow together under the banner of Christianity.

The Greek thinking that took on importance in the Middle Ages was that which culminated in Plato and Aristotle. In a school where no philosophy is taught, this is the only opportunity to acquaint the students with these fathers of Western thought. At this age Plato can be understood quite well if the basic theme of his philosophy is illustrated with his parable of the cave. Inwardly, the students understand this parable; they have noticed that the way to truth is painful and laborious. To portray the difference between Plato and Aristotle, one can bring the discussion to their political theory. Plato constructed an ideal state, while Aristotle described the constitutions of the Greek cities, searching for the idea of the state within the existing realities. Similarly, to him the Idea of each living thing is to be found within it, as its entelechy, and is accessible to the thinking mind that apprehends its outer form. In Hellenism, this "thought-seed" was scattered widely: part of it found its way into the West through Augustine, Porphyry, and Boethius, while the bulk of Aristotelian writings only later became known to the Scholastics by way of Islam.

Judaism should not be overlooked in history. While Greek thinking took the created world, the world in space, as its theme, it is to the Jews that the Occident owes the idea of world history. Where the Greeks and Romans saw history as a cycle, the Jews recognized it as the story of the Fall and Messianic redemption of humanity — as a process that has a beginning, moves through manifold crises (Flood, Confusion of the Tongues at the Tower of Babel, captivity in Egypt and Babylon), and strives towards a goal. This conception, repeated in the idea that the life of each individual is a pilgrimage towards a goal, gives meaning to history and human action. Augustine, Otto von Freising, Joachim of Fiore, and many others took up this idea of world history, so that it gained a practical significance far beyond the Middle Ages.

The historian scarcely need to be told about the significance of Roman legal concepts and the idea of the empire for the Middle Ages: the idea of renewing the empire — *renovatio imperii* — was one of the driving forces of the Middle Ages. For the teacher, however, the question arises how to summarize things of importance here in a very few lessons. One possibility is to limit oneself to the Roman constitution, describing those principles which aimed towards balance, control, and sensible selection. Among these are: collegiality (friendly relations among colleagues), annuity (one-year term of office), patricians (senate), plebeians (people's tribunes), succession of offices, and the *ius provocationis*, by which a citizen threatened with the death penalty was granted the right of appeal to the People's Assembly. Another possibility would be to describe the united Roman Empire of the year 100 A.D. as a realm of order and peace.

These three traditions of antiquity now converge in the life and journeys of the Apostle Paul. Paul was born in Tarsus as a Roman citizen of Jewish origin and Pharisean religious orientation, and grew up speaking Greek. He came to know the city life of antiquity, the racing arena and theater, the court of justice and commerce. Doubtless he read the Old Testament in Greek, but in early youth he also learned the holy language of the Jews: Hebrew. In strict manner he was instructed in the law of the Patriarchs by the Pharisee Gamaliel. The Book of Acts tells of his further path in life: the road to Damascus; conversion in the desert; first encounter with Peter; and then the great missions that take him to Cyprus, Antioch, and in Greece; to Philippi, Thessalonica, Athens, Corinth, and, above all, to Ephesus. Finally, in Jerusalem, he is taken captive and condemned to death. As a Roman citizen, however, he appeals — invoking *ius provocationis* — to the emperor, and is brought captive to Rome, where he is traditionally thought to have met his end.

It was Paul who led Christianity out of Judaism. He was able to meet the Greeks and Romans as a Greek and a Roman; he was able to speak in thoughts and pictures that were understood in the entire Mediterranean world. Thus from within the Roman Empire — slowly aging and moving towards its final decline and fall — there arose a hidden new world of Christian communities, human beings who lived out of faith, whose lives had received an entirely new meaning and purpose. What had been accessible only to a select few in the Mysteries — an unravelling of the mystery of death, a view going beyond the immediate present of earthly existence — was now experienced in communities which came together for a common meal of bread and wine. In Christianity, the whole of the ancient world finds its resolution: the Platonic polarity of idea and matter becomes the Christian contrast of God and world; individual ideas — justice, for example — become attributes of God. The pre-Christian world of the gods as well — all that was sacred in Dionysus, Mithras, and Isis — enters into Christ. After the Roman Empire has disappeared, the bishops, religious rulers of the city, take on regulating functions. The idea of Rome, born long before with the Scipios, lives on in the papacy. Bishops and cardinals assume the position of the senate. To Eusebius and Ambrose, the Roman Empire is a preliminary step towards the Christian kingdom: the Church. Finally, the idea of the goal of history, Judgment Day, is a gift of the Jewish conception of history, a conception that speaks to the feelings and gives life meaning and direction.

The Early Middle Ages —
Movement and Openness

In historical atlases the kingdoms of the Middle Ages are often recognizable as clearly defined domains; they are marked out with colored areas as though they were modern states. In reality, however, the Middle Ages, from the Migration of the Peoples on into the twelfth century, was a world in movement. This is true not only of the German emperors, who were almost always on journeys and whose lives are reflected in their itineraries: it is equally true of knights, missionaries and pilgrims, of wandering and settling tribal groups. The great outward movements that mark the decline of the old Mediterranean world are the migrations of the Germanic peoples and the spread of Islam. There is a common tendency to regard the Migration of the Peoples as having come to an end with the foundation of the Longobard kingdom. But the movement did not cease here — far from it: in 711 the Arabs overran the kingdom of the West Goths; and in 774, Charlemagne conquered the Longobards. Yet even here the movement did not stop. The history of the ninth century is determined by the voyages and conquests of the Normans and Varangians who not only made incursions into England and France, but who, as merchants, penetrated down the Dnieper to Constantinople and pressed by way of the Volga and the Caspian Sea as far as Bagdad. Only after Sicily was conquered by Roger, king of the Normans (1061), and England had fallen to William (1066) did the restlessness end. One may well ask, however, whether the Crusades that began only a little later were not another form of movement and migration.

The background of these movements and migrations shows why the various regions of Europe were not closed territories. Spiritual movements, originating in certain centers, radiated out through all Europe. Irish monks were active from England, France, and Germany all the way to Italy: Glastonbury, Luxeuil, the island of Reichenau, St. Gall, Würzburg, Vienna, and Bobbio are but a few stations of their activity. Names such as Columban, Gall, Kilian, Alcuin, and Johannes Scotus Erigena point to the diversity of their activities. Other examples of particular groups whose activities encompassed all Europe are found in the great monastic reform movements: Cluny, Citeaux, the Franciscans and Dominicans. Wandering monks carried new ideas through the whole of the Occident. Not all movements originated in the church, however.

Elusive, beneath the surface of European life lived the heretics: the Bogomils and Cathars. How this movement found its way from Bulgaria across upper Italy to France can only be surmised. Another movement is that of the troubadours. These singers of the eleventh, twelfth, and thirteenth centuries from the south of France and the north of Spain stimulated the *minnesang* in central Europe and thus in contrast to monastic culture they set an entirely different world whose roots we hardly know. Finally, it can be supposed that legends and stories were disseminated in wide areas of Europe by unknown singers. The Nibelungenlied was written down near the Danube in Austria at the beginning of the thirteenth century, but it is generally known that the Frankish legends and songs in which "der Nibelunge nôt" (the distress of the Nibelungen) originated, found their way to Iceland and were recorded there in the songs of the Edda around 1230. Still stranger in this respect is the spreading of the Arthurian legend, of which Alanus ab Insulis wrote in 1170: "To which place within Christendom has the winged fame of Arthur, the Briton, not penetrated? Who does not speak of the Arthur the Briton, for he is not less well-known to the peoples of Asia than to that of Brittany, as one hears from pilgrims who return from the eastern lands." In fact, the picture of Arthur can be found on the cathedral of Modena, built around the year 1100, as well as on a mosaic in the cathedral of Otranto, which dates back to 1166. As early as the eighth century pilgrims, minstrels, and merchants traversed Europe and the Byzantine Empire; at the time of Harun al Rashid there were even hostels for Christian pilgrims in Jerusalem. Harun himself sent the well-known delegation to Charlemagne, which indicates that he was informed of events in the Western world. Long before the Crusades, Catalonia and Sicily had been touching points with the Arab world — areas through which Arabic culture and science made their way into Europe. As early as 967 Gerbert d'Aurillac, the later Pope Sylvester II, visited Catalonia to study there. Gerbert was still a solitary figure, but after 150 years Arab culture was flowing ever more steadily through Catalonia, Sicily, and Salerno into the West.

When we approach medieval history from this aspect, it reveals itself as the history of great movements. Instead of a history that proceeds from emperor to emperor and from pope to pope, we have a real cultural history. These movements can then serve to illustrate the evolutionary stages of the medieval world. The first stage here would be the

Christian mission, which, from its starting points in Ireland and the South, gains an ever-growing hold in northwest Europe. The second stage is the monastic culture of the Carolingian renaissance, in which the combined influence of the streams from Ireland and the South finds a continuation. In many ways, these cloisters are but small domains on small clearings in a world otherwise still wild, wooded, and swampy. This is reflected in the fantasy life of the times, which was still rife with monsters, giants, and dragons — creatures that appeared not just in legends (*Beowulf*), but were shaped and charmed into pictures and sculptures as well. It is not until the high Romanesque period that these figures completely disappear. From the outside, this world was still threatened by the Norsemen who sailed up its rivers with their dragon ships. The situation is similar in the tenth century: while the western Frankish Kingdom was threatened by the Norsemen, Bavaria, Saxony, and Swabia were troubled by the Hungarians, and southern Italy by the Arabs.

The rise and spread of the monastic reforms of Cluny and Gorze finally mark a new stage of development, a stage that culminated in a separation between the spiritual and the worldly. Before these reforms, the thinking of the age was pictorial and concrete; thought and immediate appearance were not yet separate. A secular coronation was also as an act of consecration, and had religious content. The office of emperor most particularly was both a religious and secular office: the emperor was surrounded with religious vestments. Otto III even appears as an apostle; Henry II became a Holy Emperor and was even recognized as such in the Roman breviary. The might of the emperor banned the powers of darkness to the depths until Judgment Day. Thus it was also the emperor who reformed the Church from within and brought the reform to Rome. The reform of Cluny, the movement that called for freedom of the Church, changed thinking completely. A pictorial, imaginative view of the world gave way to a view based on ideas and laws as formulated in the dictatus papae. At first this meant separating and dividing: here the religious, there the secular. The emperor wields the outer sword, the Church the inner sword of the word. This separation pervades all of life: The priest, belonging to God, can no longer unite with woman, who is of this world: celibacy is introduced. The week is divided into the holy days (from Thursday evening to Sunday), during which the feud must rest, and the secular days. Moreover, this is also the time when Rome made its final break with the Eastern Church. On the 16th of July, 1054, the bull of excommunication for Michael Cerularius and his followers was placed on the altar of Hagia Sophia by papal legates under the leadership of Cardinal Humbert of Silva Candida. With this act, the West shut itself off from the East.

Now comes the beginning of theological thinking proper. The eleventh century sees the first dispute over the nature of the Holy Communion: Berengar of Tours' "De sacra coena adversus Lanfrancum." The eleventh century witnesses the first proof of God within the realm of Christianity: Anselm of Canterbury. Thus the eleventh century manifests the signs of zwîvel, of doubt. It is also in the eleventh century that Peter Abelard is born, the inventor of the dialectic method of "sic et non." All of this shows that thinking has abstracted itself from images; what takes the place of the images is analytic thinking. This insight now also enables us to throw light on the Crusades. The West, having lost the pictorial, concrete spirit of the early Middle Ages, now had to seek the spirit, to seek faith, and it sought it in faraway lands, taking the "liebe reise über see" — the "dear journey across the sea." The Crusaders who reached the holy sepulcher, however, were to find no other tidings than did the women at the empty tomb: Jesus of Nazareth, whom you seek, is not here — he is risen.

The century that follows, the twelfth, stands at first under the sign of Bernard of Clairvaux. The spirit of a high and severe asceticism, burning religious zeal, and political battle determine the character of the new monastic order. Bernard commands over popes and kings; he goes through the land working wonders, healing, reconciling, punishing. Thus, when he summoned Christendom to the Second Crusade, his word moved two kings and thousands of men. As they drew eastwards, however, the knights forgot the word of the preacher; the Crusade was a catastrophe. For the contemporaries, this was a sign, an encouragement towards entirely different ways of life. On the Second Crusade Eleanor of Aquitaine had accompanied her husband, the king of France. And she found what she had doubtless been seeking: the courtly life of Byzantium, the magic of the Orient at the court of her uncle Raymund in Antioch. Upon her return home she divorced the pious king and established her court in Angers, capital of Poitou. It was to become the center of European courtly life: here the troubadours sang and composed, here courtly romances were written. Eleanor soon married King Henry II of

174 T E A C H I N G   H I S T O R Y

England; and in 1157 her first son, Richard the Lionhearted, was born. The year 1170 found Eleanor, already divorced from Henry, in Poitiers. Future kings and dukes became proficient in courtly manners here and later modeled their own courts upon the court at Poitiers.[1]

Alongside of the ascetic monastic sphere, the worldly sphere of chivalry developed a culture of its own. Minnesang and the chansons de geste celebrated the knights of centuries past: Roland and Guillaume. This culture stressed different values than the ones known and prescribed by the church: secular, idealized love, adoration of woman, knightly form. It is this world that appears to us in the epics as the world of Arthur. To this ideal, Chretien de Troyes and Wolfram von Eschenbach add the Christian idea of the Grail. For Wolfram, this tradition was connected with the world of southern France; for by his assertion the true "aventiure" of the Grail was transmitted to him through Kyôt, the Provencal poet, who himself had found the discarded original version of it in Toledo — i.e. in the Arabic world. It is also noteworthy in this connection that Wolfram's last great epic, the *Willehalm*, concerns itself with the conflict between Christians and Arabs in southern France. At the end of the fighting, Willehalm recognizes King Matribleiz, the representative of the Arabs, as a brave and true, generous and constant man and releases him, conquered, to return to his homeland.

The twelfth century sees the ascendency of yet a third new culture: that of the cities, which succeed now in disengaging themselves partially from the spiritual dominion of the bishops. It is the patricians and the powerful merchants in foreign trade who take over the leadership here as consuls. These cities have their own constitutions, to which the leading citizens, the guilds, brotherhoods, and old families are bound by oath. In Italy the first such cities are Venice, Genoa, and Pisa, who owe their rise in good part to the Crusades, but whose interests lie elsewhere than those of the Crusaders. In Germany, the Hansa created a new economic sphere reaching from Bruges and London in the West to Novgorod in the East. The external freedom of movement enjoyed by urban traders is matched by internal freedom. At this time such freedom was a freedom belonging to the city — a corporate privilege, protection against arbitrary interference, the right to hold market, and in some places the right

---

[1] Cf. Friedrich Heer, *Mittelalter*. Zürich, 1961, p. 257-324. Regine Pernoud, *Königin der Troubadoure*. Munich, 1980 (dtv).

to choose the priest. In many towns, guilds and brotherhoods, coming together at strictly closed gatherings in intimate circles, nurtured a spiritual/cultural life of their own. The Councils of Toulouse (1229), Montpellier, Arles, and Avignon (the last in 1326) issued edicts forbidding these societies, which had bound themselves by sacred oath to mutual help and vigilance against any intrusion.[2] In addition there were numerous church guilds and brotherhoods as well, and later the Beguines and Beghards. Altogether, through the pride of their craftsmen and the worldly experience of their merchants, the cities were laying the foundation for the self-assurance and self-awareness that later blossomed in the Renaissance. This quality was particularly cultivated in those communities which maintained and defended their freedoms against both religious and secular domination.

The early thirteenth century, the period when Wolfram von Eschenbach and Walther von der Vogelweide wrote, was marked by a high degree of differentiation in social life. This also led to increasing social stratification. In the cities, besides the merchants in foreign trading and their unions, besides the craftsmen and their guilds, there was also a decidedly poor stratum, a class that can be seen already in the Pataria of Milan. In the spiritual currents that addressed themselves to the poor, distinctly non-ecclesiastical traits are evident already in the movement of the Waldensers and the Cathars. The Church responded to the problem this posed with two new orders, both of them mendicant orders. By fulfilling a vow of poverty these orders maintained credibility with the city dwellers, especially in this lowest layer. Unlike earlier monks who had built their monasteries in rural surroundings, in lonely places, and in forests, these two orders — the Franciscans and Dominicans — settled in the cities. The primary task of these new orders is no longer chiefly holding divine service, prayer, meditation on the Bible, and manual work, but rather sermon and confession. Their preaching is credible because they live in poverty. At the same time, the education of the preachers and the warding off of heresy also requires special preparation. Thus, the early thirteenth century is distinguished by the founding of universities. Bologna and Paris are followed by Oxford, Cambridge, Padua (1222), Naples (1224), Toulouse (1229), Angers, and Salamanca.

---

[2] Cf. Joan Evans, *Das Leben im mittelalterlichen Frankreich.* Cologne, 1960, p. 43-46.

Besides peasants and simple country priests, besides merchants and craftsmen, besides estate officials and knights, besides minstrels and singers, there are now also the scholars, the professors — then known as doctors.

A final picture, one that symbolizes this differentiation, is that of the Gothic cathedral. Of religious origin and symbolic form, it is the work of the cities, the master-builders and stonemasons' lodges. It is the place of the whole town community: the inhabitants of Strassburg built their cathedral after the bishop had been banished. Unlike Romanesque churches, in the Gothic cathedral figures appear as full sculptures. One sees individual human beings, prophets, knights, women, and angels, each of them well-formed and personal: people of a new era.

13

AN EXAMPLE FOR THE THEME
OF THE ELEVENTH GRADE:
THE INNER ASPECT OF HISTORY

Augustine: Christ at Work in History

During the night of August 24, 410 A.D., the Visigoth hordes led by Alaric stormed Rome the Eternal. The city was plundered for three days. News of the catastrophe spread quickly through the Mediterranean world. In their confusion people wondered how such a thing could happen. Many a Christian doubted in God's wise guidance of the world. But the heathens, whose cult was forbidden, triumphed: This is the wrath of the gods whose temple you Christians have closed, whose rites you have forbidden! The gods have withdrawn their protecting hand from the Eternal City. The news and the commentary soon also reached the North African port of Hippo and the ears of the great bishop Augustine. The talk of the heathens outraged this prince of the Church, but since their voices only became louder as the Roman Empire crumbled further, Augustine set to work. In the fourteen years between 412 and 426 he wrote the work out of which — as though rising from the ruins of Rome — the idea of a Kingdom of God developed. Since the Fall, history has been the battlefield of two kingdoms: the Kingdom of God and His angels, and the earthly kingdom where power and violence reign supreme, where human beings serve demonic gods. States lacking the idea of the highest justice are — to Augustine[1] — nothing but great bands of robbers. Robbers have their laws and their honor, too; they divide their booty according to established rules. When such a system grows in size, dominating cities and countries, then it assumes the name of empire.

Augustine illustrated his opinion with an anecdote: "Hence it was an accurate and true answer that a captured sea pirate once gave to

---

[1] In: *The City of God*, book 4, chap. 4.

Alexander the Great. For when the King asked the man how he presumed to make the sea unsafe, he replied with open defiance: And how do you presume to make the world unsafe? To be sure, because I do it with a small vessel I am called a pirate. You do it with a great fleet and are called Emperor."

For Augustine, the mark of the City of God is that in it egoism is overcome: "We see then that the two cities were founded upon two kinds of love: the earthly city upon self-love which swells even to contempt for God, the heavenly city upon love of God which rises even to contempt of self." In the City of God the kings and rulers serve their subjects with love; in the City of God human beings live in community with the saints and angels.[2] By contemplating the actual history of his own time, Augustine arrived at a memorable description. Comparing the customs of war prevalent in earlier times with those of his own, he found a growing restraint of inhuman ways; and finally, as the new quality of his own time, he discovered that "barbarian cruelty proved so mild that spacious churches were chosen as places of assembly and refuge for the people, and here no one was killed, no one carried off, indeed many were brought to safety here by compassionate enemies." "This," Augustine continues, "must be ascribed to the name of Christ and to the Christian era." If one takes Augustine at his word, the Christ impulse is at work not only in those who call themselves Christians, but seizes also the souls of barbarians and makes them gentle.[3]

This vision of history was alive throughout the Middle Ages: history is the battle between the two kingdoms, as Otto von Freising (ca. 1112-1158) also describes it in his world chronicle. What was of decisive importance, however, was that Charlemagne, who set his stamp upon the entire Middle Ages, was gripped by the ideas of Augustine. Einhard, the contemporary and biographer of Charlemagne, reports in the twenty-fourth chapter of his *Leben Karls des Grossen* (Life of Charlemagne): "The Emperor listened to a reader while he ate his meal; historical works as well as the deeds of the Ancients were read to him. The books of St. Augustine found great favor with him, especially his *City of God.*"

Charlemagne understood his own action in history and his calling as a ruler within this context. Despite all that we know about the Saxon wars and other such events, he looked upon himself as working towards

---

[2] In: *The City of God*, book 14, chap. 28.

[3] In: *The City of God*, book 1, chap. 7.

the City of God. The office of emperor was a religious office to him. The Frankish court perceived him as the new David, who — in Alcuin's words — was to defend, to teach, and to propagate the apostolic faith, and whose office it was to thus promote the City of God on earth.[4] In this spirit, the many monasteries and churches founded in this period were intended, in a rough and cruel world, to be gardens of love, places of prayer, seedbeds of culture; places in which the divine element within the human being could be nurtured, so that the Christ impulse might penetrate man, learning, and culture, and the City of God might come into being. We do not know the personal and inmost thoughts of Charlemagne, but the framework provided by these ideas was both the measure for his actions and an impulse behind them.

Experience of the World of the Saints, Angels, and Archangels — The Night-Side of History in the Early Middle Ages

If one wishes to get an "inside picture" of the history of this period, one can open the biography of Saint Ansgar. Based on Ansgar's personal notes, this biography was written — probably during the seventies of the ninth century — by Rimbert, Ansgar's successor to the office of archbishop. Ansgar was born in 801 in the northwest of France. When he was still very young, his parents decided that he should become a monk and brought him to the monastery of Corbie for education and training. Adalhart, a cousin of Charlemagne, was abbot of the monastery, which had about 350 monks. It is known that young Ansgar had seen the emperor (who had no firm seat of government but travelled from palace to palace and from monastery to monastery) as he was being led — supported right and left by a bishop — to his place of honor at the altar to partake of the eucharist at mass or in a matins service. Besides this he had doubtless heard of the emperor's plans and deeds through Adalhart, who was the confidant of Charles and entrusted with important missions. Still, it is only natural that the young pupil — now about thirteen years

---

[4] Cf. Karl F. Morrison, *The Two Kingdoms.* Princeton, 1964, p. 26-35.

of age — let up in his zeal and practice of prayer. Then he heard of the passing of the exalted emperor whom he had seen at the height of his power. The great emperor's death troubled and frightened him to the depths of his soul. Turning into himself and laboring in prayer, he exercised nightly vigils and abstinence. The celebration of Holy Pentecost was approaching once more and the night before it, as he was deeply immersed in prayer, he believed

that suddenly he was about to die and that, at the very moment of death, he appealed for assistance to the Holy Apostle Peter and John the Baptist. He was aware that his soul left his body and appeared straight away in another, exceedingly beautiful form, completely free of all mortal frailty. Then two men appeared at the very moment of his dying and wonderment. The elder had full, plain, graying hair, a reddish complexion, and serious mien; he wore a white, colorfully embroidered garment and was of short stature. Ansgar instantly recognized him as Saint Peter. The other was a young man of high stature in a silken robe, with a sprouting beard and dark, curly hair, a gaunt face and a friendly look. With certainty Ansgar took him to be Saint John. The two of them came to his side. But now his transfigured soul saw itself in an immense clarity that filled the whole world. With no effort on his part, both saints led him in an indescribably marvellous manner to the place of purgatory, as he well understood without any explanation; here they left him alone. Now he had, as he believed, to suffer many things, most of all impenetrable darkness, terrible fear, and oppression. His memory left him, and he was barely able to think the one thought, how there could possibly be such a monstrous punishment! Although in his opinion he had suffered only for three days, because of the immeasurable pain this span of time seemed to last a thousand years longer. Then at last the two men returned, however, took him again into their midst and, progressing much more joyfully than before and with a much more cheerful step, though without movement and without any bodily path, led him through a clarity that almost seemed greater. "I saw from afar" — these are his words — "various orders of saints; some stood closer to the East, some farther; all, however, looked to the East. Praising Him who appeared in the East, some lowered their heads, while others raised their countenance, spread their hands, and worshiped. When we ourselves come to the East, there appeared the twenty-four Elders sitting in their seats in a vast semicircle, as it is written in the Book of Revelations (4,4). They too looked towards the East with great reverence and offered untold praises to God. But far in the East itself there was a marvellous radiance, an unapproachable light of tremendous, immeasurable clarity. All splendor of color and all joyousness belonged to it. From it all the joyous orders of saints drew their bliss. This radiance was so mighty that I could see neither beginning nor end of it. I could indeed see nearness and farness all about, but the immensity of the light made it impossible to recognize what it concealed. I saw only surface. Immeasurable clarity poured forth from it and illuminated all the saints far and wide. And the radiance appeared to be in everyone and everyone in it. It encompassed everything, saturated and guided everyone. It covered them from above and encompassed them from below. Sun and moon did not shine here; heaven and earth were not there. Yet by no means did the clarity blind the eyes of the viewers; rather it was very agreeable to their eyes and satiated their souls most lovingly. Then an exceeding lovely voice, purer than any sound, seemed to fill the whole world; it emanated from this glory and it spoke to me: Go forth and, crowned with martyrdom, return to me! With these words all the praising choirs of saints around me fell silent and worshiped with bowed head. But I did not see any figure from which this voice had come forth. The words saddened me. For this meant that I must return to the world; nevertheless I parted from both my guides, certain of the promise of return. They had not spoken a word, neither on the way there nor on the way back, though they gazed on me as lovingly as a mother on her only son. And so I came back into my body."[5]

---

[5] Quoted from: *Das Leben des heiligen Ansgar von seinem Nachfolger Rimbert* (The Life of St. Ansgar by his successor Rimbert). W. Schamoni, ed., Düsseldorf 1965. It may be noted here that such transports taking the soul through purgatory (kamaloka) are independently reported in other sources as well. Thus, at the same time as the Grail legend was made exoteric, such reports from earlier times were written down: e.g. the *Espurgatoire S. Patrice* (Purgatory of St. Patrick) by Marie de France, around 1190, and the *Visio Tnugdali of the Priest Alber,* which was recorded in the middle of the 12th century at the Bavarian monastery of Windberg.

In this way Ansgar receives his life's task from the spiritual world by divine calling, and continues, again and again in prayer, sleep, or dream, to receive direct guidance and comfort. He is called from Corbie to Corvey, a filial of Corbie in the hill country by the Weser river; there he becomes a teacher, travels to Sweden in 829 as a missionary, and in 831 becomes archbishop in the see of the newly established archbishopric of Hamburg. While on his travels, he immerses himself daily in prayer and finds help and counsel in important decisions. Thus, when he is leaving once more for Sweden in 852, in a kind of prophetic dream his spiritual father, the long deceased Abbot Adalbert of Corbie comes to him and encourages him with these words: "Hear ye islands, and hearken ye peoples of afar! The Lord has called upon you even from your mother's womb, from the lap of your mother He has thought on your name. He has made your mouth sharp as a sword; with His hand has He shielded you and made you His chosen arrow. In His quiver He hid you and spoke to you: You are my servant; in you I shall be praised."

Thus Ansgar lived in the knowledge of being a member of a divine spiritual world. He knew that he had been called upon to travel the lands of the North and sow the seed of faith. Ansgar certainly was a particularly outstanding representative of his times. His testimony to the power of the spirit, however, does not stand alone: his life and and work fired and gave wings to others who wished to promote the Kingdom of God in a smaller way. This shows how the general idea of the Kingdom of God was understood in practice in the ninth century. It was not an historical or theological abstraction, but a vital, experiential reality. In the course of time, however, inner experience changed — at first only slowly and gradually. Looking at the nascent German Empire in the tenth century, one can recognize that Henry I, at least at the beginning of his reign, did not want to fit into the tradition of Christian rulers. In 919 he rejected coronation, anointment, and consecration by the archbishop of Mainz. It was not until 936 that Otto I took up again the tradition of Charlemagne and his Christian understanding of the throne with a solemn anointment and coronation in the cathedral at Aachen (Aix-la-Chapelle).

In the time of Henry and Otto lived St. Ulrich, Bishop of Augsburg, whose city played a special role during the Hungarian invasion of 955 and had finally laid the foundation for the victorious repulsion of the Hungarian forces. It was Ulrich who directed the defense of the city with wisdom and prudence. In the hour of battle the bishop sat high on his horse wearing his surplice. Unprotected by helmet, armor, or shield he gave his instructions without being struck by arrows or stones. This calmness of bearing and spirit of order were manifested in other of Ulrich's deeds; for he too knew that he acted upon the commission of a spiritual world. Ulrich's biographer reports the following experience out of the early period when Ulrich had just received his office:

> One night, while resting in bed, he saw St. Afra standing before him in great beauty, wrapped in a splendid robe and girded. She spoke to him: "Rise and follow me!" With these words she led him out to the field that in German is called the 'Lechfeld.' There he found St. Peter, Prince of the Apostles, with a sizable following of bishops and saints, some of whom he had seen earlier, others of whom he had never met before but still recognized exactly through divine intuition. Saint Peter held a holy synod with them, made important and innumerable dispositions and — with all due ceremony — sat in judgment over Arnulf, Duke of Bavaria, who was then still alive. Many saints complained of the Duke because of his having closed many monasteries, which he had given in fief to laity. Finally, St. Peter showed him two mighty swords, one with a pommel, the other without, and he spoke: "Tell King Henry: This sword without a pommel signifies a king who reigns without consecration of the Church; the other, with the pommel, signifies the king who holds the reins of power with divine consecration." When the synod was over, St. Afra showed him the place of encampment where King Otto later held an Imperial Diet with peoples of different lands and where King Berengar of Lombardy and his son Adalbert appeared with numerous bishops and swore allegiance to Otto. She also announced to him the coming Hungarian invasion, showed him the battlefield and promised that the victory would fall to the Christians, albeit only after a difficult struggle. After this vision she led him back again and left him as he lay in bed. When he came to himself once more, he wondered whether all this had been shown him in the body or outside of the body.[6]

---

[6] Gerhard, *Das Leben des heiligen Ulrich, Bischofs von Augsburg.* Chap. 3. In: *Ausgewählte Quellen zur deutschen Geschichte des Mittelalters,* Bd. XXII. *Lebensbeschreibungen einiger Bischöfe des 10.-12. Jahrhunderts.* Darmstadt 1973.

This report differs greatly from Ansgar's experience. Ulrich is not led through purgatory to enter into the regions of pure spirit. St. Afra, patron saint of Augsburg, leads him onto the Lechfeld, the same field where later the Hungarian battle is to take place. There a synod of departed spirits is taking place, but they are concerned chiefly with earthly affairs. In any case, however, it is clear that ordinary time has been left behind, and Ulrich is granted a view over events that are not to take place until twenty to thirty years later.

If one uses good sources — genuine contemporary reports, that is — then one can further explore indications of a relationship to the spiritual world. Thus, the Chronicle of Thietmar of Merseburg (975-1018) shows that also at the time of Otto II and Otto III, human beings were repeatedly subject to spiritual experiences, particularly meetings with the deceased. Thietmar's chronicle is of especial value because its author, who was the bishop of Merseburg, tells of his own experiences. Compared to earlier descriptions from the ninth and tenth centuries, however, it is plain that the content and fullness of the experiences is decreasing. The following report by Thietmar appears characteristic to me:

On June 21, 1012, Walthard, who earlier had for twenty-eight years filled the office of prior, was ordained Archbishop of Magdeburg. On August 12 of the same year, however, Walthard died after a short and severe illness. Not only Thietmar, but others as well pondered on the significance of this early death. Thietmar then reports that earlier, in a dream, Walthard had been promised that he would receive the archbishopric of Magdeburg, but would occupy it only for a very short time. Yet the riddle of this death leaves Thietmar no peace and in prayer he remembers Walthard. Then he recounts: "I was on watch in Meissen when, after matins on the day of the Apostles Somon and Judas (October 12), the most reverend man appeared to me. I knew the dead man well, after all, and asked him how he was faring. He replied: I have suffered my punishment as I deserved it, but now all of that is behind me. I rejoiced and said: May I ring the bells and summon the people to praise God? Walthard answered: Surely, for it is true! Then I went on: Are you aware that much gossip has turned the king against you because you are said to have undertaken much against him after your elevation? Sighing, he replied: Believe me, I beg of you, believe me, it is not my fault! But when I was about to ask him why he had died so suddenly, I awoke, and so I could never discover it."[7] It seems indicative that the dream encounter slips away from Thietmar at the moment when he wants to ask the question that really concerns him.

Thus we can see Thietmar as representative of the generation in which the age of direct spiritual experiences was entering its twilight. Up to Thietmar's time, among the tribes of northwest Europe the action of the spiritual world in earthly life was something that — while not simply a matter of course — was to be reckoned with. Even people who did not have such experiences themselves sensed the efficacy of the spiritual world through witnesses who, like Ansgar, Rimbert, Ulrich, or Thietmar, spoke of this world. These experiences were not doubted. Indeed, people also knew of encounters with demonic beings; they saw, they divined spiritual worlds as the background of earthly existence.

Only when this sensibility had disappeared in almost all strata of the population did things of a spiritual nature begin to pose a problem. Thus, starting in the middle of the eleventh century we see the pope forced to anchor his right to rule in legal ordinances. This is a sign of the progressive legalization of Christian life, a process that had begun at the time of Pope Nicholas I (858-867) with the recognition of the pseudo-Isidorian decretals by the Curia. The style of thinking was changing; in place of experience came proof. Thus, in his monologue of 1099 Anselm of Canterbury devised the first proof of God in Christian theology. Finally we see thousands of human beings — knights, burghers and peasants — setting forth on the First Crusade in search of what they have lost: direct experience of the spiritual world.[8] This is not, of course, to say that after Thietmar's time there were no longer single individuals who had a special relationship to the spiritual world. The few that there were, however, now stood out as very exceptional figures. Here one is led to think of Bernard de Clairvaux. Bernard became the leader of a whole age. His word decided many issues: during the schismatic papal election of 1130, it was his influence that decided the council of Etampes in favor of Innocent II — Bernard's verdict carried weight. Yet this figure is also surrounded with a tragic aura: it was his preaching that brought about the Second Crusade, the Crusade that foundered so terribly. It is significant that St. Bernard did

---

[7] *Thietmar von Merseburg*, Chronik, book VI, chap. 79.
[8] Cf. p. 173.

not undertake his preaching for this Crusade out of inspiration, but on the request of the pope and King Louis of France. Perhaps this is a symbol of the changed situation.

Life of the Spirit, Life of the People in the Thirteenth Century

Around the year 1200 a development came to an end that had started in the middle of the eleventh century: the old, inspired life of the spirit was now extinguished. In the twelfth century an imaginative and poetic form of thought — a form that was open to impressions from the world of spirit — had still been cultivated in various cathedral schools, the best known of these being Chartres. In the thirteenth century, pure rational activity of the kind practiced in Scholastic philosophy and theology reached its peak. In the strict artificial forms of *quaestiones* and *summae*, argumentation was formulated in precise rules; and with sharp-witted distinctions, the fine chiselling of concepts was taken to its utmost. These thought edifices are comparable in their delicate sense of measure to the Gothic cathedrals, where flying buttresses and ribs, figures and ornaments made the City of God on earth visible through light and the overcoming of gravity. Although the spiritual life of Latin Scholasticism deeply affected the general way of thinking, it was accessible only to a few thousand people who had been educated for many years at the few universities in Paris, Bologna, Oxford, Cologne, and a small number of monasteries. Thus authors of that time such as Albertus Magnus, Thomas Aquinas, Duns Scotus, or Ockham could depend upon the ability of their listeners and readers to follow their most difficult arguments. Writings went straight to the heart of the matter; for the small educated readership was equally at tuned to the "matter" and accordingly prepared.

Literature, which before had lived only in the spoken word, now took on written form, giving rise to the artful poem and the consciously created epic. Around the year 1200 the *Nibelungenlied, Parzival, Erec,* and *Tristan** were written down and performed at the courts. To be sure, even this literature reached only a relatively small circle — the knightly sphere and perhaps also the traders and merchants. It must be supposed that there was a third culture, a culture of the peasantry that expressed itself in fairy tales, legends, humorous tales and other stories. All three cultures were nourished by the tradition of the past. But this past was close-by and living: the rural world of the Gospels, the questions of ancient philosophy, and the battles of the Nibelungen were thought of and pictured in contemporary forms. Dissemination or communication of all matters was dependent upon personal contacts, personal transmission and training. A social gathering, listening to a story, had a personal impression of the storyteller; and he, for his part, looked his audience in the eye and had contact with it. The traveller coming to a small town from afar and telling of far-off events could answer questions; and the impression that he made on his audience blended with what he told. People could "size him up" and judge his report accordingly. Also the monk studying at a university learned essentially through a teacher who read to him, commented on the text, and gave the student practice in discussing it. Thus, traditional knowledge was always learned through the medium of the human being, and it was possible to apply one's own experience and one's own judgment to what one learned in this way. All forms of communication, all the content of cultural life, was immersed in the atmosphere of personal experience. It was by exercising the powers of one's own heart, mind, and soul that one found an access to difficult matters. This form of culture kept growing until the middle of the fifteenth century. The culture of chivalry, theology, and peasantry was joined by a specifically "town" culture which found expression in the *Meistersang*, the mystery plays, and in the art of the sermon — an art to which the great halls of the Gothic churches bear mute witness. In addition to the guilds there now were also lay religious movements, brotherhoods, the devotio moderna. Everything was based on human relationships: orders of monks and knights were human communities no less than universities, villages and towns. Indeed, even the state, shaped

---

* I.e. almost all the "classics" of Middle High German literature. [trans.]

by feudalism, could be described as a *state of personal associations*. The human measure held sway in everything; the world, which lay in God's hand, was commensurable. The images of the Gothic cathedrals are a reflection of this world, which is a world of human beings.

14

THE TWELFTH GRADE·

Right at the beginning of his *Reflections on History*, Jacob Burckhardt makes the remark that history is "non-philosophy," inasmuch as it merely coordinates, but does not subordinate facts. Rudolf Steiner too, who likewise did not develop a philosophy of history, notes in reference to Burckhardt that to coordinate, to cast light on historical phenomena through preceding or following events, is insufficient: "To find what explains an historical fact, we must look in the spiritual world. We must illuminate the historical facts from out of the spiritual world, otherwise they remain dead, just as objects do not shine unless we illuminate them with the light they have in common." The common light that illuminates history is the real spiritual and soul-development of humanity. This development is not an idea in the sense of the customary philosophy of history; rather it involves actual matters of fact in the soul-spiritual realm. It is in these terms that we must understand Rudolf Steiner's indication for the curriculum at the conference of April 29: "So, you have covered it all, haven't you? Now what would be needed is to give a survey in which the whole of history is put into connection. As you are aware, in my pedagogical courses I show that concepts involving causality can be grasped starting in the twelfth year of life. From then on, instruction in causality would continue right through the twelfth grade. It must be enlivened, individualized. In the twelfth grade it is a matter of going a little bit beneath the surface and seeking to elucidate inner aspects of history."

Reflecting on this statement, we are particularly struck by the words "connection," "individualize," and "inner aspects of history." The connection is the connection of development; and the best way to bring it out is by comparisons, as by illustrating the different ways people have of looking at and experiencing the world, or different ways of living together. The point here is not to make general observations, but to grasp quite individually such ways of seeing and experiencing, which means taking the destinies of particular individuals to illustrate the development — and in this case it also means doing so in such a way that the inner aspects of history are touched upon.[1]

In Rudolf Steiner's further suggestions for the curriculum, we are advised to survey the great cultures in history in such a way that their "antique period," their "Middle Ages," and their "modern era" can be recognized, and also to explore whether these cultures are fully developed or not in this sense. Steiner mentions the American culture here, which starts out with the modern age — it has no ancient period or Middle Ages. Chinese culture has no end — it has only developed its ancient period. Citing Greek history as an example, Rudolf Steiner explains what he means by antiquity, Middle Ages, and modern age: the earliest period — that of Homer — would be the antique period, the age of the great tragedians would be the Middle Ages, and the era of Plato and Aristotle the modern era. This idea confronts the historian with the task of considering these categories and determining how to deal with them. This task must be solved before it is possible to undertake this kind of presentation along with the other twelfth grade theme of a deepened, individualized survey of the whole of history.

Therefore, let a few words be said on the division into antiquity, Middle Ages, and modern era:

One might come upon the idea of taking the Cretan-Mycenaean epoch of Greek history as the ancient period or heroic age of Greece. Then the period of Dorian migration and the Homeric age would be the Middle Ages; for it is then that the legends and myths of earlier days were put into poetic form, very much as happened in the German Middle Ages. The modern era of Greek culture would then begin with Solon: it is the beginning of isonomy (equality before the law) and — with Thales — of philosophy. A view such as this neglects to see that Cretan culture and the mainland Greek culture influenced by it do not represent the beginning of later Greek culture. Particularly the culture of Crete is a culture of its own. The formation of the Greek people begins only after the Dorian immigration, very much as the development of a German people came about only after Charlemagne. If we start with the premise that antiquity, Middle Ages, and modern era are three evolutionary stages of *one* culture, then we arrive at the division

---

[1] Cf. Chapter 3: History as Soul Development.

proposed by Steiner. Looking at it in this way, we can say: In the first phase of a culture, its basic forms, contents, and themes are born. In the second stage they are taken hold of and *re-formed* by human beings. The Greek tragedians took hold of the Greek legends and myths in a new and conscious way, putting them into a structured form. Similarly, the early classical period consciously took up the legacy of the archaic period; Cleisthenes shaped Attic democracy. And finally, what human beings had formed in an artistic way was set into thoughts by Socrates, Plato, and Aristotle.

Applying this approach to Western European and German culture, we can say that the founding epoch extends from Charlemagne into the thirteenth century, while the Gothic period, Renaissance, Reformation, and Baroque work to reshape the themes of the culture, until — starting in the seventeenth century — they are consciously reflected and put into new ideal and literary form. What is important here, of course, is not that we become expert in finding parallels that exactly fit this threefold schema. What is important is the underlying fact that development *can* take this course — though it need not: that an original content is first absorbed and allowed to unfold, and that it is then given form. This forming process involves all the creative forces of the soul in assimilating the motifs of a culture. The human consciousness that is alive in this assimilation process restructures and gives shape through its own will, and it is in this shaping that it attains its sense of self. It is only then that the idea, the thought element arrives: the Renaissance and Reformation shaped culture on the level of a sense-of-self, a feeling of egohood; it was not until the time of German idealistic philosophy, however, that the *idea* of the "I" stepped forth into full manifestation, having been in preparation since Descartes.

When we consider this process still more carefully, we will notice that the formation of each culture requires a direct tradition: a people or cultural community develops what is inherent in the germ of its own culture. Yet remarkably, the products of the second and especially of the third phase can also be absorbed by other peoples and cultures. This gives rise to split cultures, a phenomenon particularly characteristic of the present time. Elements of European culture are imposed upon China and Japan — antique cultures in the sense of our definition. Or our attention is drawn to the culture in North America, which begins immediately with the adoption of modern European civilization. In such manner a picture begins to take form of cultural spheres — some complete and some incomplete — with their connections and overlappings.

These views of cultural history, however, gain meaning only through anthropological history, which forms the background of the individual cultures and reflects the meaning of historical developments. The foundations of the anthropological approach have already been discussed in the second and third chapters; here the question is what form it should take in the twelfth grade. From an external viewpoint, this approach could be linked with the four great revolutions in human history: the settlement process, the ancient cultures and the related founding of cities, the step from mythos to logos, and the revolution that is outwardly signalled by technology. There is, however, a certain danger in working with such concepts — concepts essentially taken from the realm of cultural morphology — namely that we become involved in the external symptoms of development while the inner steps of human development get lost behind the outer facts.

Hence it is essential that the themes chosen to portray the development of humanity have the necessary capacity for deepening. The great revolutions, for example, brought fundamental changes in morality, memory, world-view, relation to death, art, and mutual aid. A theme such as morality opens perspectives onto an epoch's social and historical development as well as insights into people's inner development. The settlement process, for example[2], brought a sharp distinction between good and evil. Good and evil were unequivocal: good was all that served agriculture and the community of tillers of the soil; evil was all that destroyed or hindered settlement and agriculture. In a sense, morality was completely determined from without: the conditions necessary for farming and the communal life of the farming people required quite definite behavior and attitudes — assiduous work of the soil, irrigation, respect for the activity of the other farmers, distinction between "mine" and "thine." Yet just this most simple thing could be accomplished only with the greatest devotion of all human forces. For the inner man, this unequivocal decision signified a deep incision into the whole of his being and existence. His thinking, all of his habits received a most definite stamp. The world-view of the nomads, so undetermined, so open, rich, and various in forms and meanings, gave way to limitation. Through this

---

[2] Cf. See chap. on 10th grade, p. 121 ff.

limitation, the human being shut himself off from a panoply of cosmic influences; he became a distinct, determinate being. Yet this was not an individual, personal distinctness, but a determination of behavior, understanding and habits — these being regulated by the seasonal requirements of work. Thus, the ancient Persian culture reveals a certain decisiveness, which is reflected in its understanding of death: as a later tradition shows, the Persians believed that the deceased had to walk across the chasm of death on a sword, and for the evil the sword turned up its cutting edge so that, cut in two, they would fall into the abyss.

The high civilizations of ancient times show quite a different relationship to death. The epic of Gilgamesh, on the one hand, indicates that death is becoming a mystery, a riddle. This mystery of the transience of all earthly things, however, gives rise to the impulse to explore the world of the afterlife; and so, after the death of his friend Enkidu, Gilgamesh sets out to explore eternal life. It is particularly in Egypt, then, that service of the dead clearly becomes at the same time a source of wisdom and cultural development. This wisdom reveals itself in various ways. Babylonia and Egypt know a plenitude of gods, but it is the knowledge of the planetary gods and of the zodiac, the fixed stars, that is most pronounced. Each one of these deities has something special to communicate to human beings. This differentiation finds its correspondence in the various activities of societal life: there are now kings, priests, healers, builders, scribes, warriors and hunters, craftsmen and farmers. And in a corresponding way morality and social behavior are differentiated. Morality becomes the specific efficiency and wisdom that a man displays in a particular service within the community. In Egypt, this can be seen in the idea of *ma'at*. Teichmann writes of this idea: "We can translate its name only through such paraphrases as truth, justice, or just order. It is the very breath of life both of the divine and the natural world. For our cosmos is a well-ordered one, and each being has its rightful place within it and correctly carries out his allotted tasks. Almost all artistic portrayals express the intimate connection of the ma'at with life itself by attaching to it the sign of life. The king knows the ma'at, and it is his task to make it effective here on earth, i.e. to arrange life in this world according to the laws of the divine order."

The advent of writing brought a change in the essential nature of memory. During ancient times and even into the Middle Ages, those peoples who had no writing had a totally different memory life than those who possessed it. In primeval times, memory was bound to exterior things: to places and signs that reminded people of what had happened. Then came tradition, the passing down of material couched in rhythmical language which was cultivated by the various peoples and tribes. It is to this tradition of rhythmic chant that Homer owes his knowledge of the battle of Troy, or — in our own cultural sphere — that we owe the tradition of the Nibelungen and Grail legends. This memory was superpersonal, enduring over many generations. When writing first arose in ancient Sumer, it was used not to record things of spiritual or religious importance, but to regulate economic affairs: it registered the delivery and allotment of produce. In this sphere memory needed a support. The Egyptian hieroglyphs of the early period were not at first used to support the personal remembrance of important matters. The texts in graves, pyramids, and temples were intended not for human readers, but for the gods, for whom they were an objective record of "what is, what has been, and what is to be." In the course of time the hieroglyphic inscriptions became more and more extensive and detailed and were then used in the exchange of correspondence and — quite incidentally — also as a support for the memory. The critical fact for this stage of soul development, however, was that knowledge of the cosmos was fixed for the soul in clearly defined mental pictures. It was only in Greece that this changed. First to be set down in writing, and thus fixed and published, were matters of social import: the laws of Solon and others, for example. Only then, with Herodotus and Thucydides, did the recording of earthly history begin.

One thing that is of outstanding importance in the twelfth grade is to describe the symptoms that Karl Jaspers cites as the traits of the "axial period." We are faced with the fact that in China, India, Persia, Israel, and Greece — differently in each land — a new historical impulse appears. To begin with, it is a significant fact that this impulse arises independently in the various lands. Thinking is now the medium through which human beings confront the world. Fate, nature, and the ancient myths as well are now formulated in thoughts. The people affected by the "axial period" experience their own existence in thought: They are aware of themselves as human beings. They no longer see themselves as part of the cosmos; they confront fate and seek to master it by thinking and by a conduct of life guided by thought.

When we pursue the inner motifs of history in this epoch, namely death, morality, and memory, the first thing that becomes clear is that awareness of the kingdom of the dead gradually fades. Odysseus, who lived after the Trojan war, experiences the world of the dead as a "shadowy image"; while in the Greek culture proper, only legend still tells of places where an entry to the underworld is open. The human being who lives in thought can only look at the now-closed gate. And the way he looks at the gate of death is the way he looks at nature: he knows that concealed within nature are the workings of the spiritual world, but he is able only to interpret these workings as a sign or put them into thoughts. In his biography of Pericles, Plutarch recounts that a ram with a single horn was said to have been found on Pericles' country estate. Lampon, the oracle, interpreted this to mean that the power in the state, which was then divided, would fall to the one individual with whom the ram had been found. On the other hand Anaxagoras, the philosopher of nature, dissected the head and showed that the brain of this ram did not fill the entire head but was concentrated like the pointed end of an egg towards where the root of the horn was. Thus, nature had become something that required deciphering; it had become a code that one man interpreted as a sign of the future, the other explained in terms of the past.[3]

In this period memory and conscience increasingly are experienced within: What was once the Eumenides has now become the inner force of conscience. Memory is no longer experienced as the cosmic power Mnemosyne — mother of the muses by Zeus — but as an inner space of the soul. The *Confessions* of Augustine, in the eighth chapter of the tenth book, contains a marvellous testimony to this experience. Augustine finds that the world of the senses gives him no insight into his own being, and then continues: "So I shall step beyond this part of my being and rise by degrees to Him Who who has created me. Thus shall I come to the fields and great halls of memory, where are the treasures of innumerable images that my senses have gathered together of all things. There too is stored up everything that we think, as we enlarge, diminish, or otherwise vary what has touched our senses. All that has not been swallowed up and buried by forgetfulness lies there." After this introduction, Augustine gives a detailed description of memory, portraying it as the inner space of the unending soul in which man awakens to himself. The development of this kind of inwardness from the Greek tragedians through Socrates and Plato and up to Augustine; the filling of this inner

---

[3] Dietz, Karl Martin: "Erinnerung und Wissen." In: *Die Drei* 1976, p. 666.

space (which can be taken as the mind-soul*) with the content of Christian faith: these are things that twelfth grade students are fully capable of understanding.

A third aspect of this period emerges when we look at the moral incorporation of the individual into the community. In the ancient cultures the place of the individual in the community was determined largely from without. The majority of the people lived as farmers, a lesser number were active as craftsmen, while a very small group, under the leadership of the god-king and his helpers — the priests and princes — guided the destiny of the people. It was rare that the individual had the chance to shape his own life: birth, necessity, and hierarchy determined life. In Greece and Rome as well, and particularly in the lands of the Orient, birth — i.e. the parental house into which one was born — remained a decisive factor in the outer shaping of life. Still, due to a great number of circumstances very much had changed in comparison with the ancient cultures. Externally, seafaring and trade, as well as far-ranging military campaigns all contributed to a greater mobility: The individual had the opportunity to change his position. In places where there were democratic or republican constitutions, the affairs of the entire commonwealth were discussed; the individual learned of different possibilities for public action. Even in places where no such outward possibilities existed, there were differing conceptions and views: for example, in Judaism, with the doctrines of the Sadducees and the Pharisees, or the Essene way of life. The teachings of Buddhism touched many people in India and offered them the possibility of pursuing an inner path of their own. Christianity, finally, addressed itself to everyone: slave or freeman, man or woman — anyone could become a Christian.

The way for this historical situation had been paved when the question as to good action was first posed in thought form. In the ancient cultures, obedience as such was a virtue. Obedience was expected towards one's father or elder brother, to the king and his representatives. Starting with Socrates, however, each individual was able to ask what is good. Thus, Plato developed his conception of virtue in thought form. The Stoics and Epicureans followed his example with still different conceptions. All of them formulated virtue in thoughts, yet all still had a *general* ethic in mind — the modern idea of individual action born of freedom and love, in our sense, was not yet present. Still, thought established itself as a new authority against tradition and against mere obedience. Here again we can refer to Augustine as an example: Augustine's biography is the life story of an inner search and struggle for a view of the world, the story of a human being who lived through the different stations of world-view and thought until finally, on the basis of his own experiences, he chose Christianity.

As the individual frees himself from this kind of tradition, he finds protection in the law. Earlier times also knew law, but Rome created civil law (*ius civile*) — a law of private rights that protected the individual and regulated affairs between human beings. Roman civil law was permeated with the idea of personal autonomy. It enabled the individual to determine his heirs, while also enabling the heir to give up the inheritance. Similarly, the individual had the right to make contracts freely and press legal suits. The importance of this form of law is the legal security that it provides the individual, a security based on the codification and publication of the law.

Legal proceedings were strictly regulated and followed definite forms — forms which changed in the course of Roman history. Essentially, however, the form of legal proceedings was intended to assure that both parties had their say and that a third party made the judgment. The third party, the arbiter (*iudex*), was appointed by the praetor or another magistrate, often with the approval of both parties. The verdict was guided by written law and the well-defined customs of Roman tradition.

The history of the Middle Ages can be treated relatively briefly in the twelfth grade, as it was the subject of eleventh grade history. In the context of our survey of world history, the Middle Ages provides an excellent example of the intersection of two cultural spheres: the antique legacy lives on while the modern age is in preparation. The Middle Ages transformed all the elements of antiquity that it absorbed. The legacy of Greek philosophy, which had become known through the church fathers, through Neoplatonism and Dionysius the Areopagite, was understood in the light of Christian theology. And in the thirteenth century, when it became possible to study Aristotle carefully, his ideas were added to the "sacra doctrina" and thus received a new form and meaning. Similarly, the Roman emperor (Caesar) became the Christian emperor (Kaiser), and the Roman Empire became the *sacrum imperium* — the Holy Roman Empire. Yet at the same time, under the cloak of the empire, the tribes of the Franks, Saxons, Swabians, and Bavarians lived

on during the Middle Ages. Among these tribes the old Germanic concepts of allegiance and loyalty were still alive. Freemen attached themselves in freedom to a leader (or "lord"), pledging him loyalty, counsel,
and help, while the leader promised protection and livelihood. In this
way a leader had command over free men. Out of this relationship later
evolved the medieval feudal state, in which the idea of freedom slum-
bered unseen, or sometimes — as in the Magna Carta or in the Swiss
confederacy — came out into the open.

Certainly the Middle Ages adopted Greek and Latin concepts; but
it is just as certain that the medieval mind and soul knew a yearning, an
inner seeking that was different from the thinking of the Greeks. The
direction of this aspiration can already be recognized in Scholasticism,
and manifests itself clearly in German mysticism: it seeks to apprehend
God through personal experience, to assure itself of the immortality of
the soul. This will of the soul finds clear expression in Luther's Reformation. Luther insisted that the believer can and should find his way to
God directly. Thus, in the entire Middle Ages we see the tendencies from
antiquity at work, while the spiritual aspiration of the new age is being
prepared — at first in concealment, then ever more obviously.

All of our study of world history is aimed towards an understanding of the modern era and the present time. And this is where the students' deeper concerns and questions lie, too. In order to arrive at an
inner understanding of the present time, an understanding that can be
experienced in the soul, the students need comprehensive views that help
them place figures and events. A helpful image here is the figure of Faust.
Traditional knowledge has become stale to Faust. To him it is nothing
but rummaging in words; it is dead and meaningless. Faust therefore puts
the Holy Scriptures aside for a while, "behind the door and under the
bench." He does not want to be considered a theologian any longer, but a
man of the world: now he calls himself a doctor of medicine. Faust
would like to break out of his narrow, high-domed Gothic room; he
turns to magic, but is incapable of making magic by himself. By himself,
he is no greater than his attendant, Wagner. Thus he engages and binds
himself to the devil, Mephistopheles, in order to find his way into the
world and to effectiveness in it. In doing this he has entrusted himself to
a power that is greater and more powerful than he himself, a power that
is to accompany him on the rest of his life's journey. As his second self,
Mephistopheles goes everywhere with Faust and knows what goes on

within him. Yet "Mephisto" leads Faust not only to "Auerbach's Cellar" and the "Witches' Kitchen"; in the end, he leads him into the wide world and to far-ranging activity.

The history of the modern era as well shows that its leading, determining personalities put the Bible under the door, wishing to venture into the wide world and master it. In the process, their actions and their will unleashed a force that they could control no better than could Faust the three strongmen. Even the apparently harmless art of printing within a very few decades of its invention exercised a world-wide magic, transforming the mental constitution of humanity. The effect of this seizing and transforming of the world is much more easily recognized in modern technology, which establishes itself as a power that dominates the human being, a power with such a strong inner dynamic that it can again and again unleash new and different developments. Even if most scientists agree that certain kinds of research should not be pursued further because they see what misfortune might threaten — from genetic manipulation, for example — their insight is of little use: somehow, somewhere this research will be set into motion and exploited technologically.

These two general images become more understandable when we consider the nature of the experiment. The first basis for experimentation is that mere observation of nature no longer "says anything" to the experimenter. Nature appears dead to him. Rudolf Steiner has drawn attention to this secret in the painting of the small cupola of the old Goetheanum: here, beneath the figure of Faust he painted a skeleton. Historically this is well founded; for the advent of the modern era went hand in hand with a new awareness of transience and of death, an awareness that is recorded a thousandfold in the depiction of the dance of death. Since nature is dead and mute, the experimenter must rely on his own activity. At the same time, human activity is separated from the human being in the experimental process: apparatuses and measuring instruments are constructed to carry out the experiment. This is a highly remarkable procedure. A certain apparatus, based on human thought, is constructed, and utmost care is taken to avoid any undesired natural or human influence from without. The apparatus is checked and controlled by exact calculation, and the findings are translated into the language of mathematical physics. In this way a certain knowledge of nature is gained: a knowledge that has come about through human activity, yet is at the same time inaccessible to human experience.

The human being who employs experimentation in technology and industry, or who makes use of technical apparatuses in everyday life, exercises power. But he does not experience what he is doing. A person who brings an automobile to a standstill from a speed of sixty miles per hour does not experience what happens to the tires in the act of braking. A person who fires a grenade does not feel the suffering of the victims; a person who poisons a region with chemicals does not feel what the animals and plants suffer. Nor is this without significance for social life. Depending on how it is calculated, one can say that for each inhabitant of the industrialized countries there are around one hundred invisible "energy slaves" at his side. This too is scarcely noticed — after all, who is aware that the foodstuffs we use today take four times more calories to produce than they contain?

The exercise of power through apparatuses, however, is a gesture that is by no means limited to technology and industry. Absolutism, in principle, reveals the same structure. It wishes to treat the state as a machine: the taxpayers supply the energy; the bureaucracy is the machinery that receives this energy; and the standing army is the machine that does the actual work. Here as well, it is characteristic that the fate of the subjects remains unknown and indifferent to the ruler. Modern dictatorships, with their mechanisms of enforced political alignment, centralization, intellectual standardization, and control from above show the same tendency in the use of power. Thus, we can see the experiment and the machine as historically important symptoms.

It would be a misconception to understand this modern tendency towards controlling nature and the human being as an expression of the will to freedom. It would be more realistic to look at the modern development of freedom as a process that runs counter to the striving for power. The history of freedom begins with the restriction of power; and the first step in this history is the idea of tolerance. Spiritually, the idea of tolerance is based on the relinquishment of any claim to an absolute divine, cosmic truth. No one is in possession of an all-encompassing truth; therefore it is reasonable to enter into discussion and compare various thoughts and ideas. In the early modern age, the arena for the general discussion and free publication of ideas was the Netherlands. The Netherlands granted asylum to the fugitives of the entire continent, among them Descartes, Spinoza, and John Locke. The second step in the history of freedom can be seen in the increasing recognition of human

rights. It must be realized, however, that the human rights were originally nothing other than a restriction of the power of the state: protection from arbitrary arrest (under threat of punishment if violated);
protection of dwelling-place and property; freedom of the press and of
assembly; and the right to trial by jury. All of these pushed back interference by state power. In contrast, the rights so loudly voiced today — the
right to education and the right to work — give the state more power
and rights to interfere; indeed, these rights are stylized as obligations to
interfere. In reality — as can be seen from compulsory school attendance
— the effect of such "human rights" is to destroy the freedoms: the student becomes the object of state indoctrination. The human rights were
supplemented by measures serving the separation of powers. It was mentioned above what a brilliant social invention this was for its time. Still,
the separation of powers alone is insufficient for the further unfoldment
of freedom. Mere private freedom and mere freedom of the press (which
is essentially nothing but a freedom to criticize) will surely be highly
prized everywhere — especially by those who have once experienced the
absence of these freedoms. Nevertheless, these freedoms must be supplemented today by a socially productive freedom.

Socially productive freedom takes on tasks that must be solved.
Such tasks are manifold — some can be solved by research, others by
social aid, counselling, and training. There is one domain in which many
such undertakings exist: wherever economic demand is at work, in other
words, wherever something is produced that can be sold for profit.
When it is successful, however, this kind of free enterprise is connected
with technology and relies heavily upon the "energy slaves" mentioned
above. Even under present-day working conditions, it employs people in
such a way that they can seldom understand the work they do as volun-
tary fulfillment of a socially meaningful task. Let it be said in passing that
this could certainly be changed. There are, however, also social tasks
which by their very nature can only be undertaken voluntarily; and it is
particularly serious that these tasks too are as a rule not based upon free
initiative and self-organization. Research, social work, schools, and hospitals have today all become an affair of the state. State programming and
institutionalization of aid, education, and research cause severe social
damage: responsibility and initiative are undermined; decisions are made
by administrative agencies that necessarily know less about the matter
than those who do the work; unnecessary projects are carried out while

necessary tasks are not taken in hand. Hence not only has the problem of productive freedom remained unsolved in the recent past, but the state of affairs has grown even worse.

When we have taken up questions of this sort, we have really already broached a wider theme. It is characteristic of the modern era to reflect upon social relationships (and not just upon single grievances) and to draw up global plans for better societies. Thus, Thomas More wrote his *Utopia*, Bacon *Nova Atlantis*, and Campanella the *City of the Sun*. Later, the utopias — in Rousseau's *Contrat Social*, for example — became programs, and in the French Revolution the attempt was made to realize the program. It failed. This, however, provided the occasion to reflect on how revolutions can be made, how history can be formed. This is a highly significant symptom. The German Revolution was still a "natural event" in history: no one had wanted, planned, or directed it in this form. Luther had set the stone rolling — without realizing what he had done. The English revolutionaries of 1640 entered into conflict with the king with somewhat more awareness; but they still saw themselves as reestablishing the old law of the kingdom — no one had initially aimed for what happened in 1649. Without it having been intended, the Commonwealth had been created; and since it had not been intended, there soon came the peaceful restoration of 1660, and only the stupidity of the kings provoked the "bloodless revolution" of 1688. The situation before the French Revolution was already different. There was talk of the coming revolution, and there were also ideas of what was wanted. These ideas were at first unequivocal: human rights and separation of powers. Both were in fact proclaimed, but the Revolution did not stop; it developed its own momentum and finally ate its own children. In our own century this development had come to the point where people were well-versed in revolution: Lenin, Mao, Ho Chi Minh, and others developed not only the goals, but also the strategies for revolution and for the subsequent reshaping of society. The most impressive example of a strategy for revolutionizing a society in our century was given by Mao. It is natural that corresponding counter-strategies were also conceived and carried out.

All of this shows that humanity has entered a time when it has not only become the master of nature, but also actually is beginning to plan and "make" history consciously. The only question is: do those who plan and make history really understand what history is; do they know what the human being is? When one looks at the results of the revolutions of the twentieth century, this appears highly doubtful — despite some undeniable economic successes and the political victories of the revolutionaries. For if one takes the freedom of human beings seriously, one cannot totally plan and organize either history or society.

At the same time it cannot be denied that today above all, in the face of unbounded difficulties and threatening catastrophes, the idea of total planning for society and history might seem a way out of danger. It can scarcely be expected, after all, that the problems will solve themselves in a human direction. There is a pressing need for fair distribution of the goods of the earth, for prudent dealing with the natural resources, and an end to environmental pollution and devastation. It is being recognized that technology must be held in check. Political conflicts, which have become more acute in the last decade, are in need of a solution not involving weapons. The arms race, requiring energy, manpower, and material, must be brought to an end in the near future. All reasonable people see these problems, problems that threaten to become catastrophes, but much too little happens — even relatively small conflicts fail to be solved, such as the one in Northern Ireland that has been smoldering for twelve years.

When we consider how all these problems can be approached in practice, however, it becomes clear that there is no single authority or power that is practically or theoretically in a position to effect a systematic solution of all world problems. There is no world brain capable of keeping an overview of the various difficulties, conflicts, and dangers and moving them towards solution; nor is there a world government that has the necessary power to do so. Thus simply from an external point of view, there is no possibility for total planning. The only thing possible today would be to come to an agreement about common goals. This would mean that in defining these goals, a common awareness would be gained. This common awareness, recognizing its goals as preconditions for the survival of humanity, could be the basis on which the various authorities, groups, and states could then act and make certain laws that are absolutely necessary — laws to preserve the ecological balance of the earth, for example. Under these circumstances the historical process would not be planned, but it would be suffused with awareness. To work towards this kind of awareness is practically the only possibility that exists to shape history in a meaningful way.

The task of history instruction also lies in developing such an awareness. The students must learn to recognize the unique situation of the present:

For the first time in history it is necessary for humanity to shape its own history.

For the first time, the history of all humanity is at issue and not the particular history of single nations or regions of the earth.

For the first time, the human being faces — in technology and the environment — the possibility of a self-endangerment of all humanity.

Altogether, this makes it imperative that more and more human beings see this task and take it up in its various single aspects. History instruction has a contribution to make here.

Made in the USA
Middletown, DE
22 July 2015